PLAIN TALK ON

John

by
Manford George Gutzke

ZONDERVAN
PUBLISHING HOUSE OF THE ZONDERVAN CORPORATION
GRAND RAPIDS, MICHIGAN 49506

PLAIN TALK ON JOHN
Copyright © 1968 by
Zondervan Publishing House
Grand Rapids, Michigan

Fifteenth printing October 1980
ISBN 0-310-25571-6

Library of Congress Catalog Card Number 69-11646

Printed in the United States of America

CONTENTS

Chapter 1

INTRODUCTION

The faith of a Christian centers in Jesus Christ. The Gospel of Jesus Christ tells above all else what He did, what He is doing now, what He will do; it is always dealing with the person of Jesus Christ.

The whole world by now knows about the coming of Jesus of Nazareth as a babe at Bethlehem, and that Christians affirm that God has made this same Jesus both Lord and Christ. No matter how much or how little they know about Him, whether they believe in Him or not, the name of Jesus Christ stands out in the consciousness of all people everywhere who have heard any word of the gospel message.

MEANING OF THE CHRISTIAN FAITH

All Christians trace their faith back to Him, and they rest in Him. What does "the Christian faith" mean? Men may acquire a certain view of the world as they study the Bible and grow to understand the Gospel, but this is not primarily the foundation of Christian faith. The Bible sets forth very clearly certain truths about man, his creation by God and in His image, his nature, his destiny, and his need of a Saviour; and all this is involved in, but is not the essence of, the faith of a Christian.

The Gospel is focused upon Jesus of Nazareth as the Christ of God. It is in Jesus Christ and in Him alone that men must believe, if they are to be saved. Peter said ". . . for there is none other name under heaven given among men, whereby we must be saved" (Acts 4:12). Paul wrote to the Corinthian believers that when he came unto their city and preached, he was ". . . determined not to know any thing among you, save Jesus Christ, and him crucified" (I Corinthians 2:2). Of Paul it was further said, as he went about preaching that he spoke of ". . . one Jesus, which was dead, whom Paul affirmed to be alive" (Acts 25:19b).

Today some say that this idea is too simple, or even too narrow. Simple it may be, blessedly simple: yet it is true! The shining of the sun is simple yet it is essential to life. The fact that the Gospel is simple should not lead anyone to doubt. Getting married is really a very

9

simple thing. There are ramifications, there are profound consequences; but actually it is not a complicated matter to get married. A boy and girl can accomplish it very easily. When it is accomplished, however, the fact of marriage, with all its meaning, cannot be altered.

The matter of receiving Jesus Christ is likewise a simple thing to do. Even a child can do it. But when such a decision has been made, it is final. As with marriage, though in a far deeper, holier sense, there are vast ramifications and profound consequences in this simple act of faith: accepting Christ as Saviour.

> There was a man sent from God, whose name was John. The same came for a witness, to bear witness of the Light, that all men through him might believe. He was not that Light, but was sent to bear witness of that Light (John 1:6-8).

As we proceed in our study of the gospel of John, it will be obvious that its attention is focused primarily on Jesus of Nazareth.

Almost 2000 years ago Jesus was born in Bethlehem. He lived for about 33 years, and died on a cross. At that time the cross was not a sacred symbol of atonement, but an instrument of justice used by the Romans to inflict maximum punishment upon any criminal. Jesus of Nazareth spent three years in public ministry as a teacher, all the while working signs and wonders. He claimed to be the Son of God, and allowed others to so identify Him. He was finally condemned to death because He would not deny His deity. As a matter of fact, before the high priest Jesus affirmed that He was the Son of God. Earlier He had said to others: ". . . the Son of man is come to seek and to save that which was lost" (Luke 19:10). ". . . the Son of man came not to be ministered unto, but to minister, and to give his life a ransom for many" (Matthew 20:28). And again, ". . . I am come that they might have life, and . . . have it more abundantly" (John 10:10).

IMPACT OF JOHN'S GOSPEL

It is this testimony of Jesus of Nazareth that is recorded in the gospel of John. In the 2000 years since these words were spoken by the Saviour, His message has profoundly affected human affairs. History contains the massive testimony, the impressive record of Christianity. And yet, while nations and cultures have been changed through this testimony, while the Gospel has been pervasive in the affairs of men, always, wherever it has been proclaimed, what is at the center of the historical changes is that individual men and women have come to believe in Jesus Christ as their personal Saviour and Lord.

Wherever the basic dynamic of all that is called Christian has been operative, the experience has been personal: it has happened in individuals, not to groups. Many converts may have come in a group when they came to faith, but in each case of regeneration it was the individual who lifted up his heart and yielded his life to God: the matter was a very personal one. "But as many as received him, to them gave he power . . ." (John 1:12).

I can remember the days of my unbelief, my problem was not a matter of failing to believe *in* God: I simply did not believe *there was a God*. I certainly didn't believe that Jesus of Nazareth was the Son of God. I had heard about Him, and I felt if the records were true He must have been a wonderful man; but I had no idea of considering Him being other than a man like myself. In those days, when I began to wonder if there might be something valid in the Christian Gospel, what first impressed me and what I could not exclude from my thinking, was the tremendous record the Gospel had made during these 2000 years.

A candid look at the reported facts would show that this movement started in a small province of an obscure country when citizens of a captive nation, a few Jews, under the heel of the great Roman Empire, stood up and bravely began to declare to the whole world that God had sent His Son in the person of Jesus of Nazareth into the world to seek and to save the lost. Beginning with these few Jews the Gospel of Jesus Christ has spread around the world.

The Christian faith has spread across every natural barrier: deserts, mountains, and seas have not prevented its extensions. The Christian Gospel is today preached among the Eskimos in their igloos of ice in the frozen north, and to natives in the heart of Africa, living in arbors under great jungle trees at the sweltering equator. It has been proclaimed to men of high and low degree. Kings have believed it, and peasants have rejoiced in it. Old and young, rich and poor, educated and illiterate, very clever and very simple have all listened. In all these groups some have believed! The gospel message has gone everywhere, and whoever has received Jesus Christ has experienced the joy and inward blessedness of belonging to God.

My own mind and heart was full of skepticism, yet I could not ignore this testimony of Christianity. Always in the back of my mind, and often confronting me with stubborn insistence was the clear impression that it was tremendously important — even to me — that Jesus of Nazareth was born in Bethlehem.

The witness of Christianity in the history of the world is impressive, but even more vital to faith is a study of the gospel of John. It contains a more direct witness — Jesus Christ Himself. The record of incidents involving Jesus of Nazareth, and the report of His words in teaching and in promise, show who He is, what He did, and what He will do:

> And many other signs truly did Jesus in the presence of his disciples, which are not written in this book. But these are written, that ye might believe that Jesus is the Christ, the Son of God; and that believing ye might have life through his name (John 20: 30, 31).

Chapter 2

THE COMING OF THE SON OF GOD

THE WORD (1:1-14)

> In the beginning was the Word, and the Word was with God, and the Word was God. The same was in the beginning with God (John 1:1, 2).

These first two verses of the gospel according to John, present an unusual use of what we translate in English, *Word*. In most versions of the Bible it is spelled with a capital W. Sometimes it is printed entirely in capital letters, thus: W O R D. The term used by John was a Greek word which refers to the whole realm of consciousness or to the expressed will of God. These verses could be understood in this way:

> In the beginning was [the mind of God, the will of God] the expressed idea of God, and this expressed idea of God [this will of God] actually was with God, and this idea [this will of God] actually was God. The same was in the beginning with God.

With these verses John introduces Jesus Christ. The reader may not feel sure of the total meaning of λογος, Word, if he does not understand Greek, but in reading the first two verses of this chapter of John one truth comes through clearly, this Word was with God and this Word was God.

Verse three records: "All things were made by him [by the Word] and without him was not any thing made that was made." In verse fourteen it is obvious that this refers to Jesus Christ. ". . . the Word was made flesh, and dwelt among us . . . full of grace and truth." This clearly pinpoints the fact that the birth of Jesus Christ was different from that of any other baby. About no other new-born child could such a thing be said.

John is declaring this amazing truth in all its fulness and glory: Jesus Christ actually existed before the world began. Who then was He? John makes it very clear that He was and is the Son of God, eternal with the Father. John also points out that He was the Creator. "All things were made by him; and without him was not any thing that was made" (John 1:3). This is difficult to understand with our finite minds. We cannot grasp the operation of Almighty God in the creation of the world. Christians often repeat the Apostles' Creed, "I believe in God the Father, Almighty, Maker of heaven and earth . . ." and this is true. One of the ways in which the believer understands God is to separate His person and functions. But in repeating even this simple statement of faith, the Christian is speaking of the triune God: Father, Son, and Holy Spirit. And in his gospel, John is declaring that the Son of God is the Maker of all that was created.

LIFE AND LIGHT

In preparing his readers for what he will tell them about the Son of God John goes on to say: "In him was life; and the life was the light of men" (John 1:4). These too are simple words, but their meaning is profound. We can understand them in part by our human experience, but some of their meaning goes beyond us and this world.

To read these words is something like looking at the ocean. When a person goes to the beach, he can wade in the waves which roll up onto the shore. But he can look up, letting his eyes gaze out at the skyline, away to the horizon, and his imagination makes him aware of the vast distances that cannot be seen. The ocean goes on far, far, far away and is lost from sight. A person may be overwhelmed by its immensity, and yet be very much aware that this is actually the same ocean that he is happily wading in unafraid.

"In him was life; and the life was the light of men." The life men share now enables them to move about and communicate in a known world. But what is *life?* As the ocean reaches far out of sight, so life goes on and out into eternity, beyond sight and comprehension.

The same mystery is true of light. If the lights are turned on, a person can see. If he carries a flashlight on a country path, he can walk ahead with no fear. But what makes light? Where does light come from? Genesis 1:3 reports ". . . God said, Let there be light, and there was light." The sun had not yet been created, but light was there. And what is "the light of men"? These questions lift our minds up far out of earthly existence, and focus our attention upon eternal verities.

"And the light shineth in darkness; and the darkness comprehended it not" (John 1:5). What then is darkness? To put it simply, the word *darkness* covers everything in which there is no light. It is a negative term at best: it means no light. This again brings us back to the word *light*. John wrote: "And the light shineth in darkness. . . ." In order to understand this it is important to explore the full meaning of "light." Later in his gospel, John reports the Lord Jesus Himself as saying: "I am the light of the world . . ." (John 8:12).

The meaning of the word *comprehended* is difficult to grasp in this instance, because ordinarily the word means a kind of mental exercise. Thus men talk in terms of "comprehending the lesson," or "comprehending the proposal of the committee," to indicate that the minds have grasped the facts in question. But how can darkness have mentality, that it might comprehend anything? The original Greek statement can be translated to say the darkness could not contain the light, could not overcome it. The modern translation by William Beck expressed the meaning in these words: "the darkness has not put it out."

Here is a wonderful thing! No matter how small a light may be, just a match flame shining in the dark, the darkness cannot put it out. Darkness has no power when compared with light!

John immediately claims this for Christ Jesus. He speaks about Jesus coming into the world, and says that in Him was life; and the life was the light of men; the light shines in the darkness, and nothing can put it out. John is making the bold declaration that the power of the Lord Jesus Christ can overcome anything in this world.

The Witness of John the Baptist

"There was a man sent from God, whose name was John. The same came for a witness, to bear witness of the Light, that all men through him might believe" (John 1:6, 7). The ministry of John the Baptist on this earth was to prepare people to believe in the Light of the world. "He was not that Light, but was sent to bear witness of that Light" (John 1:8).

Here John points out "That was the true Light, which lighteth every man that cometh into the world" (John 1:9), referring to Jesus Christ. So far in his report John has said several things about Jesus Christ. He has been called the Word, He was in the beginning with God, He was God, He is the true Light, and in Him was life.

Summary

Next John presents a summary of the whole witness of the Lord Jesus Christ. He came into this world, lived in it, taught in it, and eventually died in it, but the world never appreciated Him. "He was in the world, and the world was made by him, and the world knew him not" (John 1:10). Then even more personally John records, "He came unto his own, and his own received him not" (John 1:11). This is commonly understood to mean the people of His day, Israel, the Jewish people; but it need not be limited to them. "He came unto His own." His own? He made the world, it was His; He made man, man was His own. "Without him was not any thing made that was made." He came to the very thing He had made and they "received him not." Oh, the pity of it, the blind eye, the unhearing ear!

One great truth stands out. The Son of God came into this world to seek and to save the lost, and He was repudiated. He came into this world that men through Him might believe, and they turned their backs on Him. They ignored the Son of God who came in His grace to help men in trouble. That is the tragic fact which John summarizes here, at the very beginning of his gospel.

By the grace of God there were exceptions to this common attitude:

> But as many as received him, to them gave he power to become the sons of God, even to them that believe on his name: Which were born, not of blood, nor of the will of the flesh, nor of the will of man, but of God (John 1:12, 13).

What a marvelous statement! This will be demonstrated all through the Book of John, with many illustrations of people who were born "not of blood, nor of the will of the flesh, nor of the will of man, but of God."

> And the Word was made flesh, and dwelt among us, (and we beheld his glory, the glory as of the only begotten of the Father,) full of grace and truth (John 1:14).

THE MESSIAH (1:15-34)

The Jews of the Old Testament were looking for God's anointed One who would be for them the Righteous Servant, the Compassionate Saviour, and the King of Kings. They called this Coming One the Messiah, and the New Testament points out that Christ and the Messiah predicted in the Old Testament were the same person.

The Hebrew word *Messiah* means *the anointed one,* and that is exactly what the Greek word *Christ* means. Some use the word *christen* when speaking about a ceremony of dedication. This word comes from the same root as the word *Christ,* which means anointed. Anointing was used to designate a person for the filling of a certain office or position. This meant about the same as the word *installation,* or *coronation.* Sometimes the word *ordination* is used to mean the same idea.

Even though the Jewish scholars studied the Old Testament Scriptures with their prophecies and predictions about this person, and then waited for God to send His anointed One, they could not understand that the sufferings of the Messiah and the glory that was to follow could belong to the same person. Israel in the days of the Old Testament records believed in the law of God. They recognized it as the eternal requirement of God for man. They believed the law of God should be obeyed, and they knew they had failed in disobedience. Their prophets told them that God would send the Messiah who would live a perfect life, obeying God's law to the fullest extent, and who would save them out of their sins (Matthew 1:21).

These Old Testament people also believed in the mercy of God, in His long-suffering and loving-kindness. The phrase "the goodness of God endureth forever" occurs over and over again in the Psalms. The manifestations of this mercy, this long-suffering, this loving-kindness of God to His people would come, they believed, to fulfillment in the Messiah, who would bring His people back to God.

Israel believed in the sovereignty of God. They acknowledged His rule, trusted His wisdom, and accepted His Word as they knew it in the Scriptures of the Old Testament. So they looked for the Messiah who would deliver them and rule over them. Furthermore, the Old Testament prophets predicted that the Messiah would be born in Bethlehem (See Micah 5:2; Matthew 2:4-6).

At the time of the birth of Jesus Christ, the plight of the Jewish nation was acute. They were living under a conqueror. They yearned for deliverance and many felt the time was ripe for the ancient prophecies to be fulfilled, that Messiah would now come.

JOHN THE BAPTIST

During those troubled days there came into the country of the Jews around Jerusalem and in Galilee a remarkable young preacher by the name of John. He was the son of a priest. He had grown up in the rural areas, and he was clothed in the usual garments of a countryman. Mark tells that he wore clothes of "camel's hair" and a leather girdle (or jacket) such as would be worn by a man accustomed to outdoor country life. His diet seems strange to us. It consisted of locusts and wild honey. But that, too, was not abnormal. It was the food of the poor people, and John lived among the poor of his country.

John was a preacher of great power. I do not know how I can convey, in words which will linger with you, what an unusual preacher this young man was. He had evidently begun to preach when he was about thirty years of age, or perhaps a little younger, and he was a man of power and conviction. The people had become very much attracted to John. We read in one of the gospels that there "went out to him Jerusalem, and all Judaea, and all the region round about Jordan, And were baptized of him in Jordan, confessing their sins" (Matthew 3:5, 6). Jerusalem was the greatest city of the nation, and the Jews would not be likely to flock out into the wilderness of Judaea to hear any ordinary young man. But they went out en masse to hear the message of this young evangelist, John the Baptist. Some wondered whether this prominent and youthful preacher might not actually be the Messiah. Perhaps this was the one who would lead them out of all their troubles, and would effect deliverance for them!

The first fourteen verses of this first chapter of John have been dealing with "the Word of God." By this Word of God, we have seen, John, the writer of the gospel, meant Jesus Christ. Now it appears

John the Baptist esteemed Him as the Christ. "John [the Baptist] bare witness of him, and cried, saying, This was he of whom I spake, He that cometh after me is preferred before me: for he was before me" (John 1:15).

Among them who heard John preach there were some who wondered if he were Messiah and boldly asked the question. John's reply was quick and firm. "Oh no, I am not. There is One coming after me, He is greater than I am, and He is the One to whom you will want to turn." Then John spoke with even greater emphasis, "I wouldn't even presume to undo His shoelaces."

The sum and substance of what John the Baptist said about Jesus is found in John 1:16, 17:

> And of his fullness have all we received, and grace for grace. For the law was given by Moses, but grace and truth came by Jesus Christ.

This is a forceful and concise way of saying that not only was Jesus Christ greater than Moses, but that He brought a revelation of God's grace and goodness such as Moses did not know in his day.

When the Jews sent priests and Levites to Jerusalem to ask him, "Who art thou?" John answered in words of deep spiritual significance. He told them plainly he was not the Christ, but only His divinely-sent messenger.

> And he confessed, and denied not; but confessed, I am not the Christ. And they asked him, What then? Art thou Elias? And he saith, I am not. Art thou that prophet? And he answered, No. Then said they unto him, Who art thou? that we may give an answer to them that sent us. What sayest thou of thyself? He said, I am the voice of one crying in the wilderness, Make straight the way of the Lord, as said the prophet Esaias (John 1:20-23).

Very plainly indeed did John identify himself with the prophecy of Isaiah: "The voice of him that crieth in the wilderness, Prepare ye the way of the Lord, make straight in the desert a highway for our God" (Isaiah 40:3). Prepare! Cut down the hills and fill up the valleys, make a straight pathway for the Lord's coming, open up the way before Him!

God uses human pathways to help man. When His mission was to redeem the souls of men, He came in the form of a man. Even as God used this John of the desert, just so today He sends men on His errands to prepare pathways for His feet.

When John spoke of his own ministry he said: ". . . I baptize with water . . ." (verse 26). What was John saying here? It seems likely he was using *water* in the sense of cleansing. In effect he was saying, "My business is to prepare; my particular function in preparing this meal is to wash the utensils, to clean up the kettles. I baptize with water for the washing away of sins and the cleansing of hearts in preparation for the coming of the Messiah. He is coming soon and when He comes He will use the cleansed utensils. I am fulfilling the prerequisite of cleaning up the kitchen, but the Messiah will prepare you a meal — He will fill the kettle!"

THE LAMB OF GOD

". . . Behold the Lamb of God," cries John (verse 29), "which taketh away the sins of the world." This does not necessarily mean that this is John's first glimpse of Jesus. John's mother Elisabeth, and Mary the mother of Jesus, were cousins. It is entirely possible that John and Jesus knew each other in that small family circle. But it seems that John did not recognize Jesus as the Messiah until the time of the baptism of Jesus.

John makes it clear how he came to realize that this was indeed Messiah, the Son of God.

> And John bare record, saying, I saw the Spirit descending from heaven like a dove, and it abode upon him. And I knew him not: but he [God] that sent me to baptize with water, the same said unto me, Upon whom thou shalt see the Spirit descending, and remaining on him, the same is he which baptizeth with the Holy Ghost. And I saw, and bare record that this is the Son of God (John 1:32-34).

In other words: "The same One who sent me to baptize with water, thus made it clear to me that this was His Son." And so the identification is announced as John the Baptist proclaims Jesus of Nazareth as the Christ, the long-looked for Messiah.

TELLING OTHERS (1:35-42)

What seems to be God's plan to spread the good news of salvation around the world, to tell all men that the Son of God came "to seek and to save that which was lost"? Salvation is the free work of God, because of His abundant grace, and there is no question but that He has displayed His kindness and His mercy on behalf of the children of men. However, He calls upon saved souls to share the tidings of salvation with others. When sober consideration is given to this commission, it is almost frightening because of the implication of responsiblity it conveys to those who believe.

What a challenge to the heart of every Christian! The knowledge of the Gospel must be spread abroad in the world by the men and women who have experienced its power. The very heart of the gospel message is that Christ Jesus came to save men from their sins. One of the first results of this salvation in a human soul is causal. Now *that* man or woman wants to tell others. When the Lord Jesus comes into the heart of a believer, there is an immediate impulse to tell somebody about the peace of mind and joy of spirit which floods his soul, like sunlight streaming out from behind a bank of dark clouds.

The demonstration of this truth is seen repeatedly in the study of John's gospel. In John 1:35-37 there is a very interesting and important illustration of the efficacy of the preaching of John the Baptist.

> Again the next day after John stood, and two of his disciples; And looking upon Jesus as he walked, he saith, Behold the Lamb of God! And the two disciples heard him speak, and they followed Jesus.

This seems a simple, uncomplicated reaction. And it was! It happened very naturally, but how important it was! John had preached in such a way that the people who heard his message followed the Lord Jesus Christ. That is a notable result. They might have been tempted to follow John himself, or their hearts might have been hardened so they would have failed to follow anyone. They could have heard John preach, and then gone back home with hearts and lives unchanged. But these men heard *John* preach, and then they followed *Jesus!* What a tribute to John's preaching!

Apparently John did not emphasize that they had been doing wrong, although that may have been true. Apparently he did not press upon them the necessity for doing right, although they probably realized this. It seems John did not tell them the community needed their services, although that may well have been the case. He stressed none of these things. Instead, he said: "Behold the Lamb of God!" This was his topic; this was the theme of his message. He talked about salvation through Christ, with the result that these people, looking at Jesus, were constrained to follow Him. Why should the sight of Jesus, the Lamb of God, produce such a result? The Holy Spirit used John's preaching to open their eyes to understanding.

Let any man or woman, boy or girl, be helped to see and consider Jesus Christ, and He will stand before them with outstretched hands, saying "Come unto me, all ye that labour and are heavy laden, and I will give you rest" (Matthew 11:28). When a soul really sees Jesus, He will no longer be just a picture on the wall or a statue in a church, but a living, loving Saviour. His eyes will be on the sinner; His hands outstretched to help, and then, with the ears of his soul the sinner will hear Him say, "Come, follow me!"

John the Baptist preached about Jesus of Nazareth in such a way that his hearers arose and followed Jesus. Such preaching sounds like the preaching of Paul the Apostle when he went to Corinth: "For I determined not to know any thing among you, save Jesus Christ, and him crucified" (I Corinthians 2:2). This seems to be the distinctive feature. John said, ". . . Behold the Lamb of God. . . ." Paul said, ". . . know any thing among you, save Jesus Christ, and him cruci-fied." In each case the hearers were moved to faith in the Lord!

The word *Lamb* conveys the meaning of a sacrifice for sin in the ritual of the Old Testament. "Behold the Lamb of God" calls upon a person to look upon the One whom God has sent to die in atonement for sin.

RESPONDING TO THE MESSAGE

In response to this word the two disciples of John the Baptist fol-lowed Jesus. In their experience a new and thrilling fact is seen (verses 38 and 39). When a person sees Jesus Christ as the sacrifice for sin and is moved to cast all else aside and to follow Him, then the Lord becomes his teacher. He now will be guide and companion. In this case He pointed out the relationship's real significance by asking, "What seek ye?"

It would be helpful for each person who enters a public worship ser-vice to have this in mind. The worshiper could hear the Lord saying to him, "What seek *ye?*" In fact it could be good for each wor-shiper to ask himself that question as he comes before God.

The reply of these two men is a bit difficult to interpret. ". . . Mas-ter, where dwellest thou?" Perhaps they mean to say, "We would like to know what you mean. What is the source of your strength? Upon what or whom do you depend? Where is your resting place? Where do you dwell? What about your personal life, Rabbi?" This may sound presumptuous, but it need not necessarily be so.

"COME AND SEE"

The reply of Jesus Christ to these two inquiring souls is far reaching: "Come and see." There was no argument, no explanation or description, no attempt at justification. There was only this direct invitation, "Come and see."

Here is an important truth. When any person takes Jesus as Saviour and Lord, all faith is centered in Him. He wants the believer to "come and see," to share in the innermost secret of His spiritual strength. But note! He does not parade this before the world. He is not offering His ideas or proclaiming the riches of His grace nor the greatness of His power to those who do not care. There is no "casting of pearls be-fore swine" here. There is just this simple word of invitation: "Come and see."

The truth seems to be plainly put: if anyone wants to know about the Lamb of God, the way is open. The soul needs only to respond to *come, see,* and thus move into the inner circle by faith. ". . . They came and saw where he dwelt, and abode with him that day: for it was about the tenth hour" [i.e., 4 P.M.] (John 1:39). They spent the evening and the night in fellowship with Him. Something of the nature of this fellowship can be learned from its effect upon Andrew. He did not go out the next day with only the memory of a bright and happy evening. Andrew went out the next day to find his brother, Simon, because of his own deep experience. He had been with the Lord, and so immediately he sought his brother that he might share the blessing with him.

Societies of Andrew are to be found all over the country, and they render a worth-while service in urging men to seek their brothers in the flesh or their brother men to bring them to the Lord. There are churches named after Andrew, and this is good, because the name recalls the man of whom it is said, "He first findeth his own brother Simon. . . ." This is a wonderful thing!

When Andrew found Simon, what did he say? ". . . We have found the Messias . . . the Christ. And he brought him to Jesus . . ." (John 1:41, 42). There is no record of any argument or debate. There is no indication of a discussion as to what Simon ought to do. There was no attempt at an interpretation of what the situation called for, or a review of the neighborhood, with an expression of its need, nor any talk about its sinful state and what could be done. None of these things are mentioned. Such topics may be all valid, when one is trying to introduce a man or woman to Christ, but it would appear they are not the primary consideration. What is mentioned here is that Andrew had come to Jesus personally, had spent the night with Him, and had then felt under a commission to go and find his brother. Argument was not necessary. He simply said, "We have found the Messias. . . ." And he brought that brother to Jesus. That is the important thing.

> . . . And when Jesus beheld him, he said, Thou art Simon, the son of Jona: thou shalt be called Cephas, which is by interpretation, A stone (John 1:42).

Jesus pointed out the big change that would take place in Simon's heart. "Thou art called Simon . . . thou shalt be called Cephas." *Simon* means *sand,* and the name *Cephas* means *rock.* It was said later that Jesus "knew what was in man" (John 2:25). He was able to discern the unstable aspect of Peter's character: shifting, impulsive, full of weakness. A permanent building cannot be erected upon a foundation of sand. It is necessary to have rock for a sturdy, lasting structure. What Jesus really seems to be saying is, "at present you are Simon, an unreliable, vacillating individual, 'in and out,' 'up and down,' completely undependable. But I will make you a dependable man, just like a rock for strength of character."

As this study moves along into this wonderful book, it will be noted

again and again how the Lord Jesus Christ deals with people personally.
Here at the outset He invited two men to spend the night with Him,
and by that personal touch changed their lives. Andrew acted at once
on his new knowledge and went out personally to bring his brother
to Jesus. Jesus, clearly understanding Simon, dealt with him according to
his personal need. It is good to realize that this is how the knowledge of
Christ spreads to the hearts and lives of men and women today, just as it
was on that afternoon when John the Baptist directed two men to "the
Lamb of God."

PHILIP AND NATHANAEL (1:43-51)

The Scripture calls upon all believers to "Let the redeemed of the
Lord say so . . ." (Psalm 107:2). Christians are told, in this clear admonition, to testify to others. Someone might very well ask himself,
"To whom shall I 'say so'? Where shall my witness be given?" The
answer is simple. There is an old saying, "Charity begins at home."
So does Christian witness! ". . . go quickly, and tell his disciples . . ."
(Matthew 28:7), was the command of the angels. "Go and tell the
group nearest to Him, the glad, good news of Jesus' resurrection." The
principle is the same today. John reported that a Spirit-filled minister,
such as John the Baptist, could turn people to Christ. And when men
came to know Jesus, they went out to win their own family and friends.

Now in the narrative John reports Jesus Christ's personal concern
for the hearts of men. "The day following Jesus would go forth into
Galilee, and findeth Philip, and saith unto him, Follow me" (John 1:
43).

Here is a new aspect of truth. Note the use of *would*: "Jesus would
go forth," the indication of purpose and planning on His part, the implication of deliberate action. As a rule, men and women do not come
to Christ of their own volition. Someone has witnessed, seed has been
sown somewhere along the way. Since seed sown may not bear fruit
immediately, but in God's own time, someone else may reap the glorious fruition of that sown seed.

When the Lord has dealings with any person, invariably the first
word He speaks is "Come to Me," or as in the case of Philip, "Follow
Me." This seems to be always an individual matter. The Lord set out
and found *Philip,* and this is by no means the only instance where He
dealt with an individual. It is important to recognize the fact that the
individual is the basic unit of Christian experience. It is a good thing
to plan, by God's grace, to start a Sunday school in such and such a
community. However, it will be important to remember to begin that
group as the Lord leads, by seeking *individual* children, young people
and adults. In the last analysis, Tom, Dick, and Harry, and Mary, Jane,
and Elizabeth, each have to make up their individual minds to attend
that Sunday school. The founding of the school can be discussed with

friends, talked about in the city and county, but it will not mean a thing if Tom, Dick and Harry won't want to come. The individual personal response is necessary.

In telling the story of how Philip became a believer John reports a matter of possible significance when he writes: "Now Philip was of Bethsaida, the city of Andrew and Peter" (John 1:44). Now we are told where Jesus found Philip. The possibility seems obvious that when Andrew and Peter went home, they began at once to witness in that community. As their startling news was noised about, it is quite possible that Philip's curiosity was stirred and that he was actually hoping to see this Jesus about whom the whole community had begun to talk. A stone flung into a pond will cause ripples to go in all directions, eventually touching every shore.

Whatever the manner of the meeting between Jesus and Philip, it seems certain that something happened in Philip's heart. There appeared in him the same zeal that Andrew felt when he "first findeth his own brother." We read that "Philip findeth Nathanael . . ." (John 1:45). We do not know anything about their background, nor of their circumstances. It is quite possible that Philip and Nathanael were old friends, and Philip's first impulse was to find his friend and tell him. ". . . We have found him, of whom Moses in the law, and the prophets, did write, Jesus of Nazareth, the son of Joseph" (John 1:45).

John tells something about Nathanael in more detail. He reports his reply to Philip. Nathanael said, ". . . Can there any good thing come out of Nazareth . . .?" It would seem that Nathanael had thought about the things of God. Apparently he had ideas about what to expect, and it may be he had faced problems concerning his personal relationship with God. Perhaps he and Philip had discussed these matters previously. In any case, Philip found Nathanael and gave his glowing testimony: here was the fulfillment of prophecy. Here was Messiah!

In passing, realize that the added phrase, "the son of Joseph," does not indicate that Philip meant that Jesus was the physical son of Joseph. This was the common expression of the day. Jesus had grown up in the home of Joseph and Mary. Joseph would be considered as His father, even as he was His earthly guardian in the eyes of the law.

It is very significant that Philip did not say something like this: "Come and see! We have just found the most wonderful man this community has ever beheld. He has a real attitude of concern for other people, even for servants. He does not care about money or comfort. He has a good understanding about the way the government should be run, and his plans for the community are tremendous!" No, Philip said nothing like that. He did not claim Jesus to be an outstanding person. He said nothing about His morale, ethics, or plans. What he did say was, "We have found one who fulfils the Scripture. We have found the Man about whom Moses and the prophets wrote. Here is the Christ!"

CRITERION FOR RECOGNIZING JESUS

This, then, is the criterion for recognizing the Lord Jesus as Christ, believing in Him, accepting Him as the Messiah. There was no appraisal of His person or His work, but there was a conviction that Jesus Christ fulfilled the promises of Old Testament Scripture, that He satisfied the prophecies.

Nathanael's answer was one of natural scepticism. Such reaction can be heard today on every hand. The popular feeling in that community seemed to be that Galilee was an area out of which nothing good could come. Nazareth was a small city, and there would seem to be an undertone of scorn as well as scepticism in Nathanael's comment.

But Philip gave an answer which should be a guide for all who witness for Christ. He did not waste time in arguing the point, nor did he attempt to detail all the ways in which Jesus of Nazareth fulfilled the prophecies. He gave the classic reply to all sceptics: "Come and see," an invitation to observe, to witness a demonstration.

As the story is told one can see how honest doubt can be handled. At the very outset there is appreciation of integrity. Jesus recognized that here was an honest man, a good man, genuinely sincere, and as Nathanael approached He said, ". . . Behold an Israelite indeed, in whom is no guile!" (John 1:47).

There is no way of knowing to what Jesus was referring when He said, ". . . Before that Philip called thee, when thou wast under the fig tree, I saw thee" (verse 48). It is entirely possible that Nathanael had been having some spiritual experience one day while sitting in the shade of a fig tree. He may even have prayed to God about it as he meditated upon the problem. Whatever happened that day, Jesus had seen him, and had known of his experience. When Jesus said, "When you were under the fig tree, I saw you," Nathanael's scepticism was gone and he answered, ". . . Rabbi, thou art the Son of God: thou art the King of Israel" (verse 49).

It is worthy of note that Philip apparently knew nothing of Nathanael's fig tree incident. But Jesus did, and could talk to Nathanael about it. The friend who witnesses to any sceptic may not be aware of the spiritual history of that sceptic, but God knows all about him. When Philip brought Nathanael to meet Jesus of Nazareth he had done what he could. Things happened between Nathanael and Jesus that removed all doubts. Philip was not involved in that process. He had done his part when he brought Nathanael to Jesus. The Lord Himself led Nathanael to real conviction.

Chapter 3

THE BEGINNING OF JESUS' MINISTRY

THE WHY OF MIRACLES (2:1-12)

The question often raised by the unsaved, or by babes in Christ who do not yet understand much of the Word of God, is, "Why did Jesus Christ perform miracles?" These inquiring people do not question that Christ did perform the miracles, nor doubt His power so to do. They accept the fact that these miracles demonstrated control and dominion over nature and natural events. The burden of their question is, why was this necessary?

A word of admonition at this point in the study of the gospel of John would seem to be in order. Attempting to interpret a miracle by rational factors, implying that what seemed to be a miracle was a natural event which Jesus of Nazareth used for His own purposes: such unbelieving interpretation should be avoided by anyone who wants to know the real truth.

The Scriptures teach plainly that Jesus was and is the Son of God in human form while on earth, and now raised to His own place at the Father's right hand. Now Christians believe in Him and serve Him by the power of the indwelling Holy Spirit. But in the days of His flesh there were no churches, no hymns such as are sung to His praise today. There was no long history of Christian testimony. There was the Old Testament, but it hadn't been completed in the New yet. How could people then know that He was the Son of God incarnate in human flesh? He came as their Messiah, but how could they be sure? Even if they wanted to believe, then as now, scepticism reared its head. It is here that the importance of the miracles can be felt. The miracles performed by Jesus of Nazareth, while He walked among men in the days of His earthly ministry, were to demonstrate His power as the Son of God. They caused the people of that day to realize that the living God by the exercise of His will, actually controlled and manipulated the processes and forces of nature. A phrase from the lips of Nicodemus clearly emphasizes this: ". . . for no man can do these miracles that thou doest, except God be with him" (John 3:2).

It was as if the miracles, the works which Jesus performed, were His credentials, His certificate of recommendation, so to speak. They were to commend Him to the confidence of people who came to look and to listen.

To gain the confidence and to challenge the faith of the people around Him, He showed His power over nature. A man could expect this Teacher to work a miracle in his soul when he saw the exercise of His power over nature! When a man saw a power at work, suspending the natural processes, overcoming or halting the orderly working of nature, so that a miracle comes to pass, he realized that God had taken a hand and was at work through Jesus of Nazareth. The natural consequence is that such a man could trust that power to operate in his behalf. This is logical reasoning which has its place in the development of confidence even to this day.

This need for miracles is not as common today as it was then. Now people do have the Word of God in the Scriptures, including the New Testament records, and also the testimony of the centuries to the power of the Gospel of Christ. These factors help to bring conviction to men today and enable souls to trust in Him.

THE MIRACLE IN CANA

The opening verses of the second chapter of John's gospel show how Jesus was working miracles to win the confidence of people. The story is the report of a marriage in the city of Cana of Galilee. It seems to have been normal that Jesus and His family attended such an occasion. The mother of Jesus was there, and He and His disciples had been invited to the ceremony. At this time Jesus was treated like any other citizen of that community. While all the circumstances are not known, He was present as one of the guests, just like anyone else.

The narrative goes on to say, "And when they wanted wine, the mother of Jesus saith unto him, They have no wine" (2:3). The word *wanted* may well be translated *lacked*. When Mary said to Jesus, "They lack wine" there is the suggestion that she knew something of His power and it seems she had confidence that He would do something about the situation.

His answer seems almost strange. ". . . Woman, what have I to do with thee? mine hour is not yet come" (verse 4). This use of the word *woman* was not as blunt in their language as it seems in ours today. This did not indicate any lack of courtesy or grace on the part of Jesus toward His mother. In those days it might well have been counted as unfitting for Him publicly to address her as "mother." The important thing to note is His answer. ". . . mine hour is not yet come." This is as though He was saying: "Why do you call on me now? I am not yet ready for public ministry." To supply wine now by a miracle, would mean inevitably that He would receive notoriety. This would catapult Him immediately into the center of public attention, and apparently this was not what He wanted at that moment.

The record goes on to report that "His mother saith unto the servants, Whatsoever he saith unto you, do it" (verse 5). This seemed to indicate that Mary was well known and respected, or else she would not have addressed the servants this way. Be that as it may, her word to them implies that she knew more than He had revealed to others, of His power and, furthermore, He would go ahead and help them. This story shows the very real confidence which Mary had in her Son.

CO-OPERATION

There is a lesson here for all Christians. In His work in the world today the Lord needs obedient co-operation. Since He was going to turn that water into wine, why call the servants at all? Why ask their participation? The answer to that question will help to show why, today, He uses believers in His gracious love, to work for and with Him.

There were "six waterpots of stone" there, and Jesus told the servants to fill them to the brim with water. Could He not, if He were going to turn the water into wine, have brought the water in, or miraculously caused it to be in the waterpots? Perhaps so, but apparently He wanted others to share in this, and here is the lesson for Christians in this twentieth century. Through the working of the Holy Spirit, God can work in hearts and lives, bringing conviction and saving men and women, without using human agents. But apparently He chooses what must be to Him a much better way. He has seen fit to give to believers the work of plowing the field, scattering the seed, cultivating the ground, and even taking care of the crops (I Corinthians 3:6-9).

There is another lesson in this first miracle. When Jesus told the servants to fill the waterpots they did so, "up to the brim." If a believer is going to co-operate with his gracious Lord, he should do so one hundred per cent. He should "fill the waterpots to the brim" in glad and expectant obedience.

When this new wine was served, there were comments by the guests as to its quality. Yet the purpose of this work was not for Jesus merely to furnish good wine. The miracle had a more specific purpose, as verse eleven seems to imply. "This beginning of miracles did Jesus in Cana of Galilee, and manifested forth his glory; and his disciples believed on him." In the miracle He showed His power, and His relationship to God. And so His disciples found their own faith strengthened and enriched. They saw Jesus, whom they had come to obey and trust, as a worker of miracles by the power of God. This is the way men need to see Him today, as the Miracle Worker!

He works today in and through believers as they witness to His Word, to produce miracles of His grace. What greater miracles can there be than redeemed souls? Believing witnesses, believing testimony, by the power of the Spirit of God, produces by His grace great miracles in transformed hearts and lives.

CLEANSING THE TEMPLE (2:13-25)

As the narrative of the gospel of John moves along, the reader learns about the varied ministry of Jesus of Nazareth, and discovers more and more of the whole truth about Him. One aspect of His character often escapes the attention of people: the fact that Jesus of Nazareth could be intolerant. It is common to consider intolerance uncommendable today, so that there is public disapproval of a man who is intolerant, as if he were entirely wrong. This element in common outlook needs to be challenged. Would it ever be right for a Christian to tolerate sin?

An incident occurred at the very beginning of the public ministry of Jesus of Nazareth, which makes it plain that He would not tolerate any irreverence toward God. At the very outset of His approach to the mind of men, there is this judgment upon any behavior which suggests a lack of reverence. There is no place in the Word of God that one can find a shred of evidence to support any idea that God will look lightly upon anyone who approaches Him carelessly, or even casually.

This truth is clearly demonstrated in the incident reported in John 2:13-25, called the "Cleansing of the Temple." Here Jesus made it plain that the deepest honor, respect, and reverence for God, His Father is His due. The account tells the circumstances: "And the Jews' passover was at hand . . ." (John 2:13). Because this was the time of the Passover it was to be expected that Jerusalem, where Jesus was going, was filled with people. Large crowds were everywhere, and Jesus went in with them to the temple. In the temple were those that sold oxen and sheep and doves, and here the changers of money were sitting (John 2:13, 14). Strange as this may sound now there were several reasons why this could be. The Temple was not just a single edifice, but a group of buildings, something like a university campus of today. The group of buildings was considered as "The Temple," and the grounds surrounding the buildings were part of the whole complex. In the yard between some of the buildings was a place for keeping the livestock, destined for offerings. Selling sheep, oxen, and doves within this Temple area was more legitimate than it might sound to modern ears. People came to Jerusalem to worship from all over the Mediterranean world. Since sacrifices were a part of the Jewish ceremonies, and pilgrims from afar could not carry their livestock with them over great distances, they had to purchase them. Perhaps some could carry doves, but since only the poorer people offered doves, it usually happened that those who could afford to travel the long distances wished to offer a lamb or a sheep. It was natural, therefore, for them to expect to find suitable animals for the sacrifice, that, in the course of the cleansing ritual, they might offer these creatures for their sin offerings.

It was such animals that Jesus found in the Temple area. Naturally in this buying and selling of animals to be used in sacrifices, the owners of these creatures wanted to make a profit. Alert business practice prompted men to try to get as close to the place of sacrifice as possible so that when worshipers came looking for a suitable offering, these would be at hand. Thus they moved closer and closer, until they were actually using part of the Temple courtyard. It was as if, in the outer area of any church, perhaps in the foyer of the sanctuary, somebody opened a flower shop and began to sell flowers to worshipers who wanted to place flowers in the church in memory of some dear one. The presence of the money changers was also quite natural. Many of these pilgrims came from Arabia and Africa. They brought the currency of their native land. Every traveler in foreign countries knows he must exchange his American bills and coins for the currency of the land in which he wishes to make a purchase. The same situation existed centuries ago in the land of Palestine. Normally there would be a small discount for such an exchange. Money changing became a very profitable business, arousing the same sort of competitive practices that had developed in the selling of the cattle.

When Jesus came into the temple area, and entered the outer court, he found it filled with tradesmen and pilgrims. The buying and selling was brisk. The functions performed by these people were perhaps entirely legitimate, but the circumstances were not right. The salesmen were seeking great gain, profits were high, and no doubt the scene was far from conducive to any spirit of worship.

JESUS REACTS IN ZEAL

John reports about Jesus of Nazareth that

> . . . when he had made a scourge of small cords, he drove them all out of the temple, and the sheep, and the oxen; and poured out the changers' money, and overthrew the tables (John 2:15).

This certainly seems to have been violent action. It may seem strange to readers. Often people cherish a picture of Jesus as a man of gentle mien, gracious and mild. Yet this incident shows Jesus acting with stern insistence! ". . . Take these things hence; make not my Father's house an house of merchandise" (John 2:16).

It is possible that the disciples looked at the scene with amazement as they ". . . remembered that it was written, The zeal of thine house hath eaten me up" (John 2:17).

Is it necessary to think that Jesus lost His temper in this situation? No, not at all. He can be seen as fulfilling the word in Psalm 69:9 and charging these people to think about the holiness, majesty and power of His Father, and their God. There is surely a lesson for all who believe in God and who came to worship Him. In the public worship of God all should be done in humility and sincerity, never for personal advantage.

The spirit in which a man worships, the intention of his actions, qualifies whatever he may do. In the Sunday morning worship service, in Sunday school, in the midweek service, even in the meetings of the boards and organizations of any church, each believer should be asking himself, "Why am I here?" The ultimate answer should always be, to worship God in sincerity, in spirit and in truth; and in that frame of mind to serve Him to the best of ability and talent.

There is one other observation to be made. It is not unusual for some to condemn other Christians for being somewhat excited about their personal faith. Each should examine his own spiritual conduct. Each should ask himself, "Am I ever excited, am I ever aroused to outward expression, am I zealous in my worship of God? Is my spiritual mood worthy of God?" A cool, or even lukewarm attitude is not good enough.

Is it true that people of today feel excitement more than others? The same people who chide Christians for showing fervor of spirit in worship may be found "rooting" for their home team with great zeal and often with a raucous voice. Should excitement over a game (entirely legitimate in itself) be appreciated as proper sentiment, and fervor and zeal in the worship of God be condemned as undesirable?

In the incident John has reported Jesus gave an example of His zeal for the house of God. There are undoubtedly conditions today when those who honor God should express their feelings fervently and with vigor. Believers today may not use the physical means which Jesus employed that day in the temple, but believers should not be lukewarm. There is a sober passage in Revelation 3:15-18 which gives a picture of what the Lord Jesus Christ thinks of the lukewarm servant.

> I know thy works, that thou art neither hot nor cold: I would thou wert cold or hot. So then because thou art lukewarm, and neither cold nor hot, I will spue thee out of my mouth (Revelation 3:15, 16).

When Jesus turned from His work of cleansing the Temple, He found Himself confronted by Jews who asked: ". . . What sign shewest thou unto us, seeing that thou doest these things?" (John 2:18). They did not understand His reply, ". . . Destroy this temple, and in three days I will raise it up" (John 2:19). They knew that the great Temple had been years in the building. But long afterward, His disciples remembered His words and realized that He was speaking of the temple of His body, the temple of the Holy Spirit.

Here again is a lesson for believers. Since God is dwelling within the believer, in the person of the Holy Spirit, everything the Christian does should be done unto the Lord. To treat the body as belonging to any man is, actually, to be profane. That such truth was implied is indicated by the fact that after Jesus had risen from the dead, then His disciples remembered what He had said, ". . . and they believed the scripture, and the word which Jesus had said" (John 2:22). In other words, the resurrection of His body within three days reminded them of this prediction and gave them confidence. And faith in that resurrection of His body, together with confidence that He is even now at the right hand of God the Father interceding for us, produces fruit in the lives of believers as they witness for Him in daily living.

Chapter 4

THE MEANING OF SALVATION

SALVATION (3:1-13)

The third chapter of John's gospel gives the most complete explanation of salvation of any portion of Scripture. To understand it, we must make a visit with Nicodemus.

"There was a man of the Pharisees, named Nicodemus, a ruler of the Jews" (John 3:1). This simple statement has a number of important facts in it. If Nicodemus was a "man of the Pharisees," he was a member of that group of Jews who truly believed in their Scripture. The Pharisees believed the Scripture was God's Word, and they valued and honored it.

It is quite possible that referring to him as a "ruler of the Jews" implies he was a member of the Sanhedrin, and such membership indicates a high rank and standing among his people. This Council was the "Supreme Court" of Jerusalem. Any member was an able respected man in the community.

Nicodemus came to Jesus "by night." Some suggest that this was a cowardly thing to do, and criticize him because he did not come openly. Actually there is oftentimes more courage in quiet sincerity than in noisy approach. It should be remembered that when the time came for Jesus' burial, Joseph of Arimathaea and Nicodemus (called secret disciples) were the two men who buried Him. It does not reflect any great wisdom to judge by the outward appearance in any circumstance of life. I cannot accept the accusation that this man of the Pharisees came in a sort of sneaky fashion. It does not seem necessary to think that he was a furtive man, but rather his actions could show he was cautious and realistic. The night time was probably a time when Jesus was not besieged by hundreds of needy people, and so had time for the interview. Also it could be a mark of his urgent interest that he sought this interview at a time when Jesus was free to spend time in conversation with him. The fact that later Nicodemus did not confess Christ openly because he feared the Jews, could also be a matter of caution, for he knew he stood in danger of stirring up much feeling not only against himself, but also against the teacher whom he wished to question.

Nicodemus' word of greeting shows the life that Christ was living. He called Jesus "Rabbi," which means *teacher*. The use of that title was a mark of Nicodemus' esteem: ". . . Rabbi, we know that thou art a teacher come from God: for no man can do these miracles that thou doest, except God be with him" (John 3:2). Nicodemus did not comment on what Jesus said as a teacher but rather on what He did. He pointed out that no man can do the things Jesus did, without God's presence. This emphasized the fact that the credentials for authority as a teacher are the capacities for actual service! The man who has power to act, the man who gets things done, is the man who should teach, for such characteristics indicate that he has something which teachers should have to help people achieve results. Here is a reason for the miracles which Jesus performed. Any man who could work such miracles must have contact with God Himself.

John does not report that Nicodemus ever put into so many words what he wanted to know. Yet this man came with a question in his heart. John had already stated that Jesus "knew what was in man" (John 2:25), and so no doubt he was able to read the desires and longings of Nicodemus' heart. In any case He began at once to answer the unspoken question.

BEING BORN AGAIN

"Jesus answered and said unto him, Verily, verily, I say unto thee, Except a man be born again, he cannot see the kingdom of God" (John 3:3). Apparently the unspoken question in the heart of this Pharisee was something like: "What kind of person are you talking about? How do you do what you do? How can I become as you are?" Jesus met him right at the door, as it were, and said, in effect: "There is no possible way of entering into this kind of life without being born again."

Nicodemus' reply was the honest attitude of his heart. He ". . . saith unto him, How can a man be born when he is old? can he enter the second time into his mother's womb, and be born?" (John 3:4). This is an honest question in any natural approach to the subject. What does it mean to have a new birth? It is physically impossible for that child, grown to manhood, to enter again into his mother's womb, and be born a second time. This *is* bewildering to any serious mind, oriented only to that which belongs to nature.

The answer of Jesus was simple and without argument. ". . . Verily, verily, I say unto thee, Except a man be born of water and of the Spirit, he cannot enter into the kingdom of God" (John 3:5).

There is in this no condemnation of Nicodemus because he was wrong, no time spent in argument: just a plain, blunt assertion, spoken with authority. First Jesus has said, "be born again," and now He says "born of water and of the Spirit." These two words, *water* and *Spirit,* can be understood here as symbols of two accents in preaching, each legitimate, each having its part to play.

Water refers to the preaching of John the Baptist, who baptized with water. The *Spirit* refers to the preaching and teaching of Jesus of Nazareth, who baptized with the Holy Spirit. The emphasis of John the Baptist was: "Repent!" He spoke about sin, preaching that men should turn away from it with confession. Jesus preached about life in God, calling upon men to believe God and to receive the Holy Spirit.

What Jesus of Nazareth said to Nicodemus means that unless a person responds in repentance and faith he cannot enter into the kingdom of God. The soul must take John's teaching to heart and repent; he must take Christ's teaching to heart and believe what God has promised. Whoever responds in this way will have the indwelling Spirit, the kingdom of God within, a relationship of living obedience to God.

After this plain statement Jesus went on to set forth a general truth by way of explaining what is involved. "That which is born of the flesh is flesh; and that which is born of the Spirit is spirit" (John 3:6). "Flesh" defines the things which can be seen and handled: Spirit encompasses those elements of life which cannot be seen nor handled. Flesh can be sensed, Spirit is believed. When this distinction is recognized, many truths will become plain. The things of this world which you can feel, see, handle — the ordinary procedures of everyday living — are part of reality in human affairs, and are dealt with by the senses. Spiritual matters, which cannot be seen, are understood in faith according to the revelation in the Word of God. They are nonetheless real and are, in fact, much more important.

Following this, Jesus of Nazareth gave to Nicodemus what might almost be regarded as a warning.

> Marvel not that I said unto thee, Ye must be born again. The wind bloweth where it listeth, and thou hearest the sound thereof, but canst not tell whence it cometh, and wither it goeth: so is every one that is born of the Spirit (John 3:7, 8).

This can be very helpful to anyone seeking to understand what has been said. Jesus is explaining why it is so hard for anyone to grasp this aspect of the truth. Spiritual reality cannot be seen, humanly speaking, any more than the wind that blows. Men can never see where it comes from or where it goes, but they accept it as true because they are aware of its effects.

QUESTION OF A SKEPTIC

The next remark of Nicodemus is always the final question of the natural man, when he is confronted with the evidence of the new birth, of a changed life, of a new outlook on the world: "How can it happen?"

Jesus gave a challenging answer:

> . . . and knowest not these things? Verily, verily, I say unto thee, We speak that we do know, and testify that we have seen; and ye receive not our witness. If I have told you earthly things, and ye believe not, how shall ye believe, if I tell you of heavenly things? And no man hath ascended up to heaven, but he that came down from heaven, even the Son of man which is in heaven (John 3:10-13).

Here again it is obvious that Jesus presented no argument. Actually there is no reasoning one's way into the kingdom of God. Either a man comes by faith in response to God's call, or he does not enter. Jesus challenges Nicodemus to consider what he knows. "You are a master of Israel — is it possible you do not understand spiritual values? You *ought* to know, you are familiar with the Scriptures, you know the way God works."

This is the sort of consideration that is valid today: "We speak that we do know, and testify that we have seen; and ye receive not our witness." The Christian church offers evidence to the thousands who daily pass by her buildings, many of whom never come inside to learn the Gospel. It is possible that some churches do not present a significant witness, but this does not change the fact that churches in general bear witness to the reality of God, heaven, and the Gospel. It is commonly known that the Christian message insists on the necessity of the new birth. When Christians in their personal lives show the effect of being born again, their testimony is clear to the whole world.

For God So Loved the World (3:14-17)

Having emphasized that every man must be born again, Jesus now teaches that this is possible through the Son of God. And although Nicodemus did not realize it then, He was speaking of Himself. John 3:16 is one of the most loved and quoted verses in all of the Bible. Little children have memorized this passage and can quote it, even though its real meaning may go far beyond their young minds. However, in learning the words, the form of truth has become a part of their mental storehouse, and as they grow into years of understanding, the Holy Spirit can interpret it. These same words are equally beloved by mature believers almost at the end of their earthly walk. Even when their minds begin to fail, a beloved verse like John 3:16 will linger in their dimming memories to bring joy and consolation until this world passes away, and new life begins with the Lord in the house of many mansions.

While John 3:16 is in itself a wonderful statement it occurs in a larger passage that makes it clear that God will save men through His Son Jesus Christ. The word "saved" is often ignored and apparently even avoided by many who would present the Gospel, but it is a proper New Testament word that has rich meaning. In avoiding that word some will say that men are "reconciled" to God, and this is also wonderfully true! Sometimes it is said men must come into right relationship with God. And this is true. Men should thank God for making possible a way of escape from sin so that they can come to God. But why not use the good word loved by many, and say *saved?*

In concluding this passage John writes: "For God sent not his Son into the world to condemn the world; but that the world through him might be saved" (John 3:17). "Saved" is a New Testament word, and every Christian could be using it daily, in his communion with God, with thanks for this gift of grace. Salvation is *God's* work; man "is saved" on account of Jesus Christ. And for all that is done by the operation of Jesus Christ in any individual heart, it will always be proper to use this word, *saved.*

Saved is rich in meaning. One idea included in it is *salvage,* as from a shipwreck. Men are adrift, helpless and hopeless, until the outstretched hand of the Saviour has salvaged them from total loss, bringing them to eternal safety.

The dictionary defines *saved*: "to preserve by care." Here is another word picture of the blessed truth. The Saviour does indeed preserve the whole person. Paul knew this, as he wrote in I Thessalonians 5:23, ". . . I pray God your whole spirit and soul and body be preserved blameless unto the coming of our Lord Jesus Christ."

The dictionary also gives a few other aspects of the truth of the Gospel in its definitions of this word *saved;* namely, "to deliver from the punishment and power of sin, or from spiritual death." It is also possible to add an "l" making out of "saved" the word "salved" in which the healing aspect is noted. The Psalmist wrote, "Bless the Lord, O my soul, . . . who healeth all thy diseases" (Psalm 103:2, 3). The adding of the letter "l" is not far fetched, for the word *salvation* contains it!

Salvation is a wonderful word for Christians; it is at least as important a word as *creation.* Actually, *salvation* in some respects is bigger — it involves far more! God is the Creator of the physical world in which men live. God is also the Saviour of the world, especially the spiritual world. So when He effected salvation, He did something which was as great as creation, but more permanent.

This need never be a complicated matter. Jesus stated it plainly and simply to Nicodemus. The Bible always keeps it clear: "He that hath the Son hath life; and he that hath not the Son of God hath not life" (I John 5:12).

THE SON MUST BE LIFTED UP

Jesus was setting this truth before Nicodemus when He said, "And as Moses lifted up the serpent in the wilderness, even so must the Son of man be lifted up: That whosoever believeth in him should not perish, but have eternal life" (John 3:14, 15). Jesus was recalling an incident from His Old Testament, Numbers 21:4-9: "And they journeyed from mount Hor by the way of the Red sea, to compass the land of Edom: and the soul of the people was much discouraged because of the way." It was quite natural that the people became downhearted and discouraged because of the road they were following. No doubt it was a long and tedious journey and the people felt worn out.

"And the people spake against God, and against Moses. . . ." They complained about God, because His providence allowed this, and they found fault with Moses, because he was leading them in this hard and wearying way.

> . . . Wherefore have ye brought us up out of Egypt to die in the wilderness? for there is no bread, neither is there any water; . . . And the Lord sent fiery serpents among the people, and they bit the people; and much people of Israel died.

The *fiery serpents* were sent in chastisement. The judgment of God was upon the people for their wayward hearts. The result under God was actually glorious.

> Therefore the people came to Moses, and said, We have sinned, for we have spoken against the Lord, and against thee; pray unto the Lord, that he take away the serpents from us. And Moses prayed for the people. And the Lord said unto Moses, Make thee a fiery serpent, and set it up upon a pole: and it shall come to pass, that every one that is bitten, when he looketh upon it, shall live. And Moses made a serpent of brass, and put it upon a pole, and it came to pass, that if a serpent had bitten any man, when he beheld the serpent of brass, he lived.

In itself this is a simple story. Yet it is dramatic and teaches something very profound. Because of their wilful complaining the people found themselves in a state of peril. Then, by the grace of God and under His direction, Moses set before them an opportunity for life instead of death. A serpent of brass was made and put high on a pole. When an Israelite was bitten by one of the living serpents and was doomed to die because of the poison in its bite, he only needed to look at this brass serpent lifted upon that pole in the center of the camp, and he lived.

Jesus lifted this incident out of its Old Testament setting and applied it here to salvation. The Bible makes it clear that "the wages of sin is death," but it is also true that "the gift of God is eternal life through Jesus Christ our Lord" (Romans 6:23). Here Jesus uses this Old Testament illustration to teach that even if a man is truly dead in sin, facing separation from God through all the endless ages of eternity, he can repent and believe — lift up his eyes to the Saviour on the cross, believing in the atonement attained there for our redemption — and thus be saved.

THE OFFER OF SALVATION (3:18-21)

The world in which we live has certain fixed patterns, which cannot be changed, and under which men live day by day. In this universe there is a sun which rises each morning, shines during the day, and sets at night. That sun shines without the consent or approval of man, altogether apart from human judgment, or man's total understanding as to how it maintains its place in its heavenly orbit. A man may see good in it, he may think its glow and warmth worthwhile. On the other hand, he may think it is far too hot, or so bright it hurts his eyes. The man may complain that there is no heat in the sun at all on a cold, stormy, snowy January morning. Will any of his opinions make any difference to the sun? Not one particle! If the man has any intelligence at all, he will adjust his physical life to the ways of the sun: dress warmly when needed, wear light-weight clothing when the sun's rays are uncomfortably hot; because this is the only world he knows, and in this world is the sun which man cannot alter or remove. A similar situation exists in spiritual things.

Can any human being evade Jesus Christ? Can any man put out of his life the knowledge that one day he will have to account for his attitude to the Son of God? It is not possible for any man or woman to evade Jesus Christ. In the Gospel, God Himself, the Almighty One, confronts the soul of man with outstretched hand.

If two persons meet on the street, and one reaches out to shake the hand of the other, such conduct will be recognized at once as a friendly greeting, not to be ignored. That is very much the way the Gospel of the Lord Jesus Christ is presented to the soul of men. God comes with hand outstretched, and the man who turns around and walks away from God is turning his back on the greatest thing in the world, the gift of God, eternal life through Jesus Christ. No man should "play games" with his conscience about this. Any man who turns his back on God must expect to take the consequences, and it is he who is responsible for the inevitable consequences, not God. The man who ignores God, rejects Jesus Christ, is actually turning his back on the most gracious offer ever made to a human being — eternal life, joy and peace in his soul now, and blessing in the world to come.

A man does not ask to be born: he does not ask for the parents who give him many of his human characteristics. He has no choice as to his physical makeup or his personality. All of this was in God's plan for him when he was conceived and born. But he is a human being, with body, mind, conscience, spirit. There is no one else exactly like him with his own will to do as he likes. That will is the gift of God to him, and he is able to choose wrong or right, evil or good, according to his own preference. And that will entails a responsibility.

To use the language of the college campus, consideration of the claims of Jesus Christ is not an elective course. No man can take it or leave it as he pleases. It is required of him that he choose, and there is no way to avoid that responsibility.

There is much in the Christian Gospel a man may never understand until he reaches heaven. But even a child can understand this simple matter of accepting or rejecting Jesus Christ.

God is welcoming us into His family by the Gospel. It does not make any difference who or what the sinner is, God comes to him in the person of Jesus Christ, reaches out arms of love, and calls him to Himself. Nobody who hears can escape the responsibility of his answer to this call.

John expresses it very simply:

> He that believeth on him is not condemned: but he that believeth not is condemned already, because he hath not believed in the name of the only begotten Son of God. And this is the condemnation, that light is come into the world, and men loved darkness rather than light, because their deeds were evil (John 3:18, 19).

MAN'S PART

This is a categoric statement. This does not allow any neutral ground, no area for uncertainty. He that believeth is not condemned, he that believeth not is condemned already — two statements that cannot be misunderstood.

If a man enters an office building, and wants to reach the eighteenth floor, he gets into an elevator. He pushes the right button, and the car will ascend. But if he does not get into the elevator, he will remain exactly where he is. One other fact is also clear: he cannot be half in and half out. If the man is in the elevator, he can go up; if he stays out, he cannot go up. There is no middle ground. This principle is true on the spiritual plane. When a man accepts Christ, he is saved; when he rejects Him, he is lost.

It is important to remember that a man is not condemned because he fails to accept Christ. He is already condemned in the sight of God. There is no such thing as any person coming before God with a clear record, a stainless heart. Every man is a sinner, and is already condemned. From the man who believes in the Lord Jesus Christ is lifted the already-existing condemnation; the man who rejects finds the penalty of sin still there. God is just: God hates sin; but God does not hate the sinner. In His great love and mercy, He has prepared a way out of the condemnation which rests upon the human race. The acceptance of this way is within the prerogative of the individual soul.

Why would any man remain under condemnation? John offers an explanation in 3:19, 20:

> And this is the condemnation, that light is come into the world, and men loved darkness rather than light, because their deeds were evil. For every one that doeth evil hateth the light, neither cometh to the light, lest his deeds should be reproved.

It may be noted that sinful man does not love darkness rather than light because darkness in some ways is nicer to experience. That is not the reason given by John. The simple truth of this matter is that a man who is doing what is wrong does not want the light to shine upon his deeds. Everywhere in the world men commit evil at night when the eyes of other men cannot easily see them. The man who habitually practices evil does not want the light. On the other hand, the man whose life and character reflect honesty, truth, and sincerity, is perfectly willing to have his work stand the test of the bright light of God. In fact, he loves the light and revels in it.

If someone reads this book who has not made the decision to accept Christ, he would do well to remember that there is really only one question for him to answer: not who wrote the Bible, or what God is going to do with the heathen. Is he honest? Has he reached the point where he is willing to be open and aboveboard with God, to forsake the darkness, and to seek the light? Is he willing to come into the presence of a holy God, sinner that he is, and confess his sin. Is he willing to accept forgiveness and cleansing by the atonement of Jesus Christ? One fact can be known to anyone: God is waiting for him to come. It is the glory of the Gospel to let the world know that God is ". . . not willing that any should perish, but that all should come to repentance" (II Peter 3:9).

GROWTH OF A CHRISTIAN (3:22-30)

". . . Believe on the Lord Jesus Christ, and thou shalt be saved . . ." (Acts 16:31) is a good summation of the truth set out thus far in this gospel of John. This is a good beginning, but what next? When one plants seeds in the spring, he expects to wait for a given time before he will look for signs of growth, but growth will come. That is the law of nature, and therefore, the law of God. When a baby comes into the world, his mother and father can realize infinite possibilities wrapped up in that little body and mind. Normal growth and development can give real joy to all who behold it.

Christian growth has some elements which might not be expected. When I was a young Christian, it took me some time to realize that to grow deeper in my personal relationship with my Lord and Saviour I needed to grow down, rather than up. The higher I might long to grow in grace, the lower my heart must be in submission to the source of all grace and strength, the Lord Himself. I can still remember the relief it was when I finally realized that I did not need to stand on tiptoe, stretching to make myself taller than I was that I might be well pleasing in the sight of God! I learned that I could settle down on my heels, so to speak, and walk normally. He would lift me in His grace according to His blessed will, and cause me to grow in spiritual matters. No one needs to make any mistakes here. There must be no relaxation of utter dependence upon God, no neglect in studying His Word, or in praying and in looking to Him for His guidance. The secret of the matter is the touch of God's hand upon the believer, not the strength of the believer in trying to pull himself up into His will.

THE EXAMPLE OF JOHN

In the third chapter of John, there is a good illustration of this principle of Christian growth. John the Baptist had been both preaching and baptizing the people who had come in response to his message. Apparently he stirred up some controversy through his messages.

> Then there arose a question between some of John's disciples and the Jews about purifying. And they came unto John, and said unto him, Rabbi, he that was with thee beyond Jordan, to whom thou barest witness, behold, the same baptizeth, and all men come to him (John 3:25, 26).

This indicates an atmosphere, not of quiet listening to the truth as John proclaimed it, but of heated argument.

So often people say more than is true, and sometimes what is entirely false, in order to win an argument. This seems to have happened with the Jews. They seemed to be needling John! They were intimating to him that Jesus was having a much larger crowd to hear His preaching. It may well be these men were trying to arouse John to some expression of anger or jealousy. John, however, had been filled with the Holy Spirit from his birth and thus his communion with God was very real and deep. He had already learned much about spiritual growth. "John answered and said, A man can receive nothing, except it be given him from heaven" (John 3:27). This is the classic reply to such criticism! He is implying: "If I have something that counts for anything I will know it came from God. In everything I have I will look to the Lord, who gave it to me, and remember it all belongs to Him." Could there be a better response?

John then goes on and illustrates more clearly his meaning, setting forth for all time a true picture of exalting Christ and seeking to glorify Him.

> Ye yourselves bear me witness, that I said, I am not the Christ,
> but that I am sent before him. He that hath the bride is the
> bridegroom: but the friend of the bridegroom, which standeth
> and heareth him, rejoiceth greatly because of the bridegroom's
> voice: this my joy therefore is fulfilled. He must increase, but I
> must decrease (John 3:28-30).

John affirms that he never considered himself of special importance.
He uses the illustration of a wedding to prove his point. No one
expects the best man to shine in a wedding, he says. He is only inci-
dental to the occasion. There is only one person who is entering into
the important covenant of marriage with a bride, the bridegroom, and
no one is jealous of his prominence.

John goes even further. Instead of feeling neglected, ignored, or
given second place, John says he rejoices: he is truly glad for the
bridegroom. He acts as if he were saying about Jesus, "He is my
friend, and I am His friend. I am glad that He is advancing in the
esteem and estimation of the people."

In verse 30 the principle of Christian growth is stated in a very
terse and yet complete sentence. Seven words express the whole matter: "He must increase, but I must decrease." If anyone were ever to
ask the question about the substance of a believer's growth, John
has given the answer, so clearly, so positively that it hardly needs
further exposition. As the believer grows, he humbles himself. Just
as surely as his heart is truly humble in the sight of God, the believer
will surely be lifted up.

The temptation which John faced comes to many believers today,
the subtle suggestion that one should seek personal gain, that he
should take the opportunity to be more popular than other Christians.
It comes to preachers, teachers, women in their homes and men in
their offices. But God's grace can enable the Christian to do as John
did, when he reminded the people how he had told them of his position many times: "I am the voice in the wilderness, the herald, not
worthy to tie up his shoelace." Thus the Christian can give witness
to the grace of God, testifying that he is a believer in Jesus Christ,
seeking only to glorify Him in all that is done, seeking only to tell
others about Him, and to point them to the Lamb of God, who takes
away the sin of the world.

GROWTH AS A PRINCIPLE

This is the basic principle in Christian experience which never
changes. As a believer, the Christian invites Christ to live in his
heart and needs to be conscious of that fact at all times that he
may be able to "practice the presence of God" in each moment of his
daily life. Christ is always with the believer, His strength is always
available, and because of this it is possible to say "He must increase,

but I must decrease." The Christian will strive to maintain less and less of his own will as he seeks to follow in the way Christ is leading until the Lord's hand becomes more and more obvious in his life, and people will know he is serving Him. Then those that see the Christian will not glorify or praise him, but will say to themselves, "Whatever he has, I want, for it gives him peace of mind and heart, and enables him to stand up under the pressure and the persecution of the world around him."

This progressive surrender in spirit to the guidance of the indwelling Christ is the very essence of growth as a Christian. And the fact is that the initial surrender begins a circle of joy, more complete surrender, and greater joy! There is a beautiful old hymn by Monod which progresses, verse by verse, through the stages of Christian growth, ending each verse with a phrase denoting that progress. "Some of self, and some of Thee." "Less of self, and more of Thee." And finally, "None of self, and all of Thee."

THE UNIQUENESS OF JESUS (3:31-36)

In his gospel narrative John presents Jesus Christ as the One whom God has sent to seek and to save the lost. It is a matter of history that men have tried to offer other ways of access to God, but John is very clear that this is the only way. No doubt this sounds exclusive to a multitude of people outside of Christ, but the call of the Gospel is worldwide: "whosoever believeth" is universal. Whatever exclusion there may be in actuality is made by man himself. The truth is set forth very plainly by Jesus Himself. ". . , I am the way, the truth, and the life: no man cometh unto the Father, but by me" (John 14:6).

There is agreement throughout the Scripture. There is one Bethlehem story, not many; there is one Lamb of God, not several. When God spoke from heaven, He did not say, "This is one of my beloved sons." He affirmed, ". . . This is my beloved Son, in whom I am well pleased" (Matthew 3:17). Three men died on crosses on Calvary, but only one was the Saviour of the world, and ". . . when he had by himself purged our sins, sat down on the right hand of the Majesty on high" (Hebrews 1:3). God has limited Himself to one avenue of approach through His beloved Son.

"WHAT NAIL ARE YOU HANGING ON?"

Many years ago I met a young student from Occidental College in California and conversed with him about the Gospel of Christ. He caught the fact that I was relating all things to the Lord Jesus. Finally he said to me, "It seems to me that your whole witness and testimony is on very shaky foundations, your outlook is very limited."

So I asked him simply, "What is so uncertain about it?"

"Well," he replied, "you are putting everything you trust in one person, Jesus Christ. Suppose Jesus of Nazareth just isn't true, what then? It's a good deal as if you had one nail in a wall, and you were hanging all you valued on that one nail. You are putting everything, including yourself, into one great sack, and hanging yourself by that one nail on the wall. If the nail were to break, what would happen to you?"

Without hesitation I said, "If it breaks, I'm lost."

"Exactly," he replied, with an air of having cornered me very easily.

"But if the nail doesn't break," I asked, "What then?"

"Well, according to your belief, you would be saved."

At that point I asked him, "Now what nail are you hanging on?" Then I began to point out to him some of the facts concerning our Lord, reminding him that it is the nail that matters just as in his own illustration. The Gospel is one Gospel, salvation by faith in one Lord Jesus, who came into this world at one time, to seek and to save the lost.

> He that cometh from above is above all: he that is of the earth
> is earthly, and speaketh of the earth: he that cometh from heaven
> is above all (John 3:31).

Thus John is emphasizing that the Lord Jesus Christ is different from all others. He is the only One who has come from above. All other teachers are of the earth. They are earthy, sinful, thinking and planning according to their human nature, speaking according to their limited human understanding, expressing their ideas in the language of the world in which they live. But the One who comes from heaven is different.

> And what he hath seen and heard, that he testifieth; and no
> man receiveth his testimony (John 3:32).

This sounds like what John wrote earlier. "He came unto his own, and his own received him not" (John 1:11). Jesus of Nazareth testified to the Father's love, but men did not believe His witness.

This is often seen at the Christmas season. People sing carols, attend pagents, and give Christmas parties, spending much money for cards and gifts, ostensibly in the name of the Christ child, but their hearts are far from Him, and their lives do not glorify Him. They do not receive His testimony, enjoying only the gay and jolly atmosphere of the holiday season. It seems a strange thing that people find it so difficult to believe, and yet — is it? Paul gives an explanation in II Corinthians 4:3, 4:

> But if our gospel be hid, it is hid to them that are lost: In whom
> the god of this world hath blinded the minds of them which be-
> lieve not, lest the light of the glorious gospel of Christ, who is the
> image of God, should shine upon them.

John brings out another important factor here:

> He that hath received his testimony hath set to his seal that God is true (John 3:33).

This points out that believing in Jesus Christ means also true belief in God the Father.

> For he whom God hath sent speaketh the words of God: for God giveth not the Spirit by measure unto him. The Father loveth the Son, and hath given all things into his hand (John 3:34, 35).

Nothing could more clearly declare the fact that power and authority belong to Jesus of Nazareth. There was the ring of authority in all He said and did.

Another thought is conveyed in verse 35, with its expression of the deep love of the Father for the Son. This may well reflect the heavenly part of the incarnation. The Father gave all things into the hand of the Son, that the Son might glorify Him by working out the Father's redemptive purpose in the world.

John tells that the Father gave power to the Son to administer all things because He loved the Son. This was all in the sovereign plan of God, and no reasons are advanced as to why this should be so. John simply states the sovereign will of God without question or without comment.

The last verse of this blessed chapter again brings to the foreground the redemptive work of Christ.

> He that believeth on the Son hath everlasting life: and he that believeth not the Son shall not see life; but the wrath of God abideth on him (John 3:36).

This is not saying that the wrath of God is in response to this one action. It does not mean that God is so offended by the failure of a man to accept His Son that He suddenly decides to destroy that soul. God is just and righteous and hates sin. If a man refuses this forgiveness and cleansing, the man is destroying himself. The wrath of God must rest upon him, for it has always been upon sin wherever it is found. That is the reason for Calvary. God has provided the way out.

Chapter 5

JESUS AND THE WOMAN AT THE WELL

THE WAY TO LIFE (4:1-26)

Over the whole world today the chief desire of men and women seems to be to gain whatever they can for themselves. When men become prosperous, they crave yet more prosperity. Our favorite sport is a race between neighbors to get more things than the other. Women long for all of the latest labor-saving gadgets in their kitchens. The emphasis is on "things, things, things," and never on the spiritual welfare of the people in the home or in the neighborhood. A man is considered successful if he has triumphed over his rivals and is at the head of his trade or profession.

It is obvious that pride and selfishness lie at the root of all this, and so it is very natural to man. But how dangerous that it should be one of the chief characteristics of this day and age!

This is not the way of God; this is not in the Gospel of Jesus Christ. The loving Heavenly Father does not wish this straining after possessions for His children, especially those in Christ Jesus. Of course men and women are not His children until they have come to Him in the way He has appointed through Jesus Christ. But, caught up in this other search, how few people seek that way today! Men seek what they want, yet often, when they achieve what they consider life's supreme goal, they are unhappy, dissatisfied, and feel a deep inner longing for something else, not knowing it is because they have not found God.

However, the Good Shepherd is always seeking His lost sheep. This is a wonderful truth that brings the Gospel so close to our hearts. A soul does not need to enter a church building to be found by God. This fact is evident in the confrontation between Jesus and the Samaritan woman.

JESUS MEETS THE WOMAN

When therefore the Lord knew how the Pharisees had heard that Jesus made and baptized more disciples than John, (Though Jesus himself baptized not, but his disciples,) He left Judaea, and departed again into Galilee (John 4:1-3).

Jesus left the area in which He was preaching because He did not want attention redirected from John the Baptist to Himself. John had lived out Christlikeness when he had earlier said: "He must increase, but I must decrease." But the Lord must have known also that a woman in Samaria was confused and hurt by her own sins, and was ready to be freed from them. So He sought her out, traveling from Judaea to Galilee by way of Samaria.

Although it could not be avoided on a direct route between the two areas of Palestine, Samaria was not a place Jews relished going. Students of Bible history know that the Jews despised the Jews-mongrelized-by-intermarriage-with-the-surrounding-peoples, called the Samaritans, who lived within their borders.

But even in Samaria, tired travelers must rest and eat, so:

> Then cometh he to a city of Samaria, which is called Sychar, near to the parcel of ground that Jacob gave to his son Joseph. Now Jacob's well was there. Jesus therefore, being wearied with his journey, sat thus on the well: and it was about the sixth hour (John 4:5, 6).

"The sixth hour" is noontime, when the sun is high. Jesus was tired from walking, and this spot, Jacob's well, was a usual place for travelers to rest for a little while. His stopping there seems just an ordinary situation.

"There cometh a woman of Samaria to draw water . . ." This again was the routine daily task of the women of the village.

John next reports that the ordinary became extraordinary:

> . . . Jesus saith unto her [a Samaritan woman], Give me to drink. (For his disciples were gone away into the city to buy meat) (John 4:7, 8).

It was not customary for a stranger to ask a woman for any favor or service. The fact that Jesus was alone with the woman made the situation more unusual. The woman realized that the circumstances were uncommon, and her reply indicated this:

> Then saith the woman of Samaria unto him, How is it that thou, being a Jew, askest drink of me, which am a woman of Samaria? for the Jews have no dealings with the Samaritans. Jesus answered and said unto her, If thou knewest the gift of God, and who it is that saith to thee, Give me to drink; thou wouldest have asked of him, and he would have given thee living water (John 4:9, 10).

LIVING WATER

When Jesus spoke of "living water" He was referring to *running water,* running from a fountain, bubbling up, as if from an artesian well. Evidently the woman was curious as to why He should ask this of her.

She told Him He had nothing with which to draw up the water, and pointed out ". . . and the well is deep: from whence then hast thou that living [flowing] water?" (verse 11). Skepticism shows in every word, and she may even have felt sarcastic when she questioned still further, "Art thou greater than our father Jacob, which gave us the well, and drank thereof himself . . . ?" (verse 12). This does not seem to be a courteous reception, for she is practically saying, "Who do you think you are?"

The whole encounter was unusual, and one need not be surprised at her reaction to such words from a stranger, of whom she knew nothing. Jesus did not answer her questions directly, but neither did he rebuke her. He lifted the conversation to a higher level, when He said:

> . . . Whosoever drinketh of this water shall thirst again: But whosoever drinketh of the water that I shall give him shall never thirst; but the water that I shall give him shall be in him a well of water springing up into everlasting life. The woman saith unto him, Sir, give me this water, that I thirst not, neither come hither to draw (John 4:13-15).

Any distrust she felt was removed when she realized He was offering something she did not expect. In fact, she probably did not expect Him to do anything for her. The use of the word *Sir* indicated the beginning of a change in her attitude. She realized that this was no ordinary wayfarer. She asked Him for this water of which He had spoken. There is much to learn here of an effective way to deal with a sinful, hardened soul. There must be no anger at any discourtesy. We must draw the conversation to a point where it will be possible to offer something. In this manner something of the love of God may shine through into a sinful heart.

But further surprises awaited this woman at the well. She soon found out that Jesus knew much about her. When He told her to go and bring her husband, she replied that she had no husband. Then Jesus revealed to her that He knew of her sinful state. But she was not willing to discuss her own affairs with Him. Judging Him to be a religious person, she changed the subject to a religious controversy, trying to draw His attention to the differences which existed between Jews and Samaritans concerning the right place and form of worship. By bringing up one of the biggest arguments of that day, she seemed to want to distract this stranger from that which was so personal to herself.

Christ did not become entangled in any such argument; instead He made the brief, clear statement that "God is a Spirit: and they that worship him must worship him in spirit and in truth" (verse 24). We can avoid much controversy in our witnessing by remembering that ". . . man looketh on the outward appearance, but the LORD looketh on the heart" (I Samuel 16:7). It should help to keep us from getting involved in the external distractions.

The woman then told Jesus she believed in the coming of the Messiah who would reveal the truth about everything. He answered in one short sentence which conveyed all that is to be said about Him: ". . . I that speak unto thee am he" (verse 26). It is an amazing thing that Jesus who seldom identified Himself as the Christ to anyone, did it here to this poor and sinful woman of the Samaritan community. He did not reveal this at the beginning of their conversation while she was still skeptical, but rather He revealed Himself at the end, when He had brought her face to face with the fact that she was a sinner who needed the living water which so aroused her curiosity in the first place.

This incident is a pattern for all who would try to lead men and women to Jesus Christ. No doubt the Spirit of God may work instantly and a heart may respond at once. But often there can be curiosity, scepticism, or even downright antagonism to be overcome. As guided by the Spirit, it may be someone's joy and privilege to lead those who are honest gently, but firmly, to the place where they can recognize their need. Then it will be possible to present Jesus Christ as Saviour and Lord.

THE RESULTING WITNESS (4:27-38)

When the disciples returned and saw Jesus sitting at the side of the well conversing with the strange woman they did not ask for an explanation of His unusual conduct. This suggests both that He had acted independently of social tradition before, and also that they had full confidence in His wisdom and judgment. They "marvelled" at His conduct but not one questioned Him.

John does not offer any explanation but goes on to tell how

> The woman then left her waterpot, and went her way into the city, and saith unto the men, Come, see a man, which told me all things that ever I did: Is not this the Christ? Then they went out of the city, and came unto him (John 4:28-30).

Testimony of blessing received from Jesus Christ is always a matter of real importance. The Scriptures say, "Let the redeemed of the LORD say so, whom he hath redeemed from the hand of the enemy" (Psalm 107:2). Christians are to be witnesses unto Him. This whole matter of telling people what the Lord has done for a soul is far more important than many realize. It is good for the believer to tell, and it is good for others to hear, when the telling is to the praise of God. Some testimonies seem to be merely a parading of one's own works, or a glorification of self. Certainly this is of no help to anyone. Nor is it any sign of spiritual depth and maturity to testify of former sins with an apologetic note in your voice, along the line that you "hope to do better." A testimony should be a simple, factual report of what *God* has done for you: nothing more, nothing less, always given in a spirit of true humility. The glory belongs to God, and no merit should be given to the person who has been blessed.

PERSONAL TESTIMONY

Recently a man told how he had been led to accept Jesus Christ. He had gone to a well known church, and had listened to a very fine preacher. When the invitation was given, he did feel the call of God, but said to himself, "Well, not tonight: another time, not now. I do not feel in the mood for such a step just at this moment." He was leaving the church that night in the same condition in which he entered, except that perhaps his refusal would make the next refusal even easier.

Just as he was leaving the church, he met a friend who invited him to come to the home of another member for a short time. There was to be a meeting just for men, and this visitor wondered what on earth a group of churchmen would be doing in such a meeting after an evening service in a church. He was curious, and so he went along. When they reached the home, a group of some twenty-five men were gathered in the large living room. Here he was introduced to the host, and took his seat. The host took charge of the gathering. He said, "Tonight we are going to spend our time in telling what the Lord has done for us in answer to prayer. But there is one condition. Each one of you is to tell what God has done for you in the last twenty-four hours. Anything older than that is out of date for this meeting."

There was a few moments of silence, as if each man was communicating in his heart with the Lord. The visitor thought to himself, "Well, well, this will never come to pass. They are all waiting because they cannot fulfil that requirement. In the first place," his thoughts ran on, "you should never ask men to speak in public about these things: they will be embarrassed. Men won't tell about what the Lord has done, if He ever has done anything for them, and certainly not within twenty-four hours." But even as he was thinking and growing embarrassed himself, a man arose and with glowing face, began to tell of an answer to prayer. And then another and another, sometimes two or three beginning to speak at once. The visitor's amazement grew as this went on for an hour and a half. The sheer weight of this personal testimony was used by the Spirit to break through the visitor's scepticism and reservations. The reality of the Gospel became clear and he was able to personally believe in Jesus Christ and accept Him as his Saviour. He always says that he had not been won, and might never have been won at a church service, listening to a preacher. But when he was in that home, with a group of men telling of what the

Lord had done for them, he could not resist the weight of evidence and so was led to God.

Thus does the Holy Spirit lead in winning people to Christ. One never knows when testifying to his salvation, to answered prayer, to some fresh evidence of the love of God and of grace poured out in his life or upon his family, will have a favorable effect upon a listener. No doubt many have been stirred by that song now so well known.

> It is no secret, what God can do;
> What He's done for others, He'll do for you.
> With arms wide open, He'll welcome you.
> It is no secret, what God can do.

All of this illustrates what happened in the heart of that Samaritan woman as she ran back to her village crying, "Is not this the Christ?"

"I Have Meat"

After she had left the well, the disciples offered Jesus some food, and began to learn more about Him than they had known. Apparently the disciples were reverent in the Lord's presence. They did not rush in with questions of why, what, and how. Here is excellent guidance for Bible study: spend plenty of time with the Word, and wait for the Lord to speak to you as you listen.

When He refused their food, they said among themselves, ". . . Hath any man brought him ought to eat?" (verse 33). They had urged Him, but His reply confused them, when He said, ". . . I have meat to eat that ye know not of." Then He explained to them just what He meant:

> . . . My meat is to do the will of him that sent me, and to finish his work. Say not ye, There are yet four months, and then cometh harvest? behold, I say unto you, Lift up your eyes and look on the fields; for they are white already to harvest (John 4: 34, 35).

It is possible that as Jesus was saying this, he may have been looking at the men of Sychar approaching across the fields. They were coming at the bidding of the woman to hear Him. Here again is a very real application for today. There is never a time when there is not a "white field" in which to work the will of God in telling others about Him. Jesus laid down another principle about soul winning here:

> And he that reapeth receiveth wages, and gathereth fruit unto life eternal: that both he that soweth and he that reapeth may rejoice together. And herein is that saying true, One soweth and another reapeth (John 4:36, 37).

This is a great fact in the work of God in winning souls. "The fields are white unto the harvest . . ." Why? Because other men have sown the seed.

All who travel about preaching the Word know this to be true. Why is any soul seeking, ready, waiting, eager to accept? Because someone else, maybe a faithful mother in the home, perhaps a Sunday school teacher long years ago, or a pastor when that person first joined a church, sowed the seed! Whenever anyone asked to come to church or Sunday school does so willingly, one can be reasonably sure the Holy Spirit is working on some sown seed, buried deep in his heart.

This explains what is a common occurrence when an evangelist plans to hold meetings; he pleads with the Christians in that area to pray *before* he comes. He knows that much of the work of reaching the lost will be done before he arrives. It can be his joy to reap where others have sown. If others have been praying — and working — he knows he is entering into a situation where God has been preparing the way. John points out that the person who sowed that precious seed will receive blessing in the reaping, even though another does it. This is a case of each being ". . . his workmanship, created in Christ Jesus unto good works, which God hath before ordained that we should walk in them" (Ephesians 2:10).

This principle is true in so many ways. When praying is done for others, God is already working in their hearts. When someone is in need, God may already have given someone else the necessary resources to alleviate that need. The missionary goes out to the foreign field, and the believer has been blessed at home so he can support that missionary by prayers and gifts. Thus the harvest can be reaped, and the work of the Lord can be done.

SHARING (4:39-42)

Recently, when passing through a town, I stopped late at night at a filling station to buy some gas. When I pulled up at the pump and stepped out of my car, I left lying on the front seat of the car a folder marked in rather large letters, THE BIBLE FOR YOU, INC. It was a pamphlet I was using in connection with my radio program. The station attendant happened to glance into the car and saw the folder. He said, "The Bible for you?".

I replied, "Yes, sir." and began to tell him about my radio program.

The garage man said, "You mean at 11:45 each morning," making a statement, not asking a question.

"Do you listen?", I asked.

He replied, "Right along," and, reaching into his pocket, pulled out a New Testament. Holding it up before my eyes he said, "The Bible for you, right?"

Can you understand how deeply I was warmed and cheered? Now I knew I was in the presence of a fellow Christian. It made me feel warm all over to think that I was dealing with a Christian brother.

Something like this happened with the woman of Samaria. Her warmth was contagious.

> And many of the Samaritans of that city believed on him for the saying of the woman, which testified, He told me all that ever I did. So when the Samaritans were come unto him, they besought him that he would tarry with them: and he abode there two days (John 4:39, 40).

The woman's testimony was so clear and convincing that many believed on Him. Then the people begged Jesus to remain for a time, and He spent fourty-eight hours in their midst, sharing Himself with them. This resulted in even more persons becoming believers. "And many more believed because of his own word" (verse 41).

This is the sort of thing that can happen today. I am well aware of the fact that you cannot invite Jesus Christ to come, in the flesh, into your home or community. He is not in this world in His flesh now. But as Christians, we have the Holy Spirit and we have our Bibles. Your Bible is the written Word of God, as Jesus was, as John declared, the living Word of God. Just as they asked him to stay in the little town of Sychar, a person can open his Bible today and be in the very presence of the Lord Himself. It was true then: "Many more believed because of His own word;" even so it can be true today.

> And [they] said unto the woman, Now we believe, not because of thy saying: for we have heard him ourselves, and know that this is indeed the Christ, the Saviour of the world (John 4:42).

There is a deeper kind of conviction that comes to the person who reads and studies the Bible. It is a wonderful thing to have a believing preacher point you to the Lamb of God. It is also a wonderful thing to be in fellowship with other Christian people, all of whom truly believe in Jesus Christ and who witness for Him. But when this person opens the Scriptures and begins to read the Bible, he is listening to the Lord Himself, who will talk to him personally. Thus this person can come to believe in Christ because He has shown some blessed truth concerning Himself out of His Word.

This is a common experience. As believers are regular in their reading and study of the Bible, they come to know Him more and more. Many a person is able to say, "Now I believe, not because of the sayings of other people, for I do not have to depend entirely upon that. I have heard Him as I have read the Word of God; I know that this is indeed the Christ."

There is a special blessing from God upon Bible reading and Bible study. It would be wise for every Christian to join with others, of like faith, in earnest and regular Bible study. In this way faith is developed and joy through understanding is increased, because in the written

Word of God the soul hears the voice of the Lord and learns the promises of God.

GROWTH THROUGH PRAYER (4:43-54)

The growth of faith in the heart and life of a Christian is even more wonderful than the growth of a baby. Faith in Jesus Christ will grow through knowing and obeying His will. It is just as simple as that. After the new birth, faith in Jesus Christ can grow as the believing soul receives Christ's promises as true, and prays and receives answers to prayer. No doubt many believers are held back because they pray so little. Some people seem to feel that prayer should be used only when facing a desperate emergency. It is a wonderful thing to be able to pray when a man faces sudden peril or temptation! But it is even more astonishing and encouraging that one can pray to God in every situation. It is wonderful to see that faith will grow as the answers come.

Toward the end of chapter four there is another kind of faith-generating situation. In the story of the nobleman and his son, we learn that faith can be grounded in an answer to prayer (John 4:45-54).

After the two days with the Samaritans, Jesus left Sychar and went from Samaria into Galilee. This had been His plan before His trip was interrupted. Apparently at this time Jesus of Nazareth wanted to escape public attention. If He had stayed in Samaria, the people would have made much of Him. Strange as it may seem, Jesus knew the best place to go to be ignored. That place was back home (John 4:44)!

Even at that His coming attracted attention; but not for the reasons that would have made Jesus glad. They were only fascinated by His miracles.

> Then when he was come into Galilee, the Galilaeans received him, having seen all the things that he did at Jerusalem at the feast: for they also went unto the feast (John 4:45).

It appears that the Galilaeans who were at the feast had come home, spreading tales of the things they had seen and heard concerning this man from Nazareth. So when Jesus came to Galilee, there was a great company of people who came to see Him and listen to Him.

John reports:

> . . . Jesus came again into Cana of Galilee, where he made the water wine. And there was a certain nobleman, whose son was sick at Capernaum (John 4:46).

Cana is not far from Capernaum, and when this nobleman heard that Jesus was in Cana he came to see Him. His need was great. He requested Jesus to come down and heal his son, as the lad was at the point of death. This is prayer! This man, coming because his son was seriously ill, showed faith, enough to believe that Jesus would heal his child.

THE NOBLEMAN'S FAITH

The first response from Jesus of Nazareth questioned the nobleman's motive in asking for a miracle. Even to this day the Lord may test any person who comes praying for some special matter:

> Then said Jesus unto him, Except ye see signs and wonders, ye will not believe (John 4:48).

It was as if He said, "Do you want me to come down and do this so you can see some great and tremendous thing happen? Do you only want to see something unusual like the rest of the Galilaeans?" This kind of testing could have turned away a superficial or shallow person. But the answer of the nobleman shows the sincerity of his prayer:

> The nobleman saith unto him, Sir, come down ere my child die. Jesus saith unto him, Go thy way; thy son liveth. And the man believed the word that Jesus had spoken unto him, and he went his way (John 4:49, 50).

It is amazing to see the faith this nobleman displayed, as he actually turned away and started back to his home. He had not yet seen any outward result, and yet he was confident his request had been granted.

What joy the father must have experienced when his servants brought him the good news:

> And as he was now going down, his servants met him, and told him, saying, Thy son liveth (John 4:51).

The nobleman then asked when the son "began to amend." The servants told him the day before, "at the seventh hour the fever left him."

> So the father knew that it was at the same hour, in the which Jesus said unto him, Thy son liveth: and himself believed, and his whole house (John 4:53).

There is much to understand here about faith. First there the nobleman had enough faith in Jesus Christ to come for help. Then there was more faith which enabled him to turn away toward home, after coming in the first place. Finally there was growing faith, which embraced his whole family as he told them of what had happened. This demonstrates that faith will actually grow as a person receives answers to prayer.

Chapter 6

THE WITNESS OF HIS POWER

Salvation is the work of God offered to men through Christ Jesus. Its source is God alone, but He allows and requires man to play a part in it. God saved Noah from the flood, but it was necessary for Noah to build the ark and to follow God's directions about entering into it. God brought the Israelites out of Egypt, but they had to believe in Moses as their leader and march out following him. God gave David victory over Goliath, but David had to select the five smooth stones, and exercise his skill with the sling.

In the New Testament it is written God sent His Son to redeem those held in the bondage of sin, but it was to "as many as received him. . . ."

Thus it seems to be evident that while God does provide salvation, the individual must believe, must receive the free gift of God. Man must make the response, God does not compel him. This principle of the need for a man or woman to be willing to receive blessing from God in order to be blessed is set forth in the gospel of John in the fifth chapter.

HEALING AT BETHESDA (5:1-9)

The setting of the event is very interesting, with several unusual elements. It was a place which today people call a *healing shrine*. It was a place where people gathered, called the pool of Bethesda. There were two unusual circumstances concerning this pool. One was that, at certain times, an angel went down into the water and troubled it. The other was that whoever stepped into the pool first after the waters had been thus stirred up, was cured of whatever disease he had.

In seeking to understand this story it is well to remember the Bible never describes an angel. Nowhere, in all Scripture, is there a word picture of an angel. The word *angel* is actually a functional term and means *messenger*. God sent a messenger down to start the waters moving. Just how it was done is not described.

There is no indication that this was of a particular mineral content that had curative effects. There is no hint that it had some magical

56

properties for the first man who stepped in. There is no other evidence than the plain statements of Scripture. Anyone reading such a story in the Bible should not try to explain it. If he does not understand it, he can be humble enough to accept that he does not always understand the way God works.

Jesus came by one day and saw a certain man lying at the pool, who ". . . had an infirmity thirty and eight years" (verse 5).

> When Jesus saw him lie, and knew that he had been now a long time in that case, he saith unto him, Wilt thou be made whole? (John 5:6).

It seems strange that Jesus would ask, "Do you want to be cured?" He knew what was in the hearts of men. And anyone in that crowd around Bethesda knew that the sick wanted to be cured. Certainly Jesus knew it! Then *why* did Jesus ask the question? So the man could give an answer? So he could participate? So he could realize his own inability and helplessness and confess his need? Perhaps Jesus wanted to draw from the man the admission of his helplessness which he gave in verse seven: ". . . Sir, I have no man, when the water is troubled, to put me into the pool: but while I am coming, another steppeth down before me."

Then Jesus gave the most amazing instructions to a man unable to walk for thirty-eight years: ". . . Rise, take up thy bed, and walk" (John 5:8).

Do you share my feeling of awe at these words? Do you hold your breath, waiting to see what will happen?

IMMEDIATE OBEDIENCE

> And immediately the man was made whole, and took up his bed, and walked: and on the same day was the sabbath (John 5:9).

Immediately! He did not wait to act in obedience to the command from Jesus of Nazareth. This is meant to be a classic example for all who read it, all who seek to serve the Lord in any age. The story tells us this man was "impotent," meaning entirely helpless, no power at all. This is important. Men are often jammed into corners of helplessness, and the Lord Jesus is just as ready today to speak the word of command and bring them out of valleys of difficulty, if they are ready to obey that command.

In the second place, Jesus came to the man; he did not have to go hunting for Jesus. It is comforting to remember this. God is interested in men, and the Lord Jesus Christ, alive and concerned, is close beside anyone in distress.

In the third place, the man was challenged to confess his need. He had to recognize that in himself he was not able to do what was necessary. Christians today are not exempt from realizing their own inability, apart from the indwelling presence and power of the Holy Spirit.

And in the fourth place, the word of Jesus set the impotent man free, enabled him to walk instantly as he responded in faith. How great is the power and love of God for men!

THE LEADERS UPSET (5:10-16)

The ways of God, although right and good, are by no means popular with men. This incident of the lame man at the pool of Bethesda is the first record of the Jews' opposition to Jesus. One would suppose that the Jews would rejoice in the good which had come to their fellow-citizen, this life-time cripple. But instead of rejoicing, they found fault, pointing out that the healing took place on the Sabbath day. Therefore, they claimed, the healed man had no business to be carrying his bundle of quilts, which was against the law.

The reason for their opposition is plain to see. Jesus had demonstrated before their eyes power far beyond the ordinary grasp of mortal men, and naturally this attracted attention to Himself. People came in multitudes to see Him. Things did not happen around Him in the usual way. He was revolutionary in ignoring the rules, healing on the Sabbath day. This made Jesus a serious threat to the Jewish rulers. He was a threat in His ability, for He could do more than they could possibly accomplish. He was a threat in His popularity, for more came flocking to see and hear Him that ever went to the Temple. He was a threat in His example, because He actually did things on the Sabbath, of which the Jews strongly disapproved. So instead of rejoicing in the good that was done, they criticized.

To the healed man the Jews said, in effect, "You have no right to walk around the city carrying your bed. You know you should not work on the Sabbath day." But the man answered them plainly: ". . . He that made me whole, the same said unto me, Take up thy bed, and walk" (John 5:11).

It is apparent that this cripple had felt the power of Jesus. He had been directed to walk, and to carry his bed. He probably did not hesitate to obey whatever Jesus told him to do. He had not realized it was the man from Nazareth who had done this, but he did know he was healed and he would obey whatever he was told to do.

> Afterward Jesus findeth him in the temple, and said unto him, Behold, thou art made whole: sin no more, lest a worse thing come unto thee. The man departed and told the Jews that it was Jesus, which had made him whole (John 5:14, 15).

Thus Jesus not only revealed Himself to this man, but gave him further instructions. "Blessed by God," Jesus told him, "you are now to be thankful to God for it. Try not to do anything contrary to the will of God." Now the Jewish leaders had even more reasons to attack Jesus!

Here is something which is strange — really ironical. The most implacable and dangerous enemies the Lord had were among the religious leaders! They resented anything that was contrary to their ideas and schemes. They utterly disregarded the good He did, condemning Him for not following their rules and regulations.

This continues to be a common situation. It is to be found in church. Local congregational activities are conducted by Christians who are, after all, human beings. People in church, although saved and devoted to the Lord's work, can be concerned about their personal position in the eyes of others. They want to be looked up to, rated as high as others, and they tend to do things in their own ways. If another person tries some other method that is successful, such people very quickly resent what is being done by someone else. This is one of the most serious hindrances that hurts the Lord's work.

In just this way there could be an occasion like this: A Christian takes time to go around and bring a neighbor's family to Sunday school. He has to leave home a little early to do this. People ought to be glad about that. But are they? Often they criticize the worker for wasting time and gasoline to pick up children for Sunday school. To be sure this is unreasonable, but it is sadly common among religious people. We must be on guard against it. It is easy to be Pharisaical, not so easy to be Christlike.

JESUS AND HIS FATHER (5:17-31)

Jesus Christ revealed in Himself the will of God. There was nothing in His outward appearance to suggest anything special. It was not His size, nor His clothing, nor the way in which He walked. It was His manner of life, and the things He did which revealed, through Him, God's will for men. He fulfilled the law of God in all of its aspects, but this is not the essential significance of His life and work.

It was rather this, that He did what He did because God was in Him. It was not simply Jesus of Nazareth reading the laws of God as found in the Old Testament, then mustering His natural forces together and striving to follow out what He had read. He had in Himself the very life of God, and He *was* God. Thus His righteousness, His way of living, was the way of God. In Himself, Jesus demonstrated the power and strength of God, what life would be like when it is lived with God, and what work would be like when one works with God.

John 5:17-31 explains this. "I and my Father are one," Jesus said. This does not mean, of course, that God the Father was indwelling the body of Jesus of Nazareth as one person. He did not mean that at that moment His human body was a part of God in heaven. What He does mean to say is this, that He, as Jesus of Nazareth, and God as the Father in heaven, were one in the unity of the Godhead, even as Adam and Eve were one in the unity of man: as husband and wife are "one flesh." In His human form were the works of the will of God, in which both He and His Father shared in unity.

JEWS CHARGE BLASPHEMY

The very way Jesus said these things offended the Jewish leaders. They felt He was making Himself equal with God, *and He was!* But He meant more than that! He was not only equal with God, He was at one with His Father in living communion by the one Spirit that was in them.

> But Jesus answered them, My Father worketh hitherto, and I work. Therefore the Jews sought the more to kill him, because he not only had broken the sabbath, but said also that God was his Father, making himself equal with God (John 5:17, 18).

Notice the way Jesus put this. "My Father is working in all things that concern this world and its inhabitants, and I also work along with Him. Namely, I am moving right along in the way of my Father."

The reaction of the Jews was swift and sharp, for now they not only accused Him of breaking the laws concerning Sabbath observances, but also of blasphemy against God.

> Then answered Jesus and said unto them, Verily, verily, I say unto you, The Son can do nothing of himself, but what he seeth the Father do: for what things soever he doeth, these also doeth the Son likewise (John 5:19).

Such a statement blends the two and presents the Father and the Son as being in union. They are one in themselves. The Son does nothing of Himself; He does not act on His own.

Today men frequently use the word *unilateral,* meaning work undertaken or done by one person without participation of others. This is a very common human procedure and can be seen naturally in children. Any normal child has ideas of his own, and wants to carry them out according to his will. This indicates that he is truly a human being and will naturally develop in sinful selfishness.

GREATER WORKS

But as far as a Christian is concerned, the picture must be a different one. Any child of God will strive to be like the Lord Jesus, who was the only begotten Son of God. The Son does not originate actions as from His own will: He carries out the Father's plans, doing what He sees the Father do. Jesus went on in His discussion to point out even deeper truth.

> For the Father loveth the Son, and sheweth him all things that himself doeth: and he will shew him greater works than these, that ye may marvel (John 5:20).

Christ Jesus, while He was on earth performed certain miracles, such as the healing of the lame man at the Pool of Bethesda. Jesus now tells them that this is only the beginning: there will be "greater works than these, that ye may marvel." When one wonders what greater works and when, all he has to do is remember Pentecost. There thousands of hearts were touched and three thousand lives were changed. Peter arose and preached a message that was in the will of God, and as God worked in that great multitude, there occurred one of these "greater things." Peter's words brought conviction, because God was inwardly working in the multitude. Even to this day in evangelism, preaching, and personal witnessing, these "greater works" are possible as men and women are won to Christ.

> For as the Father raiseth up the dead, and quickeneth them; even so the Son quickeneth whom he will. For the Father judgeth no man, but hath committed all judgment unto the Son: That all men should honour the Son, even as they honour the Father. He that honoureth not the Son honoureth not the Father which hath sent him. Verily, verily, I say unto you, He that heareth my word, and believeth on him that sent me, hath everlasting life, and shall not come into condemnation; but is passed from death unto life. Verily, verily, I say unto you, The hour is coming, and now is, when the dead shall hear the voice of the Son of God: and they that hear shall live" (John 5:21-25).

These words sound so simple but their meaning is most profound. Because God Almighty raised the dead, the Son will raise the dead: ". . . for what things soever he doeth, these also doeth the Son likewise." This speaks of God quickening the dead, through His Word, through the Lord Jesus Christ. This is what is being accomplished through the preaching of His Word, unto this very day. ". . . they that hear shall live" because God will raise them from the dead, and the Son will do the same.

But Jesus still is not finished with His amazing recital. He continues with this teaching concerning the marvelous relationship between the Father and the Son.

> For as the Father hath life in himself; so hath he given to the Son to have life in himself; And hath given him authority to execute judgment also, because he is the Son of man (John 5:26, 27).

Here Christ indicates an amazing possibility for those who are His. Redeemed men and women, as they walk in the will of their Lord, enabled by the Holy Spirit, may also do the works of God! Not because they are doing anything in themselves will this be realized, but because the Father is working through them. No matter where a Christian is, he can be doing the very things God wants to accomplish, as he walks by faith in His way, according to His Word.

JOHN'S TESTIMONY (5:32-35)

There is another that beareth witness of me; and I know that the witness which he witnesseth of me is true. Ye sent unto John, and he bare witness unto the truth. But I receive not testimony from man: but these things I say, that ye might be saved. He was a burning and a shining light: and ye were willing for a season to rejoice in his light (John 5:32-35).

Christian life and all Christian experience is grounded in faith. When a man says he believes, he is referring to something he has not seen. If he had seen it, he would not have to affirm his belief, for he could then say he *had seen it*. But when he says he believes he is referring to something not at the moment within his range of vision. He may be speaking of something that has not yet happened, something he truly expects is going to come to pass to which he is looking forward. ". . . faith is the substance of *things hoped for,* the evidence of things *not seen*" (Hebrews 11:1). To believe means to accept as true what one not only does not see, but cannot check on.

When men and women saw Jesus of Nazareth what did they actually see? They saw a man, whom they knew to be a good man for even Pilate knew this! Hundreds and thousands saw Him work miracles. Whether they understood the miracles or not is not important, but the fact that miracles were performed was never denied. There was no question of faith involved in this, for thousands of eyes had seen the miracles performed.

What then, did they need to believe? They needed to believe He was the Christ, the long-awaited Messiah. They needed to believe that Jesus was actually the Son of God: the promised way of salvation for them. They had to accept, as trust, that God's plan of salvation was revealed in this person who walked their streets.

When we look at Jesus as He is told about in the gospels, we see a person who was outwardly human in form, but actually He was the Son of God.

In order to help the Israelites to believe this, Jesus pointed out several lines of testimony for their consideration. First He drew their attention to John the Baptist. What had John the Baptist said about Jesus? When he first saw Him, he said, ". . . Behold the Lamb of God, which taketh away the sin of the world" (John 1:29). Thus John identified Jesus as the sin-bearer and deliverer.

Now, who was this man speaking, who identified Jesus as the Saviour? These things are told about John the Baptist. First, he was a man filled with the Holy Spirit from the day of his birth. This would mean that he was constantly under the influence of God, making him an honest, sincere person. He was a dedicated man, committed to one thing only, the service of God. He was a man with a gift: he was a powerful, effective preacher of God's Word. All Jerusalem went out to hear him. Finally, he was courageous, preaching the truth, no matter what circumstances he was facing. This eventually cost him his life. This dedicated, spiritually-minded, courageous man said that Jesus was the Christ.

The Baptizer was a forerunner of the countless Christians in the world, who are sincere, genuine, Spirit-filled men and women of God. Their lives show their integrity, and they have one outstanding thing in common, their faith in Christ. What do such people say? Just what John the Baptist said so long ago: "Behold the Lamb of God." There is not a true Christian who denies that Jesus is the Christ, the Son of the living God.

Even the most skeptical mind should be impressed by comparing the character of genuine Christian men and women, with their effect upon the world today, with the character and effect of people who reject Christ, many of whom are careless, wicked, and godless. The testimony of such comparison based upon the difference in character is overwhelming.

When Jesus pointed out the testimony of John the Baptist He emphasized the great prestige John had as an honest, competent, able man, and preacher of the Word.

FAITH GROUNDED IN JESUS' WORKS (5:36-38)

Jesus told His hearers of a greater witness than the testimony of others: He challenged each person to "come and see."

> But I have a greater witness than that of John: for the works which the Father hath given me to finish, the same works that I do, bear witness of me, that the Father hath sent me. And the Father himself, which hath sent me, hath borne witness of me. Ye have neither heard his voice at any time, nor seen his shape. And ye have not his word abiding in you: for whom he hath sent, him ye believe not (John 5:36-38).

The works of Christ Jesus actually accomplish more in the way of grounding faith, than the testimony of the people who have been blessed. The consequences of preaching the Gospel are a real witness to the truth of the Gospel. In listening to a well-known evangelist or a famous preacher, one may be greatly impressed by his logic, his vocabulary, his tone of voice, or his earnestness. But in the final analysis, the most impressive factor, the thing which would most incline a person to *believe the message* is to find a real change in those who accept the message that is being preached. The actual conversion of a man or woman is often more convincing than any words the preacher may use.

Such demonstrations of power can be actually seen. Either a husband or a wife, or both, hear the Gospel, and a home, which was on the verge of being wrecked, is not broken up. The two live in reconciliation, and home and children are saved. A drug addict accepts Christ, and the habit which enslaved him is broken. A woman known to be other than of good character accepts Christ, and her whole life is changed and becomes a thing of purity and faithfulness to God. These transformations can and do happen, and they are the "greater works" promised. This is the work the Father gave Christ Jesus to complete, the accomplishing of the Father's will.

There is an old spiritual, seldom heard today, "Oh I know the Lord, I know the Lord, I know the Lord's laid His hands on me!" which emphasizes the connection grounded in personal experience. There is a sense in which the personal answer to prayer, the certainty in the heart of God's presence of His hand "laid on me," is the thing which confirms faith in a special way.

Such experiences come, for the most part, to those who read the Bible in communion with the Holy Spirit and feed on it day by day. Jesus suggested this when He said, "And ye have not his word abiding in you . . ." (verse 38). Apparently there were people there in front of Him who did not believe in Him. He was pointing out that the reason they did not believe was that they had never heard the Word of God. That does not mean that God was not dealing with them in providential ways. But it does mean they had not recognized His will for their lives. The hand of God may have been active in their affairs. God watches over all His creation, and He works with all men to turn them to Himself. But when a man refuses to heed, turns a deaf ear or a dull eye upon every attempt of God to reach him, nothing can be done. God does not force Himself upon anyone. He seeks their willing surrender of will and heart to Him.

WITNESS OF THE SCRIPTURES (5:39-47)

Jesus of Nazareth continued His teaching about the situations that would help men to believe. First He had pointed out the witness of John the Baptist. It is always helpful to note the straightforward testimony of people who have been affected by the Gospel, people who have themselves experienced the grace of God in Christ Jesus. Then He had reminded them there is a greater witness than John, in the very works which God has done. There is something so undeniable about the results of the power of God that faith is confirmed by evidence that can be seen. In verse thirty-seven Jesus may be referring to the voice from heaven at the time of His baptism by John: "And the Father himself, which hath sent me, hath borne witness of me. . . ." But now He points out something else, another factor in this matter of faith, growth in grace, belief and trust: the witness of the Scriptures.

Jesus introduced this line of thought by urging the people to *search* the Scriptures. This suggests immediately that all truth contained in the Bible is not lying on the surface to be seen in casual reading. It is necessary to compare Scripture with Scripture in order to get at the hidden truth and achieve real understanding.

> Search the scriptures; for in them ye think ye have eternal life . . .
> (John 5:39).

The Jewish people, who were criticizing Jesus and openly opposing Him, thought they could discover the things of God in their Scriptures; and they were right, this was true. Jesus went on to say that the Scriptures testified of Him, and He knew what they would learn if they would study. The word *Scriptures* and the word *Bible* mean the same: the Scriptures are the Bible, and the Bible is composed of the Scriptures. The truth about Christ Jesus is not a matter of public opinion nor of common consent. It is not learned when men look through the Bible, selecting the portions they like or of which they approve, and then take such selections as the basis of their faith about Jesus Christ. A person should humbly ask what do the Scriptures say? How does the Bible tell about Christ Jesus? The Word of God was given for the purpose of making all these things clear about His Son, Jesus Christ.

A WILLING ATTITUDE

The whole experience of coming to conviction about Jesus Christ through the Scriptures depends upon a certain willingness to come to Him. An unwilling attitude can prevent the grace of God at work. This Jesus said to Jews who stood by and saw the miracle for the lame man and other marvelous deeds. They still would not come to Him, and He points out why. To have the faith to accept Christ, there must be willingness to believe. These people did not have willing hearts.

This illustrates a very significant truth. Apparently, if any person wants popular acclaim, the approval of the people of the world, he will not seek to set his standards by the Bible. Jesus said, "I receive not honour from men. But I know you, that ye have not the love of God in you" (John 5:41, 42). Today many people fail at this point. They love the praise of men more than the praise of God. They lack appreciation of His love, and they are not at all concerned with doing His will. Seeking the praise of men they miss the blessing of God.

Jesus of Nazareth told this group of non-believing men that He came in His Father's name, and they would not receive Him. He came to do the will of His Father. What Almighty God was seeking to accomplish, Jesus came to implement, to bring it to pass. He did not come to work out his own plans. He did not come in His own name.

> I am come in my Father's name, and ye receive me not: if another shall come in his own name, him ye will receive (John 5:43).

This actually describes most of the world of sinful men and women today, ready to accept any name, any set of ideas other than the true! The preacher or teacher who comes with his own ideas is popular and of course there is a cause for this. Such a man is popular because he had expressed his own thoughts, and his hearers feel able to understand and even to argue their own ideas against his. Everything is done on the human level. It cannot be so when one is seeking to serve God. Then he must forsake his own ideas as the product of his own wicked heart and mind, and humbly accept the revelation of the Word of God.

HUMILITY NECESSARY

When a person seeks to know the mind of the Lord and will actually read the Bible, believing it to be His Word, he must humble himself. But so many people do not want to do this, even as these Jews so long ago. The faith that accepts Christ always has an element of contrition in it: the consciousness of past sin and the desire to be cleansed. The element of choice is involved since the believer must commit himself to what he reads. He told them the basic principle of His life: "I receive not honour from men." He does not look for esteem; seeks no personal prestige sought, no special position. He came humble as the obedient Son, doing nothing by Himself. His Father was working hitherto, and He worked. But for many people, this is an entirely unacceptable basis on which to live their life. It is because of this that He says, ". . . if another shall come in his own name, him ye will receive" (verse 43).

Jesus of Nazareth continues His discussion of their unwillingness to believe,

> How can ye believe, which receive honour one of another, and seek not the honour that cometh from God only? (John 5:44).

He points out it is impossible to commit oneself fully to God if one accepts honor from other people. Anyone who will accept the Word of God is not going to be honored by the people of the world. True honor comes only from God. Psychologically it is not possible for a person to surrender to the Lord if he accepts honor from other human beings. Yet there are people who will seek praise from men, and are willing to give it to men in order to receive it from them. Such persons will not turn to God.

> Do not think that I will accuse you to the Father: there is one
> that accuseth you, even Moses, in whom ye trust. For had ye
> believed Moses, ye would have believed me: for he wrote of me
> (John 5:45, 46).

Here is an amazing statement! It will not be necessary that Jesus
Christ accuse them of their unwillingness to believe. The fact is such
persons do not even accept their own consciousness and this will be
their condemnation.

The Bible testifies of Jesus Christ. Men and women today who
refuse to accept the Scriptures at face value are turning their backs upon
the Lord Jesus Christ and are bringing judgment upon their own heads.
The Bible is authentic and men need to study it faithfully and earnestly
so that they may be strengthened in faith, and may, in turn, be able
to win others.

Chapter 7

THE WITNESS OF HIS PERSON

Those who believe in Jesus Christ trust Him to do certain things, according to His promises. It is truly a wonderful blessing to be able to believe. However, many people seem incapable of believing. They do not seem strong enough. They seem unprepared, not being acquainted with the Scriptures, and having no faith in the promises of God through Jesus Christ.

FAITH IS TRUST

It is possible someone like this may actually be reading these pages. Faith always involves an element of *simple trust*. A person acts in faith when he cannot see and does not understand. Actually one may not know all the promises of God and therefore cannot rely fully upon them. But when a soul takes that first trusting step, God will respond at once, giving more faith and the assurance of His presence. The person will be strengthened by the grace of God from within to believe what is true.

The gospels record the words and work of the Lord Jesus during the years of His flesh. The reading of Matthew, Mark, Luke, and John by those who are weak in faith, or who have never taken the first step of faith in Christ, is essential. They were written so that men might both believe and find eternal life.

In these gospel narratives, it will be seen that Jesus worked many miracles, also with the purpose of instilling belief and life. They are not less effective in their testimony to Jesus Christ today, as the Bible is read. When men learn what Jesus *did,* they are able to accept in faith what He can *do* today, for anyone may insert hs own name or circumstances in the promises and claim them for himself.

FEEDING THE 5000 (6:1-14)

There is the record of a great miracle performed by Jesus in the first fourteen verses of the sixth chapter of John's gospel — the feeding of the five thousand. It is told in each one of the gospels. Any attempt to explain away this miracle, to describe it in such a way as to make it an event in which natural causes worked themselves out, is to defeat the purpose of God and is contrary to the testimony of the gospel writers.

It seems that this miracle was performed for the sake of the disciples. The answer to a question by Philip about buying bread for the multitude, carries this interesting comment, "And this he [Jesus] said to prove him: for he himself knew what he would do" (verse 6). Apparently Jesus had withdrawn from the crowd in order to teach His disciples. Great multitudes followed Him because they had seen the miracles which He had done, so that teaching became almost impossible. Jesus therefore ". . . went up into a mountain, and there he sat with his disciples" (John 6:3). The coming of such a large group of people to hear Jesus gave Him a marvelous opportunity for a demonstration, for teaching something of God's purpose and God's power. He chose this natural situation to display that power, knowing that a demonstration would enforce His teaching in a most effective way. Speaking to Philip, He raised the question of feeding this great multitude of men, women and children.

The reply of the disciples was the natural response in this situation. ". . . Two hundred pennyworth of bread is not sufficient for them, that every one of them may take a little" (verse 7). It is possible that this was a part of a fund they had, and Philip was arguing that if they spent it all, it would not be enough. Andrew, brother of Simon Peter, called attention to the only food within sight: "There is a lad here, which hath five barley loaves, and two small fishes: but what are they among so many?" (verse 9). Thus it was obvious that the prospect of feeding all this crowd was beyond their ability.

Jesus took charge. ". . . Make the men sit down. . . ." The disciples had called attention to the fact that the five barley loaves and the two small fishes were surely not enough. But Jesus quietly proceeded with the demonstration. The first thing He did was to introduce order into the confusion of the scene. No doubt this great crowd of people was milling around, and so Jesus directed that everyone should be seated. We are told there was much grass in that place, where a huge crowd could sit comfortably, and so . . .

> . . . the men sat down, in number about five thousand. And Jesus took the loaves; and when he had given thanks, he distributed to the disciples, and the disciples to them that were set down; and likewise of the fishes as much as they would (John 6:10, 11).

Much can be learned from how Jesus acted. He did not instruct a disciple to hold the few loaves and the small fish while He prayed over them. Rather He took the loaves in His own hand. Then He gave thanks to God for the food! No matter how large the crowd, nor how great the astonishment of His disciples, He took time to give thanks to His Father. Then He gave the bread and fish to the disciples. They acted as waiters, and in turn took it to all that multitude. And

> When they were filled, he said unto his disciples, Gather up the fragments that remain, that nothing be lost. Therefore they gathered them together, and filled twelve baskets with the fragments of the five barley loaves, which remained over and above unto them that had eaten (John 6:12, 13).

> Then those men, when they had seen the miracle that Jesus did, said, This is of a truth that prophet that should come into the world (John 6:14).

Apparently this demonstration had been put on that their faith might be strengthened. It is *seeing the miracle that strengthens faith,* and that is true through all Christian experience whether physical (as in the case of the bread and fish) or spiritual (as in the case of a redeemed soul).

THE IMPORTANCE OF MIRACLES (6:15-21)

In order to make any intelligent study of the book of John, or any other part of the Bible, it is necessary to accept as true the miracles which are reported.

I remember that, as a very young man, I was very skeptical about anything out of the ordinary in any report I might be hearing or reading. When I began to be interested in the Bible, and even to hope it might be true, when reading the account of a miracle, I would try to explain it away in my own mind. I would tell myself, "It did not mean just what it said, this was not meant to be taken literally." And if that did not work, I would just ignore it and try to forget that it was in the record, because my disbelief in the miracles was a real barrier to my accepting the Bible as the Word of God. I wanted to believe the Bible: but could not accept any miracle. Remember that I was as yet an unbeliever, and it was my reasoning that no one could be expected to believe such exaggerated stories, since manifestly they could not have happened. I had the feeling that these accounts were to be received as a sort of parable, created to illustrate some truth.

However, when I came to know the Gospel more fully, when I came to know who Jesus Christ was, then I saw that if I were going to accept the Lord Jesus Christ as all, I would have to accept Him as He is presented, *miracles and all.* I found, eventually, that I would have to believe in my own heart that God had raised Jesus from the dead. When I considered the condition of a body which had been in the grave (tomb) for three days, and then tried to think of it as alive again, I knew this was a miracle of the first order. Belief in the resurrection of Jesus Christ from the dead is required in any person that is to be saved (Romans 10:9). The New Testament tells of no other way to claim salvation than that. It took a long time for me to come from darkness into light, and the chief obstacle in my experience was the necessity for me to *believe*.

When I finally realized that my own thinking was weak, and I was being hindered by unbelief grounded in my natural thoughts, the Spirit broke through that mental block. And I was enabled to believe the Scriptures which say that God raised Him from the dead.[1]

This is a common experience. People can and do put up mental resistance to the truth of the Gospel. It is possible in all good conscience to feel very intelligent by simply doubting anything that involves the miraculous. For such minds the Bible is a closed book. It is as simple as that and yet tragic, for Paul says such unbelief is the work of Satan (II Corinthians 4:4).

It is possible to get an idea of how devastating such unbelief is if one thinks of cutting out of the Gospel everything that involves a miracle. There would not be much left. The Bible gives a true account of the work of God in the world of sinful men, and beyond that world, in the universe which is His creation. If a person were to take a heavy black pencil, and strike out everything supernatural, the gospel message would be blotted out entirely.

WALKING ON THE WATER

In John 6:15-21 the record is given of a particularly dramatic miracle, one certainly suited for the strengthening of the disciples' faith. Because of the action of the crowd Jesus had been separated from His disciples.

> When Jesus therefore perceived that they could come and take him by force, to make him a king, he departed again into a mountain himself alone (John 6:15).

At the end of the day His disciples went down to the sea and entered into a boat to go across to Capernaum. Since He had not returned, they went on without Him. This may well have been routine procedure but now a crisis suddenly developed.

> And the sea arose by reason of a great wind that blew. So when they had rowed about five and twenty or thirty furlongs, they see Jesus walking on the sea, and drawing nigh unto the ship: and they were afraid (John 6:18, 19).

---

[1] I might say here that my own redemption is told in a small pamphlet, *Out of Darkness,* which can be obtained from me, and which tells the story of God's working in my heart, bringing me to the final miracle of salvation through faith in Christ.

Their fright would be very normal. They saw an apparition walking on the water. The sea was very turbulent, and to see this figure approaching, so utterly out of their experience or reason, frankly terrified them.

Just a few words spoken by Jesus, ". . . It is I; be not afraid" (John 6:20), gave them assurance. Their fears subsided.

This was no spirit, it was their Lord Himself. Their confidence can be felt as John reports in verse 21: ". . . they willingly received him into the ship. . . ." Apparently they were glad to have Him, and now they felt safe. The verse concluded ". . . and immediately the ship was at the land whither they went."

The way John records this it would seem that, with the Master aboard, no problem remained, since they were immediately at their destination. Matthew's account (Matthew 14:24-33) and Mark's account (Mark 6:47-52) give more details concerning this great miracle in its power over nature. Matthew tells that

> But the ship was now in the midst of the sea, tossed with waves, for the wind was contrary (Matthew 14:24):

and Mark adds that

> . . . about the fourth watch of the night he cometh unto them, walking upon the sea, and would have passed by them . . . and they were sore amazed in themselves beyond measure, and wondered. For they considered not the miracles of the loaves: for their heart was hardened (Mark 6:48, 51, 52).

When Mark reports "they considered not the miracle of the loaves," there is the suggestion they could have been prepared to expect a miracle. If God has worked with power, believers should remember and expect great things from Him.

THE BLESSINGS OF THE GOSPEL (6:22-27)

All people who have ever accepted the Gospel know that all blessing is from God. The word "blessing" indirectly carries that meaning. When any individual comes to God through the Lord Jesus Christ, blessing is always promised. The church has long been recognized in any community as the cause of good and beneficial things. When a new church is being considered, the building of such a church is accepted by the majority of neighbors as a fine and helpful thing, because it is a symbol of blessing from God.

Just as the church is considered to be an asset to public life, so any Christian is esteemed to be a strong, positive element in good public relations, and good public works. But are these practical results the real reason why any man should come to Jesus Christ? Are these the purposes that should impel surrender to Him? As we read along in John's gospel we learn the answers.

The result of the miracle was that the people wanted to make Jesus king. This seems wonderful, but Jesus knew why they came to Him. These are the people who had been well fed even with much left over. Each man had eaten his fill. It would be easy for them to think that here was a solution to one of their great needs. If this great miracle worker were made king, they need never hunger again! Everything would be taken care of. Because of the temporal benefits, they wanted more temporal benefits and wanted them permanently. This the Lord refused to encourage.

No doubt today there are temporal benefits from the Gospel: teaching of the children, aiding of the sick, caring for orphans, helping the poor, ministering to the blind and incurable — all helpful services pertaining to the temporal life. Integrity in business, honorable dealing in government, development of temperance and self control in personal life are important. The attainment of strong family relationships to the strengthening of the community and society mean much.

It must be remembered, however, that such seeking of the temporal benefits of the Gospel is not what God intends.

> Jesus answered them and said, Verily, verily, I say unto you, Ye seek me, not because ye saw the miracles, but because ye did eat of the loaves, and were filled. Labour not for the meat which perisheth, but for that meat which endureth unto everlasting life, which the Son of man shall give unto you: for him hath God the Father sealed (John 6:26, 27).

When personal, physical benefits are received it is natural to want such blessing to continue. The poor are always attracted by an abundance of food, but the great ministry of the Gospel does not concern itself primarily with food, shelter or clothing. It does not aim first at good health, or any concern of this life. It has to do with relationship to God.

SPIRITUAL BLESSINGS

This is the lesson the world needs to learn today. In becoming a born-again child of God, personal integrity is secured, for faith in Jesus Christ breeds honesty, truth and fairness in all dealings with other men and women. It follows that if a man is truly a Christian, he will be a good husband, a fine father, a decent upright citizen, a fair, square man in business upon whom other men can depend. Such a believer will be a man who exercises his wisest judgment in political affairs as a good citizen. But that is not enough! "Labour not for the meat that perisheth"! A man does not come to the Lord primarily for these practical, although very important benefits. A man comes for spiritual values: for the assurance that if he were to die tonight, he would be instantly in the presence of God, who gives victory over sin and death. Any person who receives Jesus Christ will become a different person inwardly at once. Consequently the outward personality will be changed. There will be benefits of honesty and integrity of character, and all other virtues, not from without, but from the changed heart within, being now indwelt by the Holy Spirit.

If a person was a "worrier," he does not need to worry any longer. If a man had been inclined to a hasty or a violent disposition, with the indwelling power of the Holy Spirit such a person now can have a quiet, even temper, for the Lord is in control. There need be no more dissipation, no more outbreaking sin, for the heart is set free from the power of sin. Herein lies victory in this world, and the promises of the glory to come! And this is the real meaning of the Gospel: the soul turns to God through Jesus Christ and God works to produce outward change.

"Believe on Him . . ." (6:28-40)

This portion of John's gospel presents one of the most important discussions of Jesus' teaching. He had been telling people of the blessing they could receive if they would do the work of God in obedience to Him. They asked a very practical question: "What shall we do, that we might work the works of God?" The reply of Jesus is meaningful to this very day.

> Jesus answered and said unto them, This is the work of God, that ye believe on him whom he hath sent (John 6:29).

In plain talk, this is what God wants men to do. It is all in that phrase, *believe on Him.* This is certainly more than to *believe about Him,* which will, of course, come first. Believing "about" Jesus is not sufficient for salvation. Believing *on* Him is something quite different.

"To believe on" Him is like believing *on* a bridge, or *in* a medicine. A person commits himself to a bridge by crossing *on* it, because he believes that the bridge will hold him up and carry him safely across the river. The doctor gives a prescription; the patient has it filled, and then takes it according to directions: this is actually believing *in* the medicine. Even so in the matter of believing *on* Christ Jesus.

To "believe on him whom he hath sent" will include acceptance of Jesus as Lord in every phase of life. Not only will the believer accept that Jesus Christ died for his sin and rose again to be his Saviour, but that He will now be Lord and Master. The believer yields to Him, surrenders his will to Him, and obeys Him day by day. It will not be as if the believer were told what to do and then work to do as he had been told. It is rather that the Lord will live in our minds and hearts, through the presence of the Holy Spirit. Thus He will govern our thinking until His mind becomes our mind. ". . . But we have the mind of Christ," says Paul in I Corinthians 2:16.

Believing on Jesus Christ includes acceptance of the fact that He is alive and recognition of the person and work of His Holy Spirit. The believer realizes he is here on earth, and understands that the Lord is at the right hand of His Father in heavenly places. He has never seen Him up there but he believes it to be real. He also believes that Christ has given the Holy Spirit the power to effectively demonstrate His personality and power to all who believe. Thus he is personally related to God through Christ.

CHRIST'S CREDENTIALS

When Jesus used the phrase, ". . . believe on him whom he [God] hath sent," He emphasized the source of the power and authority He was manifesting. He was showing Himself to be the Anointed One, the Messiah of the Jewish nation. He was claiming to be the One chosen to do the will of God as the Scriptures had promised. He is the One who performs the will of God, not only in the great affairs of the world, but in the individual lives of believers. ". . . My Father worketh hitherto, and I work" (John 5:17). There are plans and purposes in the will of God which a man cannot know, but if the man believes in Christ He lives in that man by faith and works through him, accomplishing what is to be done according to the will of God. One man may have one portion of a task in his care, another may be carrying a different part of the work, but the whole task is performed as all believers yield themselves with willing hands and loving obedience. God leads, believers in Christ follow — it is as simple as that.

When Jesus had stated His significance as being the One whom God had sent to bring His blessing to His people, the crowd asked for what might be termed his credentials:

> They said therefore unto him, What sign shewest thou then, that we may see, and believe thee? what dost thou work? Our fathers did eat manna in the desert; as it is written, He gave them bread from heaven to eat (John 6:30, 31).

It was as if they said, "Our fathers followed Moses and believed in him. He gave them bread from heaven, what can you do for us?" In this reference to their history they overlooked the fact entirely that *God* gave the bread in that ancient time. The manna came from His gracious hand, and Moses was only the instrument used to work out His will among the children of Israel. In His exposition of the Old Testament record, Jesus is showing Himself as their Messiah.

> Then Jesus said unto them, Verily, verily, I say unto you, Moses gave you not that bread from heaven . . . For the bread of God is he which cometh down from heaven, and giveth life unto the world. Then said they unto him, Lord, evermore give us this bread (John 6:32-34).

A gentle rebuke can be felt here, as the Lord Jesus tells them that they are overestimating the powers of Moses. God was the one who provided the manna, not Moses! Now Jesus is pointing out to them that God is still doing the same thing. But this time He is giving the *living bread*. "For the bread of God is he which cometh down from heaven, and giveth life unto the world."

THE BREAD OF LIFE

Again Jesus used the Old Testament incident to help His people understand His procedures. He took this figure of bread and applied it to Himself. If people were to ask "What is Jesus Christ doing, so we may have reason to believe in Him?" the answer is: He is changing the lives of men and women, He is doing the work of regeneration in human hearts, He is arousing and quickening man's consciences. In other words, He is giving life — spiritual life! He is doing for the spiritual life what bread does for the physical life.

> . . . I am the bread of life: he that cometh to me shall never hunger; and he that believeth on me shall never thirst. But I said unto you, That ye also have seen me, and believe not. All that the Father giveth me shall come to me; and him that cometh to me I will in no wise cast out (John 6:35-37).

This word *bread* has a wealth of meaning contained in its five letters! It nourishes, builds, strengthens. As men grow physically on natural bread, so they grow spiritually from the Bread which is Christ Himself. Jesus said plainly He would give eternal life. He would nourish the spiritual lives of all who receive Him, would completely satisfy the soul: ". . . he that cometh to me shall never hunger; and he that believeth on me shall never thirst."

When Jesus says He is the Bread of Life, He is proclaiming the fact that He gives *strength*. He is the one who can make a person strong to do the will of God. The soul that comes to Jesus Christ will not grow faint nor weary, nor fail to obey when the will of God is known. But even before that, it is the strength that Jesus will give that causes people to respond to the call of God and come to accept Christ. Jesus promises that such as come will be surely welcomed and kept by the power of God.

At this point John reports that Jesus summarized His whole ministry.

> For I came down from heaven, not to do mine own will, but the will of him that sent me. And this is the Father's will which hath sent me, that of all which he hath given me I should lose nothing, but should raise it up again at the last day. And this is the will of him that sent me, that every one which seeth the Son, and believeth on him, may have everlasting life: and I will raise him up at the last day (John 6:38-40).

This, then, is the glorious purpose of all that Jesus came to do: it is the final resurrection of every person that God the Father in His Word has brought to accept Jesus Christ.

Salvation unto eternal life by the resurrection from the dead is the work of God through Jesus Christ, and it is the will of God that this shall surely occur in and for every soul that feeds on the Bread of Life which He has sent to men in the person of Jesus Christ.

Some Murmur (6:41-46)

Jesus offered Himself as Bread of Life. But there were many who would not accept Jesus as the only way, the only source of life and blessing.

> The Jews then murmured at him, because he said, I am the bread which came down from heaven. And they said, Is not this Jesus, the son of Joseph, whose father and mother we know? how is it then that he saith, I came down from heaven? (John 6:41, 42).

Such criticism is also recorded by the other three gospels, in Matthew 13:55; Mark 6:3; and Luke 4:22. Echoes of this are heard to this day. Some people will say, "The Bible calls Jesus the 'son of Joseph'." There were people then, and there are many now, who refuse to believe that Jesus was virgin-born. They consider Him to be the child of human parentage, like any other baby who comes into the world. So there is nothing new today in denying the virgin birth of Jesus of Nazareth. In those days they said, "We know his family, his father and his mother, we know his nature, we know how he earns his living — as a carpenter. But,

> Jesus therefore answered and said unto them, Murmur not among yourselves. No man can come to me, except the Father which hath sent me draw him: and I will raise him up at the last day. It is written in the prophets, And they shall be all taught of God. Every man therefore that hath heard, and hath learned of the Father, cometh unto me. Not that any man hath seen the Father, save he which is of God, he hath seen the Father (John 6:43-46).

"Murmur not," was a definite command with the voice of authority. Jesus went on to point out that it is not possible for any man to come to Him unless the Father draw him.

The first impression upon hearing this could be that God calls some, and does not call others, as if God were making a preferred selection. But this idea is a mistake. That is not what Jesus said.

The Call to Everyone

God calls all men, everywhere, to come to Christ. His Word is given to the whole world, just as the sun shines on all men. God is no respecter of persons. The fact of the matter is that one person will come, because he hears the call of God. Another will not hear: he ignores the call, and therefore does not come. God's reason for not drawing some is that they do not give Him a chance to do so: they refuse to listen to His Word! This truth can be felt in the case of any person who considers the story of Jesus' coming on a purely human level. Such a one might rejoice in the beauty of the angel song, the worshiping shepherds and the adoration of the wise men, and yet only see this as a beautiful picture, as an allegory.

But if any person is willing to be taught, to accept what he may not understand in the narrative of the birth, life, and teaching of Jesus then God Himself will lead that soul into eternal life.

The teaching of God will come in different ways: the providence that guides daily affairs; the thoughts that come into heart and mind as a person meditates on spiritual matters, perhaps upon a sleepless bed during the long night hours; the singing of a hymn; the clear message from God in the reading of the pages of His Word, the Bible. In some such way or ways, God will speak to the willing heart. His touch upon the soul will be unmistakable, and His call clear. Then this person will begin to know the things which are hidden from any unrepentant heart and mind.

WHAT IS REQUIRED OF MAN (6:47-71)

Thinking about God and His will is not popular among men. The "straight gate" and "narrow way" have no appeal for those of the world. To receive a blessing as something for nothing, a bonus, a generous gift — many might be interested in such a proposition. Anyone wants to be favored. Most people would like to feel themselves, in some general way, which demands no co-operation on their part, as being helped by the providence of God. But when it means yielding to the Lord Jesus Christ, turning one's life, plans, will, over to Him, few people are willing to accept Him.

Great evangelistic meetings may be held, and people will come to hear and even will come forward to receive benefits, but often they will stumble away when they find out that something is required *of them,* as well as that blessings will be bestowed *upon them.*

One of the chief excuses offered for the refusal to accept Christ as Saviour *and Lord* is, "I don't have to come just that one way — there are other ways to God." Yet the truth is that there is no other name by which men can be saved. God had only one Son, and He sent that Son into the world to live and die, to take away sins, and to rise from the dead, with forgiveness, life, and victory for all who believe in Him. Jesus presented to the people before Him this difficult teaching concerning His flesh being food and His blood being drink for the believer. Those who heard Him could not understand and would not accept this.

DENY THE FLESH

Actually the formula for the blessing of God which the Lord Jesus Christ taught is very simple: Deny the flesh, and receive the blessing of God. A well known song says, "The way of the cross leads home," and that is true. It is not only the way that Jesus took to the cross, but it is the way of the cross in the believer's soul. He must be willing to deny himself, as it is said in another gospel narrative:

> . . . If any man will come after me, let him deny himself, and take up his cross, and follow me. For whosoever will save his life shall lose it: and whosoever will lose his life for my sake shall find it (Matthew 16:24, 25).

The crucifixion of Jesus is an essential element in producing saving faith. It is not only that Jesus died for sinners, as such, but the dying of Jesus Christ fixed a pattern and a procedure for believers to follow. The Christian must partake of the death of Christ. He must be crucified with Him. Paul knew this from his own experience:

> I am crucified with Christ: nevertheless I live; yet not I, but Christ liveth in me: and the life which I now live in the flesh I live by the faith of the Son of God, who loved me, and gave himself for me (Galatians 2:20).

In teaching this truth Paul later discussed, Jesus used a very simple figure of speech — the eating of His flesh and the drinking of His blood. His hearers stumbled over this, as men and women have been stumbling over it ever since. The human heart draws back from the need of self-denial.

It is very significant that Jesus set forth no argument. He used no further words to explain what He meant. He simply set forth this truth, and challenged them to accept or reject it. He made it unmistakably plain to all that salvation was available only to those who would join Him in His death.

> . . . Verily, verily, I say unto you, Except ye eat the flesh of the Son of man, and drink his blood, ye have no life in you. Whoso eateth my flesh, and drinketh my blood, hath eternal life; and I will raise him up at the last day. For my flesh is meat indeed, and my blood is drink indeed (John 6:53-55).

There is never any way to arrive at an understanding of the operation of God's grace by human reasoning. Faith does not come by putting together many excellent or inspiring thoughts which can be understood by the average man or woman. Faith comes by hearing the things that happened to Jesus, such as His death, His resurrection, His presence now at the right hand of God. It is by considering these facts in His life, and accepting them as the call of God to "whosoever will come to Him," that the sinner will find he is enabled by the grace of God to enter into the salvation of Christ. As Jesus died, so the sinner must die to self in the presence of God. He must give up his own will and desires to accept Christ. It cannot be stated in a simpler way than this: God will raise the believer from death in his sins to a new life in Christ, even as He raised Jesus from that tomb in newness of life. The believer will be a different person with new ideas and ideals, a "new creature in Christ Jesus."

JESUS' CHALLENGE

Such ideas are incredible to the natural mind, and are only to be grasped when the mind considers another world than this. Jesus challenged His disciples to open their minds to the reality of heaven.

> When Jesus knew in himself that his disciples murmured at it, he said unto them, Doth this offend you? What and if ye shall see the Son of man ascend up where he was before? (John 6:61, 62).

It is quite possible his disciples had no conception of the fact that Jesus was not limited to this world of time and sense. He was in the presence of God all the time, and He could bring them into that presence when He talked to them. He continued His words by saying:

> It is the spirit that quickeneth; the flesh profiteth nothing: the words that I speak unto you, they are spirit, and they are life. But there are some of you that believe not. For Jesus knew from the beginning who they were that believed not, and who should betray him (John 6:63, 64).

In order to be blessed in salvation it is necessary to receive the truth as God reveals it in the Spirit. When Jesus said, "the flesh profiteth nothing," He was actually pointing out that all the ideas of men profit nothing. Ideas of philosophy, logic, art and fiction are of no value in seeking to reach spiritual truth. Such truth is revealed by God. One person can never bring conviction to another: this is the exclusive function of the Holy Spirit.

The open declaration of the need to die to self so that a person could receive the blessing of God through Christ caused many followers to drop away. Jesus used this occasion to challenge His followers to definite commitment.

> From that time many of his disciples went back, and walked no more with him. Then said Jesus unto the twelve, Will ye also go away? (John 6:66, 67).

There is no doubt He knew who would stay, even as He also knew who would betray Him, for He knew what was in the hearts of men. But He wanted to draw out His believers by this simple question. He did not make any plea, nor did He offer any argument in favor of their staying with Him. He did not say, "I do hope you will go on with Me," but simply confronted them with this challenge.

This procedure brought forth Peter's declaration, as he said,

> . . . Lord, to whom shall we go? thou hast the words of eternal life. And we believe and are sure that thou art that Christ, the Son of the living God (John 6:68, 69).

No matter how the action of the crowd in forsaking Jesus as a teacher may have affected the disciples, the issue of deciding for or against Him brought out the fact that they really did believe in Jesus.

When they were challenged as to what their own stand would be they responded with definite confession of their confidence.

Perhaps each reader should face that simple challenge now. Do you feel as Peter felt when he realized his own basic, heartfelt conviction that Jesus of Nazareth was the Son of God, the source of eternal life and of all blessing?

Have you felt the pull of popular opinion? Have you felt inclined to stay away from church, to neglect prayer, not to open your Bible day by day? If that is so why not stop for a moment, and think: is that really what you want to do? This is the time for you to fling yourself at His feet, and give Him your heart and life; saying as Peter did, that you believe and are sure "that thou art the Christ, the Son of the living God."

Chapter 8

THE WITNESS OF HIS WORK

DOING THE RIGHT

The Bible says: "To every thing there is a season, and a time to every purpose under the heaven" (Ecclesiastes 3:1 ff.). It is a well known fact that if affairs are to work out to a satisfactory conclusion, they must be undertaken at the right time.

Jesus of Nazareth described His own personal conduct by saying, ". . . My Father worketh hitherto, and I work" (John 5:17), pointing out He could do nothing of Himself. This is a very important truth and John reports that Jesus was careful in His obedience to His Father to observe this matter of doing things at the right time.

Sometimes a parent must speak to a child sternly. It may be a word of rebuke or caution, perhaps even reprimand. Yet there are times when such a word only aggravates the situation. Children need to be trained, and it is the duty of a parent to train them. But discipline should be administered, or rebuke given, at certain times. An intelligent parent will be careful to choose a proper time for such words. It may well be that to do this in front of other children, or before strangers or guests in the home will provoke a child to open rebellion, and the whole point of the needed lesson may be lost. Under other circumstances, the child could have been benefited. The words may have been right, but the time wrong.

People who cultivate gardens will know that one could take good seed, and by sowing it at the wrong time of the year, get almost no crop at all. All this will illustrate there is not only a right way for any given action, but there is also the right time to carry out the plan. This principle will also work in spiritual matters. Suppose there is a man who has received great blessing from the Lord, and is anxious to tell others. He wants to testify about what God has done for him. If he picks an unfortunate time, he will lose all the effect of his testimony.

Recently at a public service being conducted in orderly fashion, a man wanted to give a testimony. This was not the correct thing to do in that setting, and the request was denied. It not only caused an awkward situation at the time, but feelings were hurt as well. Some sanctified common sense would have prevented all the distress. That soul may have had a real testimony to give that could have been helpful, but since it was not a right time to ask, neither he nor anybody else received any blessing from the attempt.

JESUS AND THE PUBLIC (7:1-9)

After these things Jesus walked in Galilee: for he would not walk in Jewry, because the Jews sought to kill him (John 7:1).

It would seem that any man who is doing the right thing should be able to go anywhere. If a person is doing right, would God not give His protection no matter where he went? Not always. Although the Lord Jesus was perfect, and all He did was entirely in obedience to His Father, yet it was God's will that Jesus exercise wisdom in avoiding the public. The Jewish people were seeking to kill Him. Eventually they would do this, but it was not yet time for Him to offer up His life for the sins of the world, so He stayed out of that region.

His brethren therefore said unto him, Depart hence, and go into Judaea, that thy disciples also may see the works that thou doest. For there is no man that doeth any thing in secret, and he himself seeketh to be known openly. If thou do these things, shew thyself to the world. For neither did his brethren believe in him (John 7:3-5).

When His brothers urged Him to expose Himself to the public they made it sound like a reasonable suggestion, but it would have been the wrong thing for Jesus to do. He would have been unwise, for this was not the Father's time for Him to act. Their motive arose out of their unbelief and this may have been the reason for their judgment. This illustrates a very important principle for believers to heed. Christians need to control their own conduct and not permit others to guide them by issuing a challenge to action when the time is not right. Unbelieving people will come to Christians, and ask what might be called "leading questions" trying to examine the validity of the testimony of the believer. The Christian must exercise careful restraint in avoiding response to the challenge of such unbelieving questions.

The Christian's only source of wisdom and strength is the Lord as the Holy Spirit indwells his heart and teaches him day by day. The living Lord will give wisdom in such situations and make the believer cautious in utterance and in conduct.

OPPOSITION TO THE LORD (7:10-24)

Christians who gratefully rejoice in the salvation provided in Christ find it difficult to realize that many people hated Him and opposed Him in the days of His flesh, even as many do today.

And there was much murmuring among the people concerning him: for some said, He is a good man: others said, Nay; but he deceiveth the people (John 7:12).

The Lord Jesus was perfect, so that no sin dwelt in Him. He lived entirely in the will of His Father, as He went about doing good. Yet a large group of people were bitterly opposed to His ministry.

This can actually be a comfort to those who preach, teach and bear testimony to faith in Christ. When a believer seeks to serve Him, he must not be surprised if, from time to time, he runs into situations of determined opposition.

The tragic aspect is felt even more keenly because the public will listen to others.

. . . My time is not yet come . . . but me it [the world] hateth, because I testify of it, that the works thereof are evil (John 7: 6, 7).

The very people the Christian wants to help, the people for whom he puts himself out, may actually oppose him. They may turn to someone else who does nothing at all for their benefit, and may accept that individual as a friend. So Jesus found it, and so Christians find it today.

There is much to be learned in noticing this event in the life of Jesus. The average man does not resent someone quite like himself, he will not offer resistance to his own kind, but be quick and ready to resent those who are different. This is a characteristic of human nature, and certainly a Christian is vastly different from his fellow citizens. Consequently, they resent his witness, and the Christian will find himself opposed.

JESUS IN THE TEMPLE

Despite the hostile opposition Jesus of Nazareth obeyed the will of His Father, and "went up into the temple, and taught." When they heard Him teaching, the Jews were amazed, and said, ". . . How knoweth this man letters, having never learned?" (verse 15). They were astonished to see that Jesus could teach, make a public address, and speak with power and intelligence, when He had not been trained under the great teachers of that day. They rated Him as an uneducated man. But Jesus offered them an explanation of His ability.

Jesus answered them, and said, My doctrine is not mine, but his that sent me. If any man will do his will, he shall know of the doctrine, whether it be of God, or whether I speak of myself (John 7:16, 17).

In saying this Jesus was telling them that the real effectiveness of His teaching would depend entirely upon the condition of the hearts of those listening. He was not speaking out of Himself. He was speaking from the Father and saying what the Father commanded. To anyone willing, His words would be accepted as the Word of God. It angered the people when He told them that the only persons who could accept and appreciate His words were those who were also willing to obey the Father as He did. This is equally true today. The only heart which can understand the truth of God's Word is the heart willing to obey Him in all that He commands.

> He that speaketh of himself seeketh his own glory: but he that seeketh his glory that sent him, the same is true, and no unrighteousness is in him (John 7:18).

There are always two ways of teaching about Christian faith and life. One of them is to have the teacher speak out of his own mind, for "of himself" means according to his own ideas. The person who teaches only according to his own wisdom is seeking his own glory. The other way is to seek the glory of "Him that sent him," which is done by teaching the ideas given to him by God. Note Jesus' use of that phrase. He could have said "seeketh the glory of God," but instead He emphasized again that He was sent of God, stressing His relationship with the Father, and by so offering His message as having authority, such a teacher would be teaching truth that would not lead anyone astray, ". . . and no unrighteousness is in him."

This is a very significant principle which could guide a Christian even in his own private thinking. It would certainly be helpful whenever one reads a book, an article or listens to a sermon to raise the question, "Is this person just speaking out of his own mind, is he just giving his views, or is he trying to bring the message of God? Is he trying to display his own cleverness? Does he strive to build up his own ego? Is he trying to enhance his own image in the minds of the people to whom he preaches? Or is he, in humility and sincerity, with dedication of heart and mind, striving to bring to his hearers God's own word for their lives?"

JESUS TAUGHT THE SCRIPTURES

Jesus pointed out to the Jews their own inconsistency in their attitude toward Him. He came teaching the will of God. Moses in the Scriptures instructed them to receive such teaching. "Did not Moses give you the law, and yet none of you keepeth the law? Why go ye about to kill me?" (verse 19). Their denial was swift, and it came in terms of condemnation, as they said, ". . . Thou hast a devil: who goeth about to kill thee?" (verse 20). But Jesus did not attempt to answer their denial. They knew the truth of His remarks about them. Instead He went on with His discussion. ". . . I have done one work, and ye all marvel" (verse 21). Apparently that "one work" was the healing of the man at the Pool of Bethesda. This is what had aroused the Jews, because it was done on the Sabbath day. This is why they wanted to kill Him. The word *marvel* could be translated in a phrase, *all excited about it.* In the way Jesus referred to it, it seems that the healing of that man was to be seen as a case of teaching the mind of God.

Jesus then went on to justify His judgment by the Scriptures. Moses gave them circumcision, and they did not hesitate to circumcise a man on the Sabbath day. From this He argued their inconsistency: "If a man may receive circumcision on the Sabbath, that you may keep that law of Moses, why are you so angry with me because I have made a man whole on the Sabbath day? You circumcise a man that he may receive blessing; I healed a man that he might receive blessing." In their superficial judgment the one practice was right and the other wrong. This is obviously evidence of gross inconsistency and illustrates the truth that while men may rationalize in defense of their opinions, their judgments are faulty when based upon personal prejudices or preferences. It is clear that such judgment is not to be trusted.

When the heart is right with God a person will search the Scriptures, and so the mind will be sound, because it is under the control of the Spirit of God. A sincere Christian needs to rely upon God daily for guidance in his thinking, humbly seeking His will, ever willing to follow that blessed will when it is revealed in his own consciousness.

THE JEWS' DILEMMA (7:25-31)

When one remembers all the good Jesus had done, it is strange so many opposed Him, but people can be influenced by talk. They are always ready to believe the worst that is said about any person, or any given situation. And enough had been said to produce confusion:

> But lo, he speaketh boldly, and they [the authorities] say nothing unto him. Do the rulers know indeed that this is the very Christ? Howbeit we know this man whence he is: but when Christ cometh, no man knoweth whence he is (John 7:26, 27).

It seems that the people felt any action of God would be totally beyond their understanding and outside of their daily experience. At the same time, they felt they knew about Jesus since He lived among them. Thus, in the minds of many, Jesus was disqualified at the very start. They were sure that when the Christ did come, none of them would be able to understand Him or His teaching. But Jesus spoke in words they could grasp, and was living His life among them without pomp or show. From this they concluded He must be only human, and so not the One to be sent from God, the Messiah. And yet the authorities did not stop His preaching!

This dilemma is reported elsewhere in the gospel narratives. The neighbors had much the same things to say. "Who is this Jesus and what is so unusual about Him? Don't we know His mother, His brothers, His sisters, and hasn't He lived right here amongst us" (Matthew 13:54-58)? What all this is based on is their assumption that they knew Jesus Christ as one of them. When the Christ, the Messiah, comes, they certainly would not know Him intimately as they thought they knew Jesus.

As a matter of fact there was that about Jesus Christ which these neighbors and these crowds did not know. They may have heard the story of Bethlehem, in which case they would have judged Mary because they did not know of the angel, Gabriel, nor of the hand of God in her affairs. They knew Jesus grew up in Nazareth, and He was called the Nazarene. They could see His humble spirit, and because of that humility, it did not seem possible to them that this could be the Son of the living God. All their thinking was based on the humanity of Jesus, and thus they felt justified in denying that there was anything supernatural about Him. They were convinced He could not be the Christ.

All this illustrates a very important fact: it is possible to be entirely wrong in thinking about Jesus Christ, if one emphasizes the human form in which He lived, and does not accept that He was God incarnate in the form of man. A person will never understand Jesus nor be able to accept Him as the Christ, unless he gets this defect cleared away in his thinking.

Jesus Himself tried to lead them into thinking of the truth they had been missing.

> Then cried Jesus in the temple as he taught, saying, Ye both know me, and ye know whence I am: and I am not come of myself, but he that sent me is true, whom ye know not. But I know him: for I am from him, and he hath sent me (John 7:28, 29).

Thus Jesus was saying in effect, "You claim to know me as a human being. You claim that you know me as neighbor, living in a carpenter's home, growing up in your midst. But you have no knowledge of the part God, my Father, has played in my life. You think of me as Jesus of Nazareth, but you know nothing about the forces upholding me, the power which sustains me. You don't recognize that God sent me, and this is why you are in such confusion in your minds about me."

JESUS WAS UNIQUE

Recently there was published a book written for the purpose of teaching children about Jesus. A chapter in this book discussed the boy Jesus. It told the story from His birth through His childhood. The author seemed to want the children to think of Him as being a Jewish boy, picturing what His life would be like in a typical Jewish home as He helped His mother and worked with Joseph. There was no mention of Gabriel's visit to Mary, and nothing of the angels coming to the shepherds. Does not this book actually set forth an entirely distorted picture of Jesus of Nazareth?

The coming of Gabriel to Mary, the heavenly host giving their message to the shepherds on the hillside, the wise men journeying as they followed the star — none of these things would have happened at the birth of an ordinary Jewish baby. They happened to show that this was a different Child. Mary was told He would be called the Son of God. Any one who does not know and accept as true these features in the story cannot understand Jesus and will have difficulty accepting Him as the Christ, our Redeemer and Lord.

Luke tells that the aged saint, Anna, who had served in the Temple for so many years, recognized this infant as the long-awaited Messiah. Simeon, who had been in the temple service for most of his life and had been promised that he would not see death until he had seen the Lord's Christ, worshiped when he saw the Child, and gave praise to God for having let his eyes see the salvation prepared by God (Luke 2:25-35). No one could ever really know the boy and man growing to adulthood in Nazareth, unless he knew this other side of the picture. To omit the heavenly features in any account of the life and person of Jesus of Nazareth is to be left in the confusion of doubt.

There are people today who claim to have an understanding of Christian experience and talk about it as a psychological affair. They speak about it as if it were a matter of adjusting one's personality to that of Jesus. They would promote Christianity as a cultural experience or as good social relationships. Usually one does not find such people engaged in prayer and praise to God. The truth is that it is impossible to have any life as a Christian unless one enters into personal relationship with God through the atoning work of His Son, Jesus Christ and in the fellowship of the Holy Spirit.

If anyone attempts to develop Christian experience on the basis of human relationship with a great teacher, he will never have any true grasp of why Jesus came, nor of what it really means to be a Christian.

In this very incident John points out something that shows how the confusion of doubt can be cleared:

> And many of the people believed on him, and said, When Christ cometh, will he do more miracles than these which this man hath done? (John 7:31)

Here is the answer. Look not at the human form of the manifestation, but at the results of the gospel witness, wherever it is believed and accepted, in any age.

What should be done about the confusion in men's minds today? Direct attention to the gospel narratives and deal with any difficulties and differences in the minds of men in the clear light of what Jesus did and said. When people think of Jesus as only human, they miss the point of the Gospel, and fail to find the promised forgiveness and peace of mind and heart. When men and women think of the Christian life as something they do by trying to improve themselves, while ignoring the spiritual and the supernatural aspects of living in Christ, the real truth is missed.

EVANGELIZATION

Opposition to the preaching of the Gospel of Jesus Christ is current today, just as the Jewish people opposed Him in the days of His flesh. Today many prominent church leaders oppose evangelistic efforts of any kind, ignoring the fact that the message was sent for all men. The need for such preaching was pointed out long ago by the Apostle Paul.

> For whosoever shall call upon the name of the Lord shall be saved. How then shall they call on him in whom they have not believed? and how shall they believe in him of whom they have not heard? and how shall they hear without a preacher? (Romans 10:13, 14)

It is obviously necessary that men and women be *evangelized,* that is, told the Gospel of God's love, manifest in Christ, if they are to become Christians.

When a human being is born into this world, he does not know about Christ. As he grows into understanding, he must be told the good news of Jesus and His love. In the world are all kinds of people, good and bad. There are strong, true, honest people, just as there are weak, sinful, cruel people. And there are Christians, both strong and weak. But there are no Christians unless the Gospel has been preached.

The Gospel of Christ is commonly preached by evangelists and missionaries, who go out to tell sinful men that "whosoever will may come," and ". . . him that cometh to me I will in no wise cast out." Witnesses go to the ends of the earth to tell all men, everywhere, that God sent His Son into the world to seek and to save the lost. And so, around the world, there is continual activity on the part of believing people in spreading this gospel message among unbelievers.

It seems reasonable that any Christian would accept this method of reaching others for Christ. Anyone should understand the urgent need of reaching unsaved men and women. But here is the amazing fact noted above. There is opposition, strong opposition in some quarters, to such evangelistic ministry and against those who would press the claims of Christ upon those who do not know Him.

I personally can look back upon the days when I myself was an agnostic, a sincere unbeliever. When I heard of such opposition to evangelism expressed by some church people, I took it as a further sign that this message just wasn't true! This seemed obvious since people "on the inside" were promoting it. In my mind then, and to this very day, there was and is astonishment that men who claim to believe in the Gospel of the Lord Jesus Christ and to serve Him, can be actually in strong opposition to any evangelistic work.

Our generation has seen great movements of evangelism in various parts of the world with many people responding. Yet there are men in opposition who cannot claim to have won anyone to Christ. A similar situation exists about missionaries, who go around the world to tell the good news that Jesus Christ can save and will keep. Yet in some churches where nothing is being done to win souls there are movements which seek to stop this missionary thrust.

Ironic Opposition (7:32-53)

Even so in some churches today, there are people who are seeking to live closer to the Lord than they ever have before. They are studying the Word more closely to ascertain the teaching about the person and work of the Holy Spirit. Yet it is reported there are pastors and church leaders who are very much against this emphasis. Such an attitude is not new! The same sort of opposition occurred in connection with the ministry of Jesus:

> The Pharisees heard that the people murmured such things concerning him; and the Pharisees and the chief priests sent officers to take him (John 7:32).

This opposition is so ironic because the Pharisees got their name from their intense loyalty to Scripture. They were men who fully believed the Old Testament to be the very Word of God. They were strong to admonish that unless a man was fully obedient to what the Scriptures said, he could not be in the will of God. These people, who so openly announced their commitment to God's Word as they had it in the Old Testament, were the very ones who most strenuously opposed God's Son and Messenger! They did everything in their power to stop His public ministry.

There is much to be learned in observing Jesus Christ's answers to His opponents. In this case He made no attempt to evade the issue before Him. He made no attempt to placate His critics. He simply went on saying the very things He had been proclaiming before they began their opposition.

> Then said Jesus unto them, Yet a little while am I with you, and then I go unto him that sent me. Ye shall seek me, and shall not find me: and where I am, thither ye cannot come (John 7:33, 34).

In other words Jesus is saying, "For a little while I am within your reach, and then I am going back to the Father — the One who sent me. Where I am, you cannot come." This was telling this group of Pharisees that they had utterly failed to understand His purpose and mission. They had no grasp at all of where He came from, nor did they recognize the Father who sent Him, and to whom He was to return. In fact these people did not understand Him at all, for they exclaimed about what He said, and argued heatedly. It would seem that they failed utterly to understand their own Old Testament with its prophetic utterances. Not only were their eyes blinded, but their hearts were hardened.

LIVING WATER

> In the last day, that great day of the feast, Jesus stood and cried, saying, If any man thirst, let him come unto me, and drink. He that believeth on me, as the scripture hath said, out of his belly shall flow rivers of living water. (But this spake he of the Spirit, which they that believe on him should receive: for the Holy Ghost was not yet given; because that Jesus was not yet glorified) (John 7:37-39).

Here, again, Jesus stirred up controversy. The Jewish people recognized this as a promise from God, a passage from the Old Testament promising the coming of the Spirit. Some said, "This must be He." Others said, "This man might be the very Christ." And so the arguments went on. Here is a most interesting thing: they could not agree in their judgment.

> Others said, This is the Christ. But some said, Shall Christ come out of Galilee? Hath not the scripture said, That Christ cometh of the seed of David, and out of the town of Bethlehem, where David was? So there was a division among the people because of him. And some of them would have taken him; but no man laid lands on him (John 7:41- 44).

How very much like so many discussions about the Gospel today! They had their Scriptures which they trusted, and Jesus Christ fit into that prophetic picture (of the seed of David, from Bethlehem), but they did not know it. They were not even aware of the facts concerning Him which could have been ascertained without any difficulty. They were ignorant, and their arguments were developed in spite of a total lack of knowledge.

And yet the testimony of Jesus carried much weight in the face of strong opposition:

> Then came the officers to the chief priests and Pharisees; and they said unto them, Why have ye not brought him? The officers answered, Never man spake like this man (John 7:45, 46).

Evidently Jesus was so convincing that the officers who came to arrest Him were influenced to leave Him untouched. They were actually excusing themselves to the authorities for their failure to apprehend Jesus and bring Him in as a prisoner because of His words. "We never heard anyone talk like this man," was their plea: They had every opportunity. There was no show of force among the disciples with Jesus, but there must have been such an air of authority about Jesus, that these men failed to carry out their plans. That they were deeply impressed can be felt in the argument in answer used by the authorities:

> Then answered them the Pharisees, Are ye also deceived? Have any of the rulers or of the Pharisees believed on him? (John 7:47, 48)

Evidently the consensus of the leaders was entirely against Jesus, with only a few individuals willing to believe. This also has a very meaningful suggestion about conditions today. The evidence of God's presence and blessing in any learning experience is in the changed lives encountered. God can give grace and wisdom in drawing souls to Him, when the disciple is looking to receive the things of the Lord Jesus Christ, and puts his trust fully in Him, giving no heed to other voices which would seek to lead him astray.

Chapter 9

THE GLORIOUS FACT OF THE GOSPEL

CHRIST'S GRACIOUSNESS (8:1-11)

Perhaps no story told of the gracious acts of Jesus of Nazareth is more widely appreciated than the account of what happened when the women taken in adultery was brought before Him. The meaning has been widely appreciated, often expressed in hymns.

> Christ receiveth sinful men, Even me with all my sin;
> Purged from every spot and stain, Heav'n with Him I enter in.
> Sing it o'er and o'er again, Christ receiveth sinful men;
> Make the message clear and plain, Christ receiveth sinful men.

Christians delight in publishing this truth far and wide. Sin is real, and one does not need to study the Bible to realize that. On every side can be seen the evidence of the reality of sin and the power of Satan. Sin is harmful. Any conduct on man's part, any attitude which is contrary to the will of God is harmful, because it separates man from God, as well as separates man from man. Sin is unclean, and destructive of all that is good. ". . . the soul that sinneth, it shall die," is the word of the Old Testament (Ezekiel 18:4); and Paul writes: ". . . the wages of sin is death . . ." (Romans 6:23). Habakkuk says of God: "Thou art of purer eyes than to behold evil, and canst not look on iniquity . . ." (Habakkuk 1:13). Nothing too strong can be said about sin; and yet the wonder of the Gospel is that sin can be forgiven, cleansed, and forgotten by God!

> . . . though your sins be as scarlet, they shall be as white as snow; though they be red like crimson, they shall be as wool (Isaiah 1:18).

The Bible leaves no room to question that God hates sin in any form: but He loves the sinner! In fact, one of the features which marked Jesus' earthly ministry was His association with sinners! This caused Him to be brought under reproach and accusation by the Pharisees on more than one occasion. For example:

> . . . as Jesus sat at meat in the house, behold, many publicans
> and sinners came and sat down with him and his disciples. And
> when the Pharisees saw it, they said unto the disciples, Why
> eateth your Master with publicans and sinners? But when Jesus
> heard that, he said unto them, They that be whole need not a
> physician, but they that are sick (Matthew 9:10-12).

It is true that some modern translations do not carry these eleven
verses in John's gospel. They are left out, not because scholars found
fault with the teaching, but because some older manuscripts do not
contain them. Nothing in this portion is such that it cannot be substan-
tiated and supported by other Scriptures. It does illustrate this truth we
are considering, Jesus' love for everyone.

THE WOMAN BROUGHT TO JESUS

Apparently this woman taken in adultery was brought before Jesus
as a sort of "test case" for the leaders to find out how Jesus would judge
her. They felt that they could make it difficult for Jesus because the
law of Moses specified that if anyone were taken in the act of adultery,
such a one should be stoned to death.

At this time Jerusalem was under the control of the Roman government, and Rome had certain laws, one of which was that sentence
of capital punishment, was reserved for the Roman courts only. The
Jews could inflict punishment up to a certain point, but they were not
allowed to inflict the death penalty without the consent of the Roman
courts. If Jesus judged in literal compliance with the law of Moses He
would offend the Roman rulers.

With this malicious intent the scribes and Pharisees brought this
woman before Jesus.

> And the scribes and Pharisees brought unto him a woman taken
> in adultery; and when they had set her in the midst, They say
> unto him, Master, this woman was taken in adultery, in the very
> act. Now Moses in the law commanded us, that such should be
> stoned: but what sayest thou? This they said, tempting him, that
> they might have to accuse him . . . (John 8:3-6).

WRITING IN THE SAND

The procedure by which Jesus handled this situation is famous and
has become a classic in wisdom. When the woman had been brought
before Him, Jesus quietly stooped down, and with His finger, wrote in
the sand. How many speculations there have been as to what words
He wrote! But nobody knows; conjecture and imagination will not
help. As they continued pressing Him for His judgment, Jesus showed
that He was aware that the fate of the woman was of no concern to
these men. They could have handled her judgment without approaching Him. Calmly He said,

. . . He that is without sin among you, let him first cast a stone at
her. And again he stooped down, and wrote on the ground (John
8:7, 8).

The account does not say that Jesus refused to look at them, it
simply says he left them alone. This gave time for God to speak to
them individually. Their response seemed to show that they had some
respect for Him, even though they were trying to trap Him; it is
evident that they paid attention to what He said:

And they which heard it, being convicted by their own conscience,
went out one by one, beginning at the eldest, even unto the
last: and Jesus was left alone, and the woman standing in the midst
(John 8:9).

There is nothing in the record to indicate that He was known to
the woman — He may have appeared to her simply as a responsible
teacher of truth. It is possible that her use of the title "Lord" did
not have any deep personal connection. John simply reports:

When Jesus had lifted up himself, and saw none but the woman,
he said unto her, Woman, where are those thine accusers? hath
no man condemned thee? She said, No man, Lord. And Jesus
said unto her, Neither do I condemn thee: go, and sin no more
(John 8:10, 11).

Does this mean Jesus condoned sin? Anyone knows better than that!
Does this mean He approved of her sin? That need hardly to be
denied. In a short time He was to die for the sins of all the world,
this poor woman's included. Then what does His reply mean?

GOD'S ATTITUDE TOWARD SIN

Here Jesus is revealing God's attitude toward sin and the sinner.
Make no mistake, don't ever wonder about it, there need be no doubt
that God hates sin. But let us cherish this glad fact and tell it to
others: God loves the sinner! When Christ Jesus looks at sinners, He
sees them as He did this woman. He sees them as the persons for
whom He shed His blood.

What a glorious word of comfort for all believers! There is no Christian who is not conscious of sin within. Even Paul cried out,

O wretched man that I am! who shall deliver me from the body
of this death? I thank God through Jesus Christ our Lord . . .
(Romans 7:24, 25).

A person must think of his past life and himself standing one day
in the presence of God. Perhaps some sin has been troubling him, or
there is something in his record which haunts him. If any one should

read these lines being thus troubled by conscience, he need only believe in the Lord Jesus Christ, believe in the forgiveness of sin. Think of this woman and of Christ's attitude toward her.

Believers should keep in mind that He wants to set them free forever from the dead works that hinder them. Anyone can have perfect freedom and liberty to turn to Jesus Christ, remembering that when He sees the sinner, He does not think of the sin, but of the sinner's need of forgiveness, and He will deliver him from sin.

THE LIGHT OF THE WORLD (8:12-20)

When Jesus was describing His ministry here upon earth, He said, "I am the light of the world." No one who looks at Jesus as being only a man can ever realize the truth about Him. This gospel of John begins by saying that ". . . the Word was with God, and the Word was God," referring, of course, to Jesus of Nazareth as THE WORD. That opening statement goes on to say that "In him was life; and the life was the light of men." To understand what Jesus meant it is important to consider what is the normal function of light: what does it do?

The first thing light does is to *reveal*. Whatever is in a room will show up when the light is turned on. When there is daylight, one can see whatever is in the yard. It does not add anything; it merely discloses whatever is present. Paul wrote ". . . for whatsoever doth make manifest is light" (Ephesians 5:13).

When Jesus said "I am the light of the world," He was saying "I myself show the true meaning of life in this world." In these words He challenged man to consider that in Himself is to be seen the truth of the creation. Does any person really want to understand living in this world? He will have to look at Jesus. When he looks at the Christ, he will be looking at One who came into this world to die, in order that he might be raised from the dead. This points to the amazing truth, that the physical world is not the final stage in God's plan. Something comes after the physical.

It is obvious that in this world the physical is first: the natural begins life. But looking at Jesus reveals that the natural must die and be raised from the dead into a new life by the power of God. This is the truth of the plan of the whole universe. When God made the world, He did not make it with the idea that this world as it is seen in the physical form, with trees, birds, flowers, sea, sky, and people, was to be everlasting. The world as it is, with both its physical appearance and sin, was never designed to be the last stage.

The Lord Jesus Christ was the Lamb slain before the foundation of the world. God, in creating the world and making man in His own image out of the dust of the ground, planned that the flesh was to die, but the resurrection of man into newness of life would bring him into the fulness of His plan for him. Thus the Gospel proclaims that when anyone is raised from the dead, as Christ was, he will have the life in him that His Son manifested. This means that God Himself will live in His creatures in the new world. This is the tremendous truth that is revealed in Jesus Christ. This world is not final. Even sin cannot end everything here. God can raise the dead and will raise the dead. In so doing He will redeem the sinner into eternal life through Christ.

It is to be noted that just before Jesus said, "I am the light of the world," there were two major actions on His part. One was the healing of the lame man by the Pool of Bethesda, and the other was the forgiveness of the sin of the woman taken in adultery. In these Jesus Christ is seen overruling the weakness of the lame man and overruling the sin of the woman. This is a promise of what is in God's plan as both these aspects of human nature are left behind. In the resurrection power of Jesus Christ, the believer is lifted beyond weakness and beyond sin. In this sense the believer is actually *delivered* from both weakness and sin. This is the real truth of the Gospel and a part of the meaning of the words of Jesus: ". . . he that followeth me shall not walk in darkness, but shall have the light of life."

PHARISEES BELITTLE JESUS

The Pharisees evidently realized how profound were the implications of what Jesus was saying. They could not deny what Jesus had done, but they could question what He taught. They sought to belittle His teaching by challenging its authority on the basis that He was making claims for Himself without any support from anyone else.

> The Pharisees therefore said unto him, Thou bearest record of thyself; thy record is not true (John 8:13).

The scribes and Pharisees applied an accepted principle to His teaching. They pointed out that there should be the testimony of at least two, whereas Jesus was defending Himself by His own words alone. The answer that Jesus gave was very revealing: He claimed that since the living God was with Him in all He did, there were actually two Persons agreeing in His utterances.

> Jesus answered and said unto them, Though I bear record of myself, yet my record is true; for I know whence I came, and whither I go; but ye cannot tell whence I come and whither I go . . . for I am not alone, but I and the Father that sent me. It is also written in your law, that the testimony of two men is true. I am one that bear witness of myself, and the Father that sent me beareth witness of me. Then said they unto him, Where is thy Father? Jesus answered, Ye neither know me, nor my Father: if ye had known me, ye should have known my Father also (John 8:14-19).

There is something to be noted in that Jesus did not here use the word *God* as in a general way He might speak of *God, the Creator*. He used the word *Father* as the One who commissioned Him. The meaning of God which Jesus is stressing is that God is the One by whom He had been begotten: God the Father, who sent Him, and lived within Him. When Christians call God *Father,* they need to remind themselves that they are using the word which means they have been born of the Spirit and are truly His sons and daughters.

JESUS' WAY (8:21-27)

The only way to secure the blessings and benefits of having God as your Father is through personal relationship with Jesus Christ. This is the meaning of what Jesus said to the Jews who opposed Him.

> . . . for if ye believe not that I am he, ye shall die in your sins (John 8:24).

Even today there are some people who have the misconception that because Jesus died for all, all men are saved. It is true that "God is not willing that any should perish," but no one should forget the words of Jesus when He warned:

> Enter ye in at the strait gate: for wide is the gate, and broad is the way that leadeth to destruction, and many there be which go in thereat: Because strait is the gate, and narrow is the way, which leadeth unto life, and few there be that find it" (Matthew 7:13, 14).

This statement should make it impossible for any man who reads the Bible to hold any such error.

Jesus went on to contrast the thinking of the public who were opposing Him, and the truth in Himself, clearly showing the difference. He said, "I go my way," as if that were different from what others might think. Then He added, ". . . ye shall seek me, and shall die in your sins; whither I go, ye cannot come" (verse 21). This was an open declaration of difference. "I go my way," that is, in the spiritual world: "Ye shall seek me," that is, in the natural world, "and shall die in your sins" being still in the natural world. No word here of eternal life through the Son coming to every man by the grace of God! Remember here Jesus was speaking to human beings and makes no reference to them as children of God. He was the Son of God and had in Himself the very life of God. They were human, with all of the evil inherent in human nature, and they were trying to find out about Him on the level of earthly knowledge. "Ye shall seek me," on their level of human living from their earthly point of view, and "shall die in your sins." They would go on as they were the rest of their days and they would eventually face death without hope. Unregenerate people cannot inherit the kingdom of God. They cannot share in the blessings given to those who accept Christ and put their lives in His keeping.

THE WAY IS SPIRITUAL

This certainly needs to be emphasized. "I go my way": this is the spiritual, this is living the life of God, having God live within. "Ye shall seek me": trying with the understanding of the flesh to find the truth in Christ, looking upon Jesus as a human being, as a mere man, refusing to accept His oneness with the Father. These people did not die in their sins because God had become impatient with them, but because they were still in the flesh. The new life had been offered to them, and they had rejected it. They had chosen to remain in the natural realm, and this was the great difference.

Jesus continued to expound on this vast difference:

> . . . Ye are from beneath; I am from above: ye are of this world, I am not of this world (John 8:23).

Here the difference is in their origin. They were earthly, striving for selfish ends, and the things that perish. Their outlook on life was marred by sin. Their destiny before them was to be destroyed. Such people are never able to understand Him.

When Jesus said, "Ye shall die in your sins," He was not imposing any punishment: this was not His condemnation: it was a simple statement of fact. Just as believers in Christ live in the spiritual realm, and will never see death, so these Pharisees and others with them went to death, because it was the natural end of their earthly existence. An opportunity had been offered for change, but they had not taken it. And so their life pattern was also the pattern of their end — death in sin. There was no relief in sight for them, nor could there be, unless they turned from their ways to accept Him.

This is actually the gist of the whole gospel message. This is the very meaning of what Christians preach. The Lord Jesus Christ now lives in the spiritual world with His Father. He lives in the hearts of believers by the Holy Spirit, whom He sent to be their Companion. When a person believes in Him and receives Him as Saviour from sin and its penalty, he becomes a child of God by the new birth, born "of water and the Spirit," and is now a new creature in Christ Jesus. He now has two natures within him, the old man, in which he was born physically, and the new man, in which he is made alive in Christ Jesus. By dying in and to the flesh, he can be delivered from the sins of the flesh and by receiving the Holy Spirit he can have peace, joy, and victory as he trusts in His Saviour and Lord.

The Unique Humanity of Jesus (8:28-32)

Today a great deal is being said about the humanity of Jesus, even in Christian circles, and this is a place where it is necessary to be very careful. It is true He wore a human body for about thirty-three years, in which He limited Himself to human situations down here: He suffered as men suffer, and was "in all points tempted like as we are, yet without sin" (Hebrews 4:15). But the actual fact of the matter is that Jesus Christ did not live in His human form as ordinary human beings live. Even in His human manifestation, He said "I do nothing of myself." Could anyone else say this of himself? ". . . God was in Christ, reconciling the world unto himself . . ." Paul writes in II Corinthians 5:19. His death was not the result, primarily of the sentence passed upon Him: for He went to that death willingly. The plan of salvation was God's plan. God sent His Son into this sinful world, God guided and directed Him, and God eventually brought Him face to face with the crucifixion. Jesus Himself spoke plainly of His unique role in His earthly career:

> Then said Jesus unto them, When ye have lifted up the Son of man, then shall ye know that I am he, and that I do nothing of myself; but as my Father hath taught me, I speak these things (John 8:28).

Lifting up refers to the crucifixion. He Himself promised that if they destroyed the temple of His body, He would rebuild it — raise it up — in three days. His resurrection is a very significant part of the story of Calvary. He promised that when He was crucified, then they would know that He did nothing of Himself, that then the truth would be fully known.

What could be more meaningful in an astonishing way than *that God would raise Jesus from the grave!* And what does that mean for believers in Him? It means that God will intervene in behalf of His own: He will take a hand in the affairs of men when they put their trust in Him. This is exactly what is expressed in the Gospel for all to understand. The revelation began with the cross of Calvary where God made manifest His power and plan in the Resurrection in such a miraculous way.

Until the time of His death, a person might think of Jesus as merely human, a man endowed with the gift of healing, doing astonishing things. But when one is confronted by Calvary, and sees Christ on that cross, one begins to understand that He did not die there in His own strength as a human being. He did not die there because human beings put Him there or because there was no way of escape possible. He died as a part of God's plan as well as His own, in obedience to the Father. He died in order that He might be raised from the dead and so might be able to raise believers with Him.

> And he that sent me is with me: the Father hath not left me alone; for I do always those things that please him (John 8:29).

Never alone — God always with Him! Later John used this kind of language when talking with His disciples.

> I will not leave you comfortless: I will come to you (John 14: 18).

Here is a great truth: God in and with His Son; and God in and with His adopted sons, the believers in Christ Jesus, by His Holy Spirit. The power of this truth is truly remarkable, as Jesus went on to point out,

> And ye shall know the truth, and the truth shall make you free (John 8:32).

This will be freedom in God, not license; but true freedom to do His will, as He enables.

A CONTROVERSY (8:33-59)

When men think about the Christian life and consider the fruit of the Spirit, they have in mind love, joy, peace, longsuffering, gentleness, goodness, faith, meekness, and temperance. Certainly no one would be opposed to such characteristics in their friends or relatives! Most favor these manifestations of the Spirit, glad for other people to experience them, and glad to have them themselves. Yet there is to be found definite resistance to the truth of the new life in the believer.

What actually produces this manifestation of the new life in the heart and life of a believer is the Holy Spirit. Yet the very mention of the Spirit of God seems to stir up opposition and antagonism. In the church itself some of the most serious animosity occurs along this line. This is similar to the fact that some church leaders, as already noted in this study, will oppose evangelistic activity. It is this same group of people often who oppose the deep truth of the indwelling Holy Spirit. It would seem almost as if, in pride, they resent any intimation that they are not quite all right, just as they are. These people cannot accept the idea that it would be to their advantage to be changed, but seem determined to oppose any truth that would make them different.

In the days of Jesus of Nazareth there were various people in Palestine. In this motley population there would surely be some who knew about the things of God. There were the scribes, scholars in the law, persons whom you could count upon to be trained in understanding the Old Testament. Then there were the priests, active in the Temple, actually spending their time in "full time service for the Lord." Then there were the Pharisees, a group of men of a certain school of thought who especially honored the Scriptures as the Word of God and undertook to keep His laws exactly as set forth. And yet all these people: scribes, priests, and Pharisees were on the defensive when they came in touch with Jesus and His teaching.

When Jesus taught the simple principle, "Ye must be born again," they could not accept it. When He talked with Nicodemus, a "ruler of the Jews," He made it clear that all men needed to be born again, regardless of their station in life. But the Jews felt this was not necessary. In order to justify themselves in their position, they argued against all that Jesus was teaching and doing, challenging and opposing every idea He set forth.

This portion of John's gospel (John 8:33-59) is a long record of controversy. The opposition to the teaching of Jesus was carried on from many angles. It was not an argument in order to discover truth. It was not a friendly discussion, such as people of like minds might have as they seek to make some matter clear. This was a series of arguments in which men sought to block the truth! They raised questions which they expected would show plainly that the things Jesus had been preaching simply could not be true.

IMPLICATIONS OF CHRIST'S TEACHINGS

They complained when He said those who trust in Him would be "free." They resented the implications of this teaching. They refused to admit they were in any kind of bondage.

> . . . We be Abraham's seed, and were never in bondage to any man: how sayest thou, Ye shall be made free? (John 8:33).

The Lord Jesus answered them by saying that ". . . Whosoever committeth sin is the servant of sin" (verse 34). They could understand that a man who is a servant is not free to do as he pleases — he is a slave. "And the servant abideth not in the house for ever: but the Son abideth ever." The Son of the household may come and go as it pleases him, and "If the Son therefore shall make you free, ye shall be free indeed" (John 8:35, 36). If they had the freedom of the Son by being born again, they would be actually free from sin.

There is a deeper meaning here than lies on the surface. Jesus is telling these men that in the natural life, as human beings, they are in the flesh. In the flesh there is sin, and it is impossible for them to free themselves from sin. A man can no more free himself from sin than he can free himself from the skin which covers him. But there is one thing which can be done, and that is, to die to the flesh. If a man follows the instructions of Paul the Apostle, ". . . reckon ye also yourselves to be dead indeed unto sin," he will be "alive unto God through Jesus Christ our Lord" (Romans 6:11). If this is done, sin no longer has any claim upon the man.

These Jews, resenting this view of themselves replied that they had never been in bondage to anybody. Jesus replied that it was not a case of their being in bondage to any person, it was bondage to sin which held them fast. So long as they were in the natural body, they were the slaves of sin, but He was ready to set them free from that bondage by teaching them that they might be born again and received as children of God.

As Jesus went on with His teaching He admitted that He knew of their claim to be the children of God because they were of the seed of Abraham, but He challenged that claim as being untrue. In rejecting Him they did not act in line with Abraham, nor did they act as children of God. Actually their conduct was such as would belong to the children of the devil. When they replied, ". . . we have one Father, even God," Jesus said unto them, "If God were your father, ye would love me . . ." (verses 41, 42). The very fact that they opposed Him showed they were not the children of God, who had sent Him and was working in Him and through Him.

As He continued this whole line of teaching the Jews simply rejected Him altogether. ". . . Say we not well that thou art a Samaritan, and hast a devil?" (verse 48). This was language designed to insult and disparage Him. But Jesus shows His humility by patiently continuing the discussion. He simply stated, ". . . I have not a devil; but I honour my Father, and ye do dishonour me" (verse 49).

As Jesus went on with His message he made further mention of Abraham as having rejoiced to see His day. The Jews were not able at all to follow the spiritual aspect of what Jesus was teaching. They felt the words of Jesus were ridiculous because Abraham had been dead many centuries before. It is very illuminating to see that Jesus did not explain away those spiritual statements. He simply repeated them and then accepted the consequence of the flat rejection of Himself and His teaching.

Chapter 10

THE SOURCE OF SIN

THE MAN BORN BLIND (9:1-7)

John tells the story of the man who was born blind and how Jesus healed him. When they saw what was done, His disciples asked Him why the man before them had been born blind. They wanted to know if it might have been sin on the part of the parents, or the man's own sin. Jesus was emphatic in His reply:

> . . . Neither hath this man sinned, nor his parents: but that the works of God should be made manifest in him (John 9:3).

The disciples had asked the natural question. In the answer of Jesus there is much to be learned about the meaning of calamity. It is natural to feel that suffering is punishment for sin. The heart of a man in trouble finds it natural to think *It is because I have done something wrong*. But this is not always true.

Some years ago I stayed overnight in a home that had been saddened by the tragic death of the only son. He had been a member of the Air Force. Having completed his term of duty, he was ready to come home and was waiting at the military base for transportation. He went for a plane ride with a friend, just to pass the time. That plane crashed, and the young man who had gone through years of military service without injury, was killed. His parents were crushed. He was their only son, and when I visited in their home a year later, the heaviness of their grief was still with them. After some hesitation the mother asked me a natural question: "Did our son lose his life because of something that we did? Is this because of something his father did, or did I do something wrong?" With this story in John in my mind I was so glad to be able to answer her with, "No, no, no!"

Just recently I had a telephone call from a listener to our radio program. She was greatly grieved because her only daughter had just fallen into shame and trouble. What was making her heart ache was the fact that years ago, when she was a young woman, she herself had done wrong. She asked me, "Is my daughter now suffering and in trouble because of the sin I committed long ago?" Because of this story in John's gospel I was able to say, "No, no, no!"

The mother of the young airman said, "You talk as if you were sure about that."

I said I was, and hoped to convey that to her. She wanted to know how I could possibly be so sure. Was it not true, she reasoned, that if we did wrong we would be punished?

I said to her, "Of course, all trouble comes from sin and all distress comes from sin: all the misery in this world is undoubtedly due to the fact that there is sin here." After emphasizing that one day God *will* judge, one day He will punish, I went on to say this is not the day of judgment. This is the day when God is showing His grace to the whole world.

WORK TODAY

As John tells the story there is another lesson to be seen in this incident. Jesus made the remark: "I must work the works of him that sent me, while it is day: the night cometh, when no man can work" (John 9:4).

Is one time as good as another for work? If there is something that should be done today, won't tomorrow do just as well for it? If there is need to pray, to read some of the Word of God, to visit a friend, would it not be just as well to do it some other time as now?

I was rebuked once by a fine Mexican Christian for using the words *soon* and *some day* in regard to the Lord's work. He said these words were not the language of the Holy Spirit. When I looked at him in surprise, he said, "Today is the day. *Today* is the Holy Spirit's word! If there is a job you must do, do it today. Don't put it off!"

The actual opening of this blind man's eyes illustrates yet another truth.

> When he had thus spoken, he spat on the ground, and made clay of the spittle, and he anointed the eyes of the blind man with the clay, And said unto him, Go wash in the pool of Siloam, (which is by interpretation, Sent). He went his way therefore, and washed, and came seeing (John 9:6, 7).

This question is natural, "Do we ever have any part in getting answers to prayer? If the result is going to come from God, does He not do the whole thing?" Sometimes it seems that way. As Jesus went about doing the works of God, there were occasions when He said, "Be clean." In the case before us, however, Jesus made clay, and anointed the eyes of the blind man and sent him to wash in the Pool of Siloam. The man went, did as he had been told, and came back seeing. Here it would seem the man had some part to play in getting the answer from God.

A Choice

It seems that when there is anything as wonderful as a promise of eternal life, offered freely to men, that people would want to receive it. Yet deep down in every human being there is a willfulness, a desire to go one's own way. When a person senses that coming to the Lord and receiving Jesus Christ means that he has to give up his own will that person may rebel.

People do not like to be forced to choose. When a man is offered this free gift of God oftentimes he does not want to be responsible for turning it down. Instead, he tries to find fault with the offer. He intimates that there is something not quite right about it. John reports several instances of this sort of response.

Pharisees Critical (9:8-41)

After this healing, the restoring of sight to a man blind from birth, the Pharisees began at once to complain that Jesus had been wrong. They were particularly critical of the procedure that Jesus followed. They did not want to acknowledge the claims made by Jesus in any way at all, and they took any opportunity to hold fast to their position. The tragedy of the whole matter was that they reduced a great miracle to no significance (for them, at least!) by their criticism of procedure and their destructive arguments.

Years ago, in the city of Winnipeg, Canada, the whole community was deeply stirred by an unusual incident. A couple of boys had gone down the river on a raft. Suddenly they were in grave danger of drowning. Other boys nearby saw the danger, rushed down to a boat they knew about. They leaped into the boat, and went out to rescue the two frightened small boys. When the rescue party brought them safely to shore, the owner of the boat accused the boys of stealing his boat! This created such a reaction in the community that the owner of the boat finally had to leave the community. Of course the charge of stealing the boat was utterly ridiculous. Yet the same type of unreasonable opposition to the Gospel occurs today.

Persistence

It is remarkable how persistent the opposition against Jesus was. First of all, they questioned the man whose sight had been restored, asking him how his eyes were opened. When he told them, they asked where the man was who had done this work. The once-blind man said he did not know. Then they asked again how the healing had been done. Of course the Pharisees really did not want to know this, they were looking for a way to find fault. When they heard He had done this deed on the Sabbath day, they immediately announced that this man was not of God because He had not kept the Sabbath day.

The reaction of the man who had been healed was quite different. He said: "Well, if He is wrong, and such a sinner, how could He open my blind eyes?"

The Pharisees then questioned the parents, for they did not accept what the son said, thinking he was a liar. They asked if this was their son. In this manner they showed their suspicion for they went on to say to the parents, ". . . who ye *say* was born blind?" (verse 19). Thus they showed they were ready to accuse the parents of not telling the truth. The answer was definite:

> . . . We know that this is our son, and that he was born blind:
> But by what means he now seeth, we know not; or who hath
> opened his eyes, we know not: he is of age; ask him: he shall
> speak for himself (John 9:20, 21).

Because the blind man's parents would say nothing about what happened the Pharisees were unable to get any information on which to build their accusations against Jesus except the healing on the Sabbath day. When they tried to make the man himself admit that it had been evil for Jesus to cure him on the Sabbath day they received his final word of testimony, the classic rebuttal, ". . . one thing I know, that, whereas I was blind, now I see" (verse 25).

Following their failure to secure an accusation against Jesus, the Pharisees expressed their chief claim: ". . . we are Moses' disciples." Now pride rings through those four words! The same sort of opposition occurs today. People who oppose strong gospel preaching will turn to the record of some great man in church history, and say, "Well, now, we are of his following, we will think as he did, we will do things his way, and if you don't do it his way, you are wrong." In this way such persons can feel justified in their opposition. But now as then it is the personal testimony that really counts. "Once I was blind — now I see!"

BELIEF

There is one more aspect of this story that is very comforting. After the Pharisees had cast the man out, Jesus heard of it and went to see him. When He found him He asked about his faith. Jesus then revealed Himself to the former blind man. No doubt with great joy, he said, "Lord, I believe," and he worshiped him.

The educated Pharisees, despite their sophisticated interest in the things of God, remained in their unbelief but this sincere individual with his humble response to the actual realities of the Word and the work of God came to know Christ personally.

Chapter 11

THE GOOD SHEPHERD

A WIDE GULF (10:1-10)

There is a wide gulf between Almighty God in His holiness on the one side, and natural man in his sin on the other. The situation can be pictured as a wall or a fence separating God and man. If there were a door in the wall, the question could be asked: "Why is that door important?" The answer is "Because the wall is there." If there were no separation, if no wall, then no door would be needed. The door has significance because the separation is real.

What makes the door valuable? When is it important? The answer is simple. The door is both important and valuable when it is used, and persons go through. If no one uses the door, it might as well be a solid wall. There is no possibility of finding any joy in the statement of Jesus Christ, ". . . I am the door . . ." (10:7), unless the door is being used as an entrance into the presence of God.

John 10:1-6 is something of a parable, in which Jesus says that if someone does not enter in by the door of the sheepfold, but climbs up some other way, he is a thief. But Jesus goes on to say that he who enters in by the door is the shepherd of the sheep. The shepherd uses the door to lead his sheep in to shelter and out to pasture.

> . . . and he calleth his own sheep by name, and leadeth them out. And when he putteth forth his own sheep, he goeth before them, and the sheep follow him: for they know his voice. And a stranger will they not follow, but will flee from him: for they know not the voice of strangers (John 10:3-5).

"I AM THE DOOR"

Continuing to use this figure of speech Jesus plainly identifies Himself as the door:

> Then said Jesus unto them again, Verily, verily, I say unto you, I am the door of the sheep (John 10:7).

Apparently the people did not understand what Jesus was trying to teach them, and so He states the truth again.

> All that ever came before me are thieves and robbers: but the sheep did not hear them. I am the door: by me if any man enter in, he shall be saved, and shall go in and out, and find pasture (John 10:8, 9).

There can be no doubt that Jesus was proclaiming the way a person can come to God. He in Himself is the only way: He is the door.

To say that *Jesus is the Son* of God is a profound statement indeed. This means not only that He has come from God, but that He was sent by God, and that God has committed all judgment to Him. God has given Him power to raise the dead; He has given His Son the right to give eternal life to anyone who believes. So when Jesus says, "I am the door," He is saying, "I am the door through which you can come to receive the blessing of God."

But there is more to salvation and its blessings than just coming to Jesus Christ. He said the believer ". . . shall go in and out, and find pasture." It is not that a person comes to Jesus just once. He does come to Him the first time, but then he is able to "go in and out," and come, and come, and come.

Living in faith is like the marriage relationship. When a young couple gets married, they have a wedding day of much excitement and joyous celebration. But that day of celebration is not the last day! It is only the beginning. It would be a sad story if it were the last day. It is the days that follow, which are bright and rich with promise as they live with each other, and grow to know each other more deeply, that make the wedding day so important.

So it is with coming to the Lord Jesus Christ. The sinner receives forgiveness, is accepted as a child of God, and from then on puts his trust in the Lord Jesus. It is then that He can live as he goes in and out of that precious door and finds pasture.

CONFIDENCE (10:11-18)

What does it mean to have confidence in the Lord Jesus Christ? Why should a man trust himself to Him? The truth will appear when one asks why should anyone trust anybody. Why trust a doctor? a mechanic? a banker? This whole matter of having confidence in someone usually develops if that person does what he is supposed to do.

When the question arises about having confidence in a doctor, one does not mean to trust him to work in the garden. Nor does one trust him to repair the engine of the car. Nor does it mean that one would consult him about some real estate purchase. He is a physician and is trained to deal with physical problems. When the matter of confidence in a doctor is brought up, the issue involved is his skill in dealing with problems concerning physical health.

When a man's car needs repairing, does he select the garage because it is painted red? or green? or because the building is long and narrow, or perhaps high and wide? Is it not true that he pays attention to the reputation of the quality of work the mechanics do in that garage?

So when one considers the question of confidence in the Lord Jesus Christ, it will be important to have in mind what work He offers to do. Such assurance is not based not only upon appraisal of His personal character as such, nor is it by understanding the source of His wisdom or power, but also by noting the consequences and the results of His working in the lives of human beings.

No doubt one of the reasons why people have difficulty in believing on the Lord Jesus Christ, putting their confidence in Him, is because He offers to forgive them *freely*. There are individuals who know deep down in their hearts that they are not worthy to come to Him, and they cannot believe it is true that He is willing to forgive them. If a man is to have confidence in Jesus Christ, he must accept as a fact that through Jesus, Almighty God will receive him and forgive him.

No one ever receives the blessing of God because he is worthy of God's regard. The blessing of God in the forgiveness of sins is not a matter of God rewarding a person for good behavior. The believer receives God's blessing because of God's grace.

> He that spared not his own Son, but delivered him up for us all, how shall he not with him also freely give us all things? (Romans 8:32)

In order to have confidence in anybody, so that one can fully trust that person, there must be evidence that he can actually do what he promises. Fortunately this is the glorious record of the Lord Jesus Christ.

THE GOOD SHEPHERD

Jesus uses the figure of the Good Shepherd in referring to Himself, and points out another reason for having confidence in Him. Notice how He begins:

> I am the good shepherd: the good shepherd giveth his life for the sheep (John 10:11).

The use of the phrase, *good shepherd,* implies that believers can rely upon Him to care for them. The basis of that confidence is in the statement that He ". . . giveth his life for the sheep." This refers to His death on the cross, when He literally gave up His life that believers in Him might have eternal life. He went willingly to that cross for each one of His own.

By way of emphasizing His trustworthiness Jesus contrasted Himself with someone utterly unworthy of trust or confidence. He talks about the *hireling,* a person who would not be very careful of the sheep. The hireling works only for his wages. He takes the place of the shepherd, but he is not the true shepherd. ". . . he that is an hireling, and not the shepherd, whose own the sheep are not, seeth the wolf coming . . ." — he sees the danger, he feels the threat! The proof of the unworthiness of this man is seen when the wolf comes, and he runs away. ". . . the wolf catcheth them, and scattereth the sheep" (verse 12).

> The hireling fleeth, because he is an hireling, and careth not for the sheep (John 10:13).

This points the finger directly at the ground on which believers can put their confidence in Jesus Christ. He puts Himself into the situation of the sinner and lets it hurt Him, in order to save that person. Anyone may have this experience of somebody coming and wanting to impress him with his trustworthiness as helper. But such a one will run away the moment danger strikes or unpleasant matters arise.

In contrast Jesus expressed the truth about Himself:

> I am the good shepherd, and know my sheep, and am known of mine (John 10:14).

Believers can trust a Good Shepherd like that. There is mutual love and esteem between such a shepherd and sheep. What loving fellowship believers can have with their blessed Lord! He truly knows each believer. Christ Jesus is constantly thinking about and cherishing the Christian.

DYING FOR THE SHEEP

> As the Father knoweth me, even so know I the Father: and I lay down my life for the sheep (John 10:15).

These are related facts. When Jesus says, "As the Father knoweth me . . ." He means the Father has confidence in Him, is trusting in and depending upon Him. In the same way He has confidence, is trusting in and depending upon the Father. Jesus as the Son responds to the Father and obeys Him, carrying out the Father's will. It was in the Father's will that the Son should lay down His life for the sheep. Jesus connected these things, putting them together so that no mistake need be made in understanding His personal, obedient, willing relationship with God His Father and His personal, self-denying sacrifice of Himself for the sheep. This is what the Father sent Him to do!

Jesus pointed out the wide range of His purpose in a simple statement:

> And other sheep I have, which are not of this fold: them also I must bring, and they shall hear my voice; and there shall be one fold, and one shepherd (John 10:16).

This makes it plain that, in addition to coming to His own nation, the Jewish people, He was going to go out into all the world to call people from all nations to put their trust in Him. His aim is to bring all the sheep into one fold. He has never expressed the aim of bringing all nations together: but He is calling believers as His sheep *out of all nations,* bringing them together into the one fold.

> Therefore doth my Father love me, because I lay down my life, that I might take it again. No man taketh it from me, but I lay it down of myself. I have power to lay it down, and I have power to take it again. This commandment have I received of my Father (John 10:17, 18).

Thus did Jesus point out how this work of redemption was to be done. First is the fact that He is going to lay down His life for the sheep; and second that He is laying down His life that He might take it again. This also is part of the work of redemption. The focal point in the whole procedure is the new life which is possible after death. The Son of God brings His first life, His human nature to the cross, and lays it down that He might be raised from the dead. This opens the way for those who put their trust in Him, to rise to new life with Him.

In these words Jesus uttered a classic statement, indicating that His death was voluntary, intentional, and planned for a specific purpose. Human instruments accomplished it, but it was always clearly in the will of God. Jesus died as He did "on purpose," the purpose being the redemption of all who put their trust in Him. ". . . No man taketh it from me . . ." He said. The death of Christ was not an unfortunate accident. It was not because rough Roman soldiers nailed Him to a cross.

No, human beings did not force Him to death. He accepted the cross, as He said, ". . . I lay down my life. . . ." He gave it up: He had power to lay down that life and take it up again, praise God!

This whole discussion enables the believer to have complete confidence in the Lord Jesus Christ, setting out the grounds upon which anyone can incline his heart to trust Him. The Son of God came to suffer and die in order that the people He loves might be saved.

A DIFFERENCE OF OPINION (10:19-42)

Is it necessarily bad to have differences of opinion about the Word of God and Jesus Christ? This depends upon the difference itself. As Jesus went about His teaching and preaching. ". . . There was a division therefore again among the Jews . . ." (verse 19). The Jews were informed concerning the Old Testament. They probably did not know it all, just as many Christians do not know the entire Bible too well. But these leaders of the Jewish nation had been instructed in their own Scriptures, and it was because of this that their differences of opinion arose concerning Jesus:

And many of them said, He hath a devil, and is mad; why hear ye him? Others said, These are not the words of him that hath a devil. Can a devil open the eyes of the blind? (John 10:20, 21).

The strongest evidence in the appraisal by one person of another in the ministry of the Gospel, is the results which follow the presentation of the truth. There will be preachers whose doctrine is difficult to understand and with whom it is not possible to be in complete agreement. Some may present ideas of such a nature that many will not follow along with them. But if these witnesses are being used of God to turn men and women from their wicked ways to know Christ, others should stop short in criticizing them or condemning them.

Guidance for such judgment seems to be clear enough in the discussion above concerning grounds for confidence. When men ask "Is your physician good? Is he reliable?" a convincing reply is not based on the fact that the doctor has red hair, light brown eyes, and is tall and handsome. What people *do* care about, in the last analysis, are the results of his practice. What happens to his patients? Is he able, by his diagnosis and prescription, to bring healing to many? Then men can judge him on the basis of his professional skill.

Some of the Jewish people said Jesus was "mad," and others said, "Wait a minute, nobody who can restore sight to a man born blind can be crazy." Such difference in judgment may sound strange about Jesus Christ, but it will help to remember that these men did not have knowledge of what has happened since the crucifixion and resurrection of Jesus: the glorious centuries of reaching the lost and winning them to Jesus Christ in the history of the church.

"Look at What I Do"

With only their own observations they became so tangled up in their own arguments that finally they came to Jesus with a blunt question:

Then came the Jews round about him, and said unto him, How long dost thou make us to doubt? If thou be the Christ, tell us plainly. Jesus answered them, I told you, and ye believed not: the works that I do in my Father's name, they bear witness of me. But ye believe not, because ye are not of my sheep, as I said unto you (John 10:24-26).

It is very significant to note that when faced with this question Jesus requested the pragmatic test. They asked, "Art thou the Christ?" And in effect He replied, "Look at what I do." He took no time in arguments for the validity of His stand. He simply pointed to the results. This profound principle should be applied whenever there is question about trustworthiness or confidence. This is the good way to answer such questions as, "Is that Sunday school teacher good? Can that man preach? What about the methods of that church leader?" The effective answer to such pointed questions would be to look at the results achieved. Are boys and girls being led to know Christ? Are souls being saved under the preaching of the Word of God? Are there RESULTS from any given ministry?

But Jesus knew the questions asked were not really sincere. He pointed out the actual reason for the unbelief of the Jews. It was not a matter of lack of understanding. It was a lack of interest and desire. He told them, ". . . Ye believe not, because ye are not of my sheep . . . My sheep hear my voice, and I know them, and they follow me." And this points to an important truth. Any man or woman who begins to argue about Jesus Christ, who gets into a controversy, who is not willing to follow the Gospel, may well be a person who will not and cannot know the truth. The fact is that it is necessary to accept Jesus as Saviour and Lord before one can understand.

Jesus stressed the fact that His sheep know His voice and follow Him: they obey Him, He knows each one by name and cares for them. But those who are not of His flock cannot expect this gracious provision, this loving care, this companionship with Him. It is a wonderful blessing to belong to the Lord.

Jesus went on with glorious words concerning the sheep whom He loves and for whom He cares:

> And I give unto them eternal life; and they shall never perish, neither shall any man pluck them out of my hand. My Father, which gave them me, is greater than all, and no man is able to pluck them out of my Father's hand. I and my Father are one (John 10:28-30).

Instead of settling their controversy, this reply angered the Jewish rulers. They recognized God, the Father, but the real point at issue was whether or not Jesus was the Christ, the Son of the living God. His linking of Himself with God the Father in this way, "I and my Father are one," was what enraged them. Their reaction was natural. When a person is wrong, and cannot win the argument in reason, he is inclined to become violent. ". . . the Jews took up stones again to stone him" (verse 31). This is shocking, and yet it is very revealing. This was the proof of their deeply rooted unwillingness to believe in Jesus at all. It was not a matter of lack of understanding. When insinuation and accusation failed to succeed in discrediting the testimony of Jesus then they resorted to violence.

Jesus Himself directly challenged their motives in their opposition.

> Jesus answered them, Many good works have I shewed you from my Father; for which of those works do ye stone me? The Jews answered him, saying, For a good work we stone thee not; but for blasphemy; and because that thou, being a man, makest thyself God (John 10:32, 33).

Thus the ground of their hatred was clearly exposed. Jesus did not concede any validity to their opposition. When the argument was at an end, and they sought to take Him, He escaped out of their hand, He went away to the place where John at first baptized and stayed there. It is significant to note the glorious fact, "And many believed on him there" (verse 42). The whole controversy about the authority of Jesus of Nazareth ended in this note of victory.

Chapter 12

JESUS AND LAZARUS

"Why?" (11:1-17)

A common question in the heart of a Christian who is in distress is, *"Why did God allow that to happen to me?"* In the raising of Lazarus there is a clear-cut teaching about this problem which Christians face.

First John gives us an insight, as it were, a bit of a glimpse, into a certain family in Bethany, whom the Lord Jesus loved: a home in which He was welcome. There were two sisters in that home and a brother, Martha, Mary, and Lazarus. A parenthesis in verse 2 tells us that "It was that Mary which anointed the Lord with ointment, and wiped his feet with her hair, whose brother Lazarus was sick."

Lazarus had become seriously ill, and the family turned to Jesus for help. ". . . his sisters sent unto him, saying, Lord, behold, he whom thou lovest is sick" (verse 3). This is revealing for two reasons. First, they said in their message, ". . . he whom thou lovest. . . ." This was an indication of the relationship of affection and regard which existed between Jesus and this family. In the second place, there is here in simple terms the true form of prayer. That is the kind of praying believers should practice.

Sometimes prayer is considered to be merely the means of getting a certain result. A person will go ahead with a new procedure, and then ask the Lord to bless his actions. Oftentimes a person can be, with reference to prayer, much as a patient who goes to a doctor, tells him what kind of medicine he needs, and then asks the physician to give him the written prescription for that medicine! A person can go to prayer with a preconceived notion of what the answer should be, come into the holy presence of God, and ask Him to do whatever seems to be good. This of course, misses the essence of prayer. The thing to do in believing prayer is to come to God with whatever request, *if it be His will.*

In this case, these two sisters simply sent word to Jesus, whom they loved and trusted, and told Him their brother, ". . . he whom thou lovest is sick." They did not feel it necessary to tell Jesus what to do.

116

It is significant that the man who was sick *was beloved of the Lord*. Sickness is not a sign of alienation from God. Sometimes people try to insinuate that if a person is ill, he must be out of the will of God. Sickness is no evidence that God has turned His back on a person.

But there is more to be learned here that is strange and astonishing!

> When Jesus heard [the news about Lazarus], he said, This sickness is not unto death, but for the glory of God, that the Son of God might be glorified thereby. Now Jesus loved Martha, and her sister, and Lazarus. When he had heard therefore that he was sick, he abode two days still in the same place where he was (John 11:4-6).

Note that the first thing Jesus said, when He heard of the illness, was that it was not unto death. He assured the disciples this would not result in the permanent death of Lazarus at this time. John has clearly affirmed that Jesus loved the members of this family, they were His dear friends. Jesus said plainly this was not a matter of death. Yet He stayed two days where He was and thus allowed time for Lazarus to die! One would have expected Him to go at once to Bethany and heal His dear friend. He deliberately delayed His response to this prayer for help from two good friends! Was this delay an indication of indifference upon the part of Jesus, the Son of God? No! Of course it was not that. But believers should study this account closely for here is a clue to understanding the problem of delayed answer to prayer.

In His Will

A Christian may come to God with a problem, and may feel it would be wonderful to have an immediate answer, because it would strengthen his faith. Sometimes this happens, and the Christian will thank and praise God for the answer. But there are times when answers to prayer are delayed. What then? The Christian must wait, assured that Christ has his best interests at heart, even as He had Lazarus'. Jesus set out for Bethany.

> . . . Master, the Jews of late sought to stone thee; and goest thou thither again? Jesus answered, Are there not twelve hours in the day? If any man walk in the day, he stumbleth not, because he seeth the light of this world. But if a man walk in the night, he stumbleth, because there is no light in him (John 11:8-10).

By way of explaining His action in starting this journey Jesus set forth a general truth: the best traveling is done in the daytime. It is always dangerous to wait too long. Better to start out in daylight. In other words, prompt action in response to the will of God, when He calls, is important. The believer should not wait. Action must be taken when God's will is made known: and it must be done, regardless of any seeming hindrances. In the face of opposition the Lord will still be guiding: He will not be changed. The best time to respond is when the call comes.

> These things said he: and after that he saith unto them, Our friend Lazarus sleepeth; but I go, that I may awake him out of sleep (John 11:11).

Jesus knew Lazarus had died, and yet He had delayed His going. Jesus was acting according to His own knowledge of what was to come. This particular death, real though it was, was temporary: now He was going to "awake" His friend from that sleep of death. There is a difference between *death* and *sleep,* but Jesus used these words interchangeably . A person naturally awakes from sleep. The Lord knew that His friend Lazarus had died, and He knew also that He was going to bring Lazarus *back to life.* But in order to emphasize the temporary condition of death He used the word *sleep* in a broader context.

In this account there is an interesting light thrown upon the character of Thomas, who is often spoken of as "the Doubter." But here is a different side to his personality:

> Then said Thomas, which is called Didymus, unto his fellow disciples, Let us also go, that we may die with him (John 11:16).

Thomas' understanding of Jesus words was limited, it is true, but there is evidence here of real courage. The disciples had just reminded Jesus that the Jews had tried to stone Him in the very region to which He was intending to go. Thomas said the others knew that in all probability if they went along they would share in any subsequent stoning attempt. But Thomas spoke up, and said, "Let us go, that we may die." Even though Thomas was a pessimist (and even after the resurrection that frame of mind still had him in its grasp) yet at this point he was willing to die with his Master. Whenever the disposition of Thomas to doubt is brought to mind, it should be remembered that at the same time he was a believer who was willing and ready to die with His Lord.

LAZARUS IS RAISED (11:18-46)

The resurrection of Lazarus is one of the most significant miracles recorded in the gospel of John or in all of the Bible. Miracles, as recorded in the Bible and especially in the four gospels, not only show the *power* of God who is able to do these things, but also reveal the *plan* of God as these great things are accomplished.

The various miracles Jesus did do not show anything in particular about His patience, His meekness, or His humility. They reveal the power of God! They show what God can do, what He will do, and His control over the forces of nature.

The believer who studies this miracle of the raising of Lazarus from the grave will be challenged to know more about God and about the will of God as He chooses to work in and through His people. The believing heart craves this knowledge, but one needs to stand still and let the Spirit speak. This kind of knowledge is not grasped easily: it is not so much for those who run, as for those who wait upon God through the Spirit. The possibilities for answer to prayer are tremendous.

Seldom would anyone in teaching the Gospel select the story of raising a man from the dead. To the natural heart and mind of man, such is not only improbable, but incredible! And yet here it is, set forth in unmistakable terms, in the Bible. Why did the Holy Spirit include this story here? It does seem incredible, and that may be just why it is recorded. Such an event will strengthen faith. The actual fact of the matter is that what God will do for any man or woman is incredible to the natural heart of any human being.

MARTHA AND JESUS

In this account of the raising of Lazarus there is the actual resurrection of a frail, human body, which had been in the tomb for so long that the sister, Martha, actually protested to the Lord about exposing the corrupt condition of that human form.

> Then Martha, as soon as she heard that Jesus was coming, went and met him: but Mary sat still in the house. Then said Martha unto Jesus, Lord, if thou hadst been here, my brother had not died. But I know, that even now, whatsoever thou wilt ask of God, God will give it thee. Jesus saith unto her, Thy brother shall rise again. Martha saith unto him, I know that he shall rise again in the resurrection at the last day. Jesus said unto her, I am the resurrection, and the life: he that believeth in me, though he were dead, yet shall he live: And whosoever liveth and believeth in me shall never die. Believest thou this? She saith unto him, Yea, Lord: I believe that thou art the Christ, the Son of God, which should come into the world (John 11:20-27).

It should be remembered that Martha was a true believer in Jesus. It is true that she was a person who could become overburdened with details, and oversensitive because of her active program of household chores, but this same woman was a true believer in all she knew about Jesus of Nazareth. Revelation about the truth in Christ was not then complete; but that she recognized His relationship to His Father is clear.

In this time of bereavement, when they were mourning the passing of their only brother, she heard that Jesus was approaching the house, and she ran out to meet Him. She was the first one to greet the Lord, and the evidence of her faith is to be seen as she said, ". . . Lord if thou hadst been here, my brother had not died." No doubt she meant that Jesus would have healed him. This shows a very real faith, for what she was actually saying was that Jesus had power, and that God would answer the prayers of His Son.

Jesus gave her assurance, ". . . Thy brother shall rise again." Here is an illustration of how easy it is to attach the wrong meaning to the right words. Martha at once acknowledged her faith in the fact that ". . . he shall rise again in the resurrection at the last day." But she did not understand this resurrection of which Jesus is speaking would take place now. Then came those wonderful words of promise which have been such comfort to the faithful of every age, ". . . I am the resurrection and the life; he that believeth in me, though he were dead, yet shall he live: And whosoever liveth and believeth in me shall never die." Martha's answer revealed her limited expectation, before the event of Calvary and our Lord's own resurrection, yet demonstrated her faith in Him, ". . . I believe that thou art the Christ, the Son of God, which should come into the world."

MARY AND JESUS

> . . . she [Martha] went her way, and called Mary her sister secretly, saying, The Master is come, and calleth for thee. As soon as she heard that, she arose quickly, and came unto him. Now Jesus was not yet come into the town, but was in that place where Martha met him. The Jews then which were with her in the house, and comforted her, when they saw Mary, that she rose up hastily and went out, followed her, saying, She goeth unto the grave to weep there. Then when Mary was come where Jesus was, and saw him, she fell down at his feet, saying unto him, Lord if thou hadst been here, my brother had not died (John 11:28-32).

Mary used the very words which Martha had said to Jesus. This shows that the two sisters shared the same faith. In facing the illness and the possible death of their brother, they had sent a message to Jesus which was like a prayer. There is no report of how His continued absence affected or troubled the sisters. But apparently their faith had not wavered. First one, then the other, affirms that faith in Jesus. Jesus simply went on with what He was going to do. The result would speak for itself as to His meaning about the resurrection, and as an answer to their prayer.

In giving his account John records a small incident which has been of comfort and solace to countless men and women through the centuries since:

> When Jesus therefore saw her weeping, and the Jews also weeping which came with her, he groaned in the spirit, and was troubled, And said, Where have ye laid him? They said unto Him, Lord, come and see. Jesus wept (John 11:33-35).

Jesus knew what He was about to do, yet He wept! He groaned and was troubled in spirit — in sympathy for their suffering, in companionship with them in their time of bereavement and heartache. What a solace to all who have stood by the open grave, or returned to the little raised mound in the cemetery in days and weeks after the precious earthly remains were laid away! Jesus wept! Jesus cared, and sorrowed, but knew, even as He weeps with the bereaved today and shares their sorrow, what He will do on that great resurrection day.

LAZARUS AND JESUS

> Jesus therefore again groaning in himself cometh to the grave. It was in a cave, and a stone lay upon it. Jesus said, Take ye away the stone. Martha, the sister of him that was dead, saith unto him, Lord, by this time he stinketh: for he hath been dead four days. Jesus saith unto her, Said I not unto thee, that, if thou wouldest believe, thou shouldest see the glory of God? (John 11: 38 - 40)

In this passage there are five important words: "Take ye away the stone." They had placed the stone on the tomb, and Jesus now called upon them to remove it to open the tomb. It is significant for believers to remember that the Lord may call upon them for their co-operation, for their response, before they know fully what He will do. Here was something the sisters could do, and in spite of Martha's most natural reluctance, this is what they did. There is no account of the joy which followed but the lesson is plain for all who read the story:

> . . . And Jesus lifted up his eyes, and said, Father, I thank thee that thou hast heard me. And I know that thou hearest me always: but because of the people which stand by I said it, that they may believe that thou hast sent me. And when he thus had spoken, he cried with a loud voice, Lazarus, come forth. And he that was dead came forth, bound hand and foot with graveclothes: and his face was bound about with a napkin. Jesus saith unto them, Loose him, and let him go (John 11:41- 44).

Thus the miracle was done openly, for all the people to see. As Jesus prayed to His Father, He made clear that it was done in this fashion that any willing soul might believe that God had sent Him. This is undoubtedly one of the reasons why this was written for the learning of believers for all time to come.

THE RESULTS (11:47-57)

In this passage there is an excellent illustration of the way truth and its open demonstration affects different people. Jesus had called upon God openly, in a voice which could be heard by all who were standing around that tomb, and God had answered in open fashion. The dead man came out, walking into their midst wearing the very clothes they had themselves wrapped around his lifeless body. The resurrection of Lazarus was carried out purposely in this spotlight of public scrutiny. Naturally this miracle must have been tremendously impressive. It must have astonished and awed the watchers, having a big effect upon their minds and hearts. And yet not every one was affected in the same way.

> Then many of the Jews which came to Mary, and had seen the things which Jesus did, believed on him. But some of them went their ways to the Pharisees, and told them what things Jesus had done (John 11:45, 46).

How true this is today! Many people who see the results when the Gospel is preached in truth and in the power of God believe and glorify His Name. But there are always some who will be incorrigible in the face of any true miracle or manifestation of the power of God. No matter what the revelation, some people will have other things in mind, and simply will not accept the implications and follow through to find peace of heart and mind with God. And so there were some at the grave of Lazarus who reported to the authorities that Jesus had done what they considered to be dangerous to their religion.

Wherever there is organization there must be leaders. When there are leaders some people rise to higher places of prominence than others, and so there is temptation to exercise vanity and pride. This is a real problem Christians have faced in every age.

At all levels of church affairs bishops and elders, stewards and deacons, and church officers generally, both men and women, are inclined to favor a rigid insistence on order. They want to keep things as they are with no changes. In this way they can be sure of holding their own positions indefinitely. It is characteristic of church history that church organizations tend to grow, to become more and more elaborate until they are a burden and a hindrance to the spiritual life of the people involved. This sort of situation developed at this time in the career of Jesus of Nazareth. Opposition to Him was not so much inspired by any animosity to Him personally, but His way of doing things seemed to threaten the status quo, and endanger the position of some of the leaders.

A Caucus

> Then gathered the chief priests and the Pharisees a council, and said, What do we? for this man doeth many miracles. If we let him thus alone, all men will believe on him: and the Romans shall come and take away both our place and nation (John 11: 47, 48).

In today's politics, such a meeting would be called a caucus: the gathering together of certain persons who think alike to make plans to control something or someone.

This caucus, this gathering of the chief priests and the Pharisees, was planning to control Jesus of Nazareth, not to promote the work of God. They recognized the fact that if they permitted His activities to continue, Jesus would soon have everybody following Him, because He was making such a tremendous impression on the people. But one of them, Caiaphas, the high priest, said to them, ". . . Ye know nothing at all" (verse 49). He went on to say:

> Nor consider that it is expedient for us, that one man should die for the people, and that the whole nation perish not. And this spake he not of himself: but being high priest that year, he prophesied that Jesus should die for that nation; And not for that nation only, but that also he should gather together in one the children of God that were scattered abroad (John 11:50-52).

This political principle is often set forth: sacrifice the individual for the sake of the group as a whole. Anybody who studies history will agree that it is the person who is doing things differently, who is making changes, who is promoting progress, who is in danger of being put away. The leaders have fixed ideas: they want to keep on doing as they have always done, saying that this is the way to true progress.

It is significant that Caiaphas actually said more than he realized, more than he knew: God was speaking through his lips, for he prophesied that Jesus should die for the nation, and for men and women everywhere in every subsequent age and nation! This man unwittingly uttered the express plan and purpose of God. Caiaphas spoke from his limited and sinful point of view, and it could be said that he "meant it for evil," but his words actually promoted God's plan, and God "meant it for good."

In all this there is a truth to be seen entirely apart from what happened to Jesus of Nazareth. Evil leadership is always under the control of God. Regardless of what happens God always brings His will to pass. Recent events in world history illustrate this very truth. Where is Hitler? What happened to Mussolini? They were powerful, evil, clever men, and God permitted them to exert power for a time, but in His time they were each destroyed. The divine purpose may be hidden, but believing hearts need never despair, God is forever on the throne!

> . . . from that day forth they took counsel together for to put him to death. Jesus therefore walked no more openly among the Jews: but went thence into a country near to the wilderness, into a city called Ephraim, and there continued with his disciples (John 11:53, 54).

This was certainly not because Jesus Christ was afraid, but as a matter of strategy. He wanted to avoid open conflict because the time had not yet come, in the will of God, for Him to be shown to the people.

John notes that at the time these events occurred the Passover was near. Crowds were going up to Jerusalem, and the people sought Jesus. They wondered if He would come to the feast. The chief priests and the Pharisees had given strict orders that if anyone saw Him, they were to be informed, so that they might arrest Him. But it was not yet God's time for the Son of God to be delivered up, and so Jesus went on His way and continued for a time in seclusion with His disciples.

Chapter 13

JESUS AND HIS FOLLOWERS

DIFFERING ATTITUDES (12:1-11)

Amid all the confusion of the many different voices in the world today in matters that pertain to the Gospel, of the many contrary opinions heard about the Word of God and the will of God, there is one question which can clear the air: *What do you personally think about Jesus Christ?*

In this portion of his gospel story John presents different attitudes toward Jesus. Six days before the Passover, Jesus went to the home of Lazarus, Martha, and Mary. He had always been a welcome friend, but now He was the One who brought Lazarus back to life, and He was made especially welcome.

> There they made him a supper; and Martha served: but Lazarus was one of them that sat at the table with him. Then took Mary a pound of ointment of spikenard, very costly, and anointed the feet of Jesus, and wiped his feet with her hair: and the house was filled with the odour of the ointment. Then saith one of his disciples, Judas Iscariot, Simon's son, which should betray him, Why was not this ointment sold for three hundred pence, and given to the poor? This he said, not that he cared for the poor; but because he was a thief, and had the bag, and bare what was put therein. Then said Jesus, Let her alone: against the day of my burying hath she kept this (John 12:2-7).

We know about several persons: Martha served. Lazarus sat at the table. Mary anointed Jesus' feet, and Judas Iscariot criticized her act. Each of these persons, in his or her conduct, reflected a certain inward attitude toward the Lord.

The first three, Lazarus, Martha, Mary, each had a proper attitude which was expressed in their conduct. No doubt it gave Martha considerable satisfaction and was quite probably an outward expression of her inward faith to prepare and serve the meal. Lazarus could have been given no greater honor than to sit at the King's table among such a company of people. But particular attention must be given to Mary who demonstrated in such notable fashion the love and worship of a loyal heart.

A Woman's Love

Who should be esteemed as the most famous woman in the history of the world? Probably Mary should be so considered:

> Verily I say unto you, Wheresoever this gospel shall be preached throughout the whole world, this also that she hath done shall be spoken of for a memorial of her (Mark 14:9).

Mary took something *of her own.* Mary paid the full price of the spikenard. This was something belonging to herself, and was very precious. No doubt it was the very best she could get, and she planned to bring this precious thing to Jesus as a gift. In this simple account of the act of a woman's love and gratitude, there is a pattern for satisfactory service to the Lord at any time. The believer may bring the best he has and offer it to Him personally as a gift of love. This will be adequate in every situation. The actual cost of the gift is not important, but it should be precious in order that it might reflect sincere love.

A housewife in her own home may have ample opportunity to serve the Lord. She can follow this simple pattern. The very best she may have personally to offer may be her faithful service in the place where He has put her.

An office worker may wonder about her daily tasks. Her service may be not in a church office, but in a commercial organization with no apparent way of bringing an offering to her Lord. But she can do her best work in that office, turning out work that is as good as she can make it. By rendering faithful and honest service, day after day, offering her diligence as an offering of praise to God, she can be giving her witness to her faith in Christ. In her daily tasks she can do it all as unto the Lord. This is truly the source of, and the nature of, acceptable true service of the Lord.

Judas

Mary's gift was actually criticized by Judas Iscariot. Her judgment was questioned. "Why wasn't the ointment sold for three hundred pence, and the money given to the poor?" Judas had apparently done nothing himself for the poor, or for Jesus, but he felt free to criticize and to find fault with someone who was presenting a gift.

This attitude is repeated over and over even among Christians. A person who does nothing in the Lord's work may feel free to criticize the one who is hard at work for Him. Any number of people who never go to church feel entirely free to criticize what is being done in the church at any time. This is much the same as persons who never read the Bible, who know nothing about what it contains, who tell the world the Bible contradicts itself and cannot be trusted.

John points out plainly that Judas was not actually concerned about the poor. Judas spoke as he did because he was the "treasurer" of the group: he carried the money bag. John adds that he was a thief. Did John mean necessarily that Judas had stolen money from that bag? It would have been hard to steal from the group, and it seems quite unlikely that Judas had been guilty of embezzling any funds. But why, then, call him a thief? Could a person be a thief who has never stolen? Is it not true that if he had been an honest man, he would never have stolen? Apparently Judas was a thief all the time. The wicked, sinful intent was there, and only opportunity was needed to bring the act of theft.

What a contrast between the attitudes of Jesus and Judas toward Mary! The Lord pointed out with appreciation that she was anointing Him for His burial. This may not have been foreknowledge on Mary's part, but it was a clear indication of the love and gratitude which filled her. Although Mary was criticized by fellow disciples, she was understood and appreciated by the Lord whom she served, to whom she gave this valuable gift. This observation can comfort hearts today as believers strive to bring Him their very best in service. Someone may misunderstand, others may criticize, but the important thing is that the Lord knows, cares, and accepts such adoration and gifts.

What was her secret, this woman who showed such devotion? How did she know this kind of action would please her Lord? This sacrificial gift was not offered because she thought it would be regarded as good, nor that people would praise her. She brought it because she loved Jesus. This is that Mary who sat at His feet and worshiped Him as her heart took in the gracious words that fell from His lips.

TRIUMPHAL ENTRY (12:12-19)

What is commonly called the *Triumphal Entry*, was Jesus' coming into Jerusalem, sitting upon a colt. Men, women and children welcomed Him. Some went before Him, strewing His way with flowers, taking branches of palm trees to wave, and crying, ". . . Hosanna: Blessed is the King of Israel that cometh in the name of the Lord" (verse 13). Such a reception must have seemed unusual even in that day.

How many in that crowd that day were in the huge crowd later shouting "Crucify, crucify!" This was one of the strange contradictions in the events which occurred in Jerusalem at the time of "The Triumphal Entry." Some of the leaders were planning to kill Him. Generally speaking, the public was paying no attention to Him. In the midst of that very situation, crowds of people came to greet Him as He rode in on the colt.

Something like this happens when people say they do not believe in the miracles. Yet with warm enthusiasm they will endorse the teachings of Jesus! How peculiarly the human mind works!

John tells the story this way:

> On the next day much people that were come to the feast, when they heard that Jesus was coming to Jerusalem, Took branches of palm trees, and went forth to meet him, and cried, Hosanna: Blessed is the King of Israel that cometh in the name of the Lord. And Jesus, when he had found a young ass, sat thereon; as it is written, Fear not, daughter of Sion: behold, thy King cometh, sitting on an ass's colt (John 12:12-15).

It was the common people with the waving palm tree branches, and the cries of "Hosanna!" that greeted Him. Here Jesus was fulfilling Old Testament prophesies, predictions that are important.

MEANING IN THE FUTURE

> These things understood not his disciples at the first: but when Jesus was glorified, then remembered they that these things were written of him, and that they had done these things unto him. The people therefore that was with him when he called Lazarus out of his grave, and raised him from the dead, bare record (John 12:16, 17).

Even when Jesus was riding along on that colt, with the palm branches and the garments strewn along the road in front of Him, it appears that His disciples did not realize just what this meant. But when Jesus was glorified, they remembered! After His death, resurrection, and ascension, when He was again with His Father at the right hand of God, then those loyal and devoted disciples remembered all He had said, and each incident which had happened in this whole affair. It should be helpful to every reader of the Bible to remember that those disciples actually walked beside Him as He rode on that colt, yet failed to understand what was happening until after He was glorified. Even now people may read the Bible and not grasp its meaning at the time, but later when they have seen His glory and have received Him into their hearts and have had the witness of the Spirit of God, the fulness of the revelation may come as a glorious blessing.

What then is the spiritual condition of man? What about teachers and preachers who talk, teach, and preach about Jesus of Nazareth as a good man, think of Him only as a human being, giving Him only human powers and understanding? What shall be thought about such people? It seems reasonable they have never seen Jesus Christ in His glory, they have no conception of His present position. The sad aspect of this is that there will be many, many passages of Scripture forever closed to all such persons. And this means that persons who hear them will never know the glorious truth revealed about Jesus Christ.

Despite opposition and objection by the leaders, many came to meet Him, because they had heard of miracles He had done. At the same time the Pharisees were deeply concerned, for they said,

> . . . Perceive ye how ye prevail nothing? behold, the world is gone after him (John 12:19).

Would that more people would "go after Him" today!

DYING TO LIVE (12:20-36)

Dying to live is a strange expression, and yet it lies at the very heart of the Christian Gospel. Dying to live — this is the route for the believer in Christ. Man's mortal enemy on earth is death, and the fear of death grips all men. Probably the greatest desire that is natural to man is to cling to life. He wants to live successfully, richly; but most of all, he wants to live! The basic threat of sin is, in the last analysis, the fear of death. And yet the one door which leads to life and glory is the denial of self unto death!

Worship in the Old Testament centered around the slaying of the lamb of God, and implied the life available by the grace of God. That grace of God is operative today, but it is effective only in such persons as will deny themselves unto self-crucifixion. The Lord Jesus said, ". . . If any man will come after me, let him deny himself, and take up his cross daily, and follow me" (Luke 9:23).

Gentiles did not know the Old Testament culture, the Gentile mind is apart from that which was trained in Old Testament truth, promises, ritual, sacrifices, and so this doctrine of dying to live seems very strange. The whole truth implied in the Old Testament is shown in the work of Jesus when He went to Calvary, died for our sin, and was raised from the dead. The whole truth is right there before us. Calvary is absolutely essential in order to have the Resurrection take place. There is no way of entering into eternal life, except a man die. A man *must be born again*.

COMING TO SEE JESUS

The Greeks in the next story John tells, however, were worshiping during the Passover, so they were familiar with the Jewish rituals and their meanings. It is as if John was guided with *us* in mind as he records Jesus' words about dying to live.

> And there were certain Greeks among them that came up to worship at the feast: The same came therefore to Philip, which was of Bethsaida of Galilee, and desired him, saying, Sir, we would see Jesus. Philip cometh and telleth Andrew: and again

Andrew and Philip tell Jesus. And Jesus answered them, saying, The hour is come, that the Son of man should be glorified (John 12:20-23).

The city of Bethsaida had a large Greek population. Philip had lived in that city and so could speak Greek, and probably had many Greek friends. Perhaps these were his friends who made the request to see Jesus. They wanted to get to know Him, to understand Him, to *see* Him. When Jesus heard of their coming and their interest He made this significant statement, ". . . The hour is come, that the Son of man should be glorified." Note how this is related to the coming of the Greeks. The idea of glorifying means that He should be brought to the fulfillment of His mission upon earth.

Glorification is like harvest time. When the wheat is finally ripe, the apples are ready to be put in the barrel, the grapes are ready for the basket: this is the harvest time. And this is the fulfillment of all the farmer has done during the season.

Now these Greeks appear asking for the privilege of entering into whatever Jesus was doing. The Gospel needed to be *demonstrated* to them. What He had to show them was something almost too incredible to accept: that a man should die and live again! When they came saying: "We want to know the truth that is in Jesus," Jesus said to His disciples, ". . . The hour is come, that the Son of man should be glorified." The hour is come! The time is here! The Son of man must go through death in order to live and thus openly demonstrate the real way of God. To be glorified, the Son of man must die, be raised from the dead, and live in newness of life.

Verily, verily, I say unto you, Except a corn of wheat fall into the ground and die, it abideth alone: but if it die, it bringeth forth much fruit. He that loveth his life shall lose it; and he that hateth his life in this world shall keep it unto life eternal. If any man serve me, let him follow me; and where I am, there shall also my servant be: if any man serve me, him will my Father honour (John 12:24 - 26).

GLORIFICATION

Here a profound and most important truth in the Gospel is set out in simple fashion. Everybody knows that in order to raise a crop, whether it be beans, potatoes, or flowers, the seed must be put into the ground and die. It comes apart, it decays; but out of it comes a plant. The plant that rises up out of the ground does not look like the seed that went into the ground! It is of the same stuff, however. Now Jesus is saying that He must go to the cross, as wheat must go into the ground, to die. Buried in both means being raised in "newness of life," by the power of God. This is what happens in the glorifying of Jesus Christ, the fulfillment of God's purpose in Him.

Jesus went on in His discussion to show still more truth. He pointed out that a person wanting to hold on to life in this world is going to lose the very thing he tries to grasp, but if a man hates his life (that is, becomes willing to give it up, to deny any love for it), that man shall "keep it unto life eternal." The farmer who is willing to throw the wheat into the ground where the kernels will disintegrate will have even more wheat. A man must follow Jesus if he would truly serve Him. But just what is embodied in that word, *follow?* It means a man will go with Him to the cross, to the death of self and sinful human nature, in order that he may be raised from the dead. The Father will be honored by the raising of the person from the dead into the new life, the resurrection life of Jesus Christ.

The profound importance of this is felt when Jesus says, "Now is my soul troubled; and what shall I say? Father, save me from this hour: but for this cause came I unto this hour" (verse 27). By way of announcing His own commitment Jesus prays, "Father, glorify thy name."

> Then came there a voice from heaven, saying, I have both glorified it, and will glorify it again. The people therefore that stood by, and heard it, said that it thundered: others said, An angel spake to him. Jesus answered and said, This voice came not because of me, but for your sakes. Now is the judgment of this world: now shall the prince of this world be cast out. And I, if I be lifted up from the earth, will draw all men unto me. This he said, signifying what death he should die (John 12:28-33).

In these words Jesus pointed out that Satan would be defeated. Also the manner of His death was made clear: "if I be lifted up," means being crucified on a cross. The people understood His meaning, and this led to more questioning of the truth of His teaching.

> . . . We have heard out of the law that Christ abideth for ever: and how sayest thou, The Son of man must be lifted up? who is this Son of man? (John 12:34).

Jesus did not answer their question immediately. A wise teacher will appreciate the opening which a question affords, but he will use the opportunity as it suits his purpose. The answer to their question involved the Resurrection, and this needed to be demonstrated before men could understand what it meant. One day these very people would see that He died and then that He was raised from the dead. They could know how He could die and then live, and how believers, after that too, may die and then live.

At this time He gave excellent guidance to those who heard.

> . . . Yet a little while is the light with you. Walk while ye have the light, lest darkness come upon you . . . (John 12:35).

What the learner, the disciple must do is to go along with the truth as far as it is seen, looking unto God, who will show further truth in Christ, step by step, as He feels the disciples are ready for it. The willing believer will accept what he can understand and believe, strive by His grace to walk in it, thank Him for it, and press onward!

ISAIAH'S PREDICTION TRUE (12:37-50)

It is almost a shock to read of the disheartening and tragic unbelief that persisted despite all Jesus had done:

> . . . though he had done so many miracles before them, yet they believed not on him (John 12:37).

In this incident it is reported that Jesus "did hide himself from them." The resulting uncertainty actually fulfilled the prophecy of Isaiah, ". . . Lord who hath believed our report? and to whom hath the arm of the Lord been revealed?" (John 12:38 and Isaiah 53:1)

The Jews had seen many of the miracles but were not fully impressed. They failed to see the deeper significance underlying the act of mercy and grace which brought sight to the blind and cleansing to the leper. Saving faith is grounded in more than the demonstration of great power. What is needed is the witness to the heart, which these people did not receive. They saw the miracles but they did not believe in Jesus as Christ.

> Therefore they could not believe, because that Esaias said again, He hath blinded their eyes, and hardened their heart; that they should not see with their eyes, nor understand with their heart, and be converted, and I should heal them (John 12:39, 40).

Some were not hardened to that extent, however:

> Nevertheless among the chief rulers also many believed on him; but because of the Pharisees they did not confess him, lest they should be put out of the synagogue: For they loved the praise of men more than the praise of God (John 12:42, 43).

HINDRANCES

Apparently there were men, leaders of the people, who actually believed, but who would not confess Him for fear of persecution. They were afraid of being put out of the synagogue. They loved to have men speak well of them, seeming to care little what God thought of them.

This whole incident in which the reaction of the Jews is set forth reveals a sad sobering truth. A man can have confidence in the Gospel to the extent that he believes that Jesus Christ is the Son of God and yet that person might be hindered from committing himself to

Christ. Why? Because he is thinking of others and their opinions. It is possible for a man to argue with himself along this line, telling himself that he ought to attend church, he should go to prayer meeting, he should read his Bible, and he should yield himself to the Lord, and yet in his mind there may be hindrances which hold him back.

> Jesus cried and said, He that believeth on me, believeth not on me, but on him that sent me. And he that seeth me seeth him that sent me. I am come a light into the world, that whosoever believeth on me should not abide in darkness. And if any man hear my words, and believe not, I judge him not: for I came not to judge the world, but to save the world (John 2:44 - 47).

Jesus of Nazareth was trying to help these people. He was pointing beyond the miracles to the power which made them possible. He told them that those who believed Him were actually believing on Him that sent Him. One need not live in darkness if one sees that God was working in Jesus of Nazareth according to His eternal purpose. This is what creation means. God did not make the world in order to destroy it, and when Christ Jesus came to do the will of God He was aiming to accomplish what God purposed in the Creation.

> He that rejecteth me, and receiveth not my words, hath one that judgeth him: the word that I have spoken, the same shall judge him in the last day. For I have not spoken of myself; but the Father which sent me, he gave me a commandment, what I should say, and what I should speak. And I know that his commandment is life everlasting: whatsoever I speak therefore, even as the Father said unto me, so I speak (John 12:48-50).

The words which fall from the lips of Jesus are really the words of God, and anyone who hears them is responsible before God for what he does with them. Jesus of Nazareth did not speak out of Himself from His own understanding. He spoke the words of God, ". . . he [God] gave me a commandment, what I should . . . speak. . . ." And this "commandment of God" will lead the soul to everlasting life if a person responds in obedience.

The Lord Jesus had called men to Himself as He began His public ministry. But He calls men at any time to put their trust in Him, to yield their wills to Him, and in this He gives certain promises. He urges confidence in these promises because God Himself is working through Christ Jesus. This is the power of God that saves the believing soul. It is the power of God that will keep the soul in the midst of temptation. By believing the word of Jesus Christ the person is actually believing the word of God. Christ Jesus has power to do wonderful things as men trust Him, for the power of God is at work through Him to all who believe.

Chapter 14

THE COMING BETRAYAL

In his gospel account John reports one incident after another in the public ministry of Jesus of Nazareth to show the truths that Jesus taught. The limited discussion in this volume can do no more than touch upon the profound truths He demonstrated. It will not be possible to do full justice to this record nor to come to a perfect understanding of each truth. Each incident can be noted and studied in passing but it will take prayerful meditation to grasp the deeper truth involved. Even so His teaching is so plain and clear that anyone reading John's report will have sufficient understanding to put his trust in Him, the Lamb of God that taketh away the sins of the world!

JESUS WASHES HIS DISCIPLES' FEET (13:1-17)

The washing of the disciples' feet was teaching the need of humility in those who have committed themselves to follow Jesus of Nazareth, the Christ of God. The truth emphasized is very important and the account of the whole affair is so graphic that it makes the lesson very clear.

John begins his account with a simple statement of the situation as it existed at that time, pointing out that ". . . Jesus knew that his hour was come that he should depart out of this world unto the Father, having loved his own . . . he loved them unto the end" (verse 1). Jesus knew ahead of time that He must leave His disciples, and He wanted to prepare them to face whatever issues might arise in the days ahead. And certainly the drastic events immediately following proved the need of such preparation.

> And supper being ended, the devil having now put into the heart of Judas Iscariot, Simon's son, to betray him; Jesus knowing that the Father had given all things into his hands, and that he was come from God, and went to God; He riseth from supper, and laid aside his garments; and took a towel, and girded himself (John 13:2 - 4).

Jesus suggests an insight into the origin of evil conduct. Judas may well have entertained the thought of betraying His Master, but this passage seems to say that in addition to whatever attitude he may have had in mind, Satan had given him the idea that now was the time to carry out this act of betrayal. The Greek brings out the use of a much stronger word than the English translation. The Greek expression implies that Satan *threw it* into his heart, as one takes a stone and throws it with some force into a lake. It was as if Judas had suddenly been obsessed with an overpowering impulse to betray Jesus.

The calm attitude of Jesus can be taken as a manifestation of the peace of God that passes all understanding. No doubt Jesus knew of the evil thoughts in the heart and mind of Judas. He knew also that the end of His earthly life was fast approaching. But He showed no sign of being disturbed. He arose from the table, and "laid aside his garments." He probably wore a cloak or cape over His clothing, as was the manner of teachers of that day. This would be the kind of garment to hinder Him if He were going to attempt a task normally considered the work of a servant. He laid aside that outer garment and took a towel and put it about His waist. This was a servant's costume. In modern phraseology, He put on an apron, and tied it in place.

> After that he poureth water into a basin, and began to wash the disciples' feet, and to wipe them with the towel wherewith he was girded (John 13:5).

Back in the days when Jesus walked the roads of Palestine, this was not a strange courtesy to offer a guest. People wore open sandals. The streets or roads were unpaved, and a man walking any distance would find his feet dusty, dirty and hot when he reached his destination. According to the customs of that day, in the case of an honored guest, a servant would bring a basin of water to rinse the dust from the feet of the guests.

Jesus took the basin and the towel to perform the menial task, going around the circle of guests, as any servant would do it. The act in itself was not unusual. The unusual aspect was in the fact that Jesus, the Master, did it.

PETER'S REACTION

When Jesus came to Peter to wash his feet, Peter protested. It was as if he had said, "I am unworthy, you cannot do that to me, Lord!" But "Jesus answered and said unto him, What I do thou knowest not now; but thou shalt know hereafter" (verse 7), indicating the act itself was more meaningful than it appeared to be. Peter could not understand at that moment, but some day full understanding would be his. But even this assurance did not satisfy Peter; he protested even more firmly.

> Peter saith unto him, Thou shalt never wash my feet. Jesus an-
> swered him, If I wash thee not, thou hast no part with me. Simon
> Peter saith unto him, Lord, not my feet only, but also my hands
> and my head. Jesus saith to him, He that is washed needeth not
> save to wash his feet, but is clean every whit: and ye are clean,
> but not all (John 13:8-10).

Peter's exclamation, "Thou shalt never wash my feet!" was not necessarily any sign of arrogance. If a person paid a personal visit to an
important man, perhaps a government official or a well-known author,
and that important man upon greeting his visitor at the door asked for
the privilege of hanging up his hat and coat, many a person out of
respect would say "Oh, no, I will hang them up myself. You should
not be doing that for me." This could have been the way Peter felt
at that moment. Jesus' reply indicates that it will be necessary in
spiritual living to accept humbly what the Lord is willing to do for the
believer and in the believer, and then to strive faithfully to fit into the
plan of God.

In making this statement Jesus used two different words for *wash*,
which convey quite different meanings. When translated carefully Jesus is saying in actual fact that a man who has bathed (i.e. been to a
public bath house and has had his bath for the day), then walked
home along the dusty roads does not need to bathe all over again,
because of his dusty feet. He needs only to have his feet rinsed, as
the second word would indicate, "but is clean every whit," that is, entirely clean after the rinsing of the feet. He is telling Peter that a
whole bath is not needed at this point, only rinsing of his feet. This is a
clear illustration of the common spiritual experience of a Christian:
even when one is believing in Christ for the forgiveness of sins it is
necessary to confess one's sins day by day.

HUMILITY

But the main thrust which makes this whole incident tremendously
significant today was its emphasis upon humility:

> If I then, your Lord and Master, have washed your feet; ye also
> ought to wash one another's feet. For I have given you an
> example, that ye should do as I have done to you (John 13:14,
> 15).

Jesus knew He was soon to leave them to face the world alone. He
knew there would be real opposition from the very beginning, and
that some of it would come from people close to each one of the
disciples. It would be very important for strength to face the world.
They must have consideration, one for another, in order to help each
other. What a lesson for today! Christians must be willing to stand in

the place of servants to others, no matter what their station in the world. The road of humility is still the road to power with men and with God.

BETRAYAL (13:18-30)

Betrayal of a friend is certainly one of the most despicable actions known to man. And when that Friend is the Lord Jesus Christ, it is difficult to understand how a man could carry such an action through, if he had ever known the Lord. For anyone who knows anything about Jesus of Nazareth it seems incredible that Judas, who walked the roads of Galilee with Jesus, who had been a part of the inner circle, and had enjoyed close fellowship with his Lord could then betray Him. But he did sell his Master to His enemies, and has become the symbol of treachery all over the world.

Jesus was not taken by surprise in this unhappy event: actually He knew what would happen. He said beforehand,

> I speak not of you all: I know whom I have chosen: but that the scripture may be fulfilled, He that eateth bread with me hath lifted up his heel against me (John 13:18).

Here Jesus gives expression to the sorrow in the heart of God as He looks down upon the rebellion of sinful men: This is a word of lament found in all Scripture. And because He knows this, Jesus wants to make it clear to His disciples that His betrayal is no surprise to Him, so that when it happens, they will remember that He knew ahead of time. This will give them more confidence in Him and in His promises.

> Verily, verily, I say unto you, He that receiveth whomsoever I send receiveth me; and he that receiveth me receiveth him that sent me (John 13:20).

In these simple words Jesus pointed out the significance of the witness of Christians. When the Lord Jesus Christ sends a Christian out to witness for Him, and that Christian's message is received, it is as if the hearer were receiving the Lord Himself. And if a person will so receive Him, it is as if he received God the Father. It will be quite true to apply this to a teacher in the Sunday school, a preacher in the pulpit, a parent in the home, or a humble witness in the office or shop. Whenever a believer tells the Gospel to anyone, this means more than just one person talking to another. The Word that is spoken by the witness is the word of the Lord Jesus Christ. When a Christian conveys His message, although the lips of the believer are actually saying the words, it is as if the Lord Himself were talking to that individual! If that person accepts what he is being told, it will be as though he had received the words of the Lord Jesus Christ. This means he had received what God said to Him: it is just as important as that. When Judas betrayed Jesus of Nazareth he was *denying* the Gospel; even so when any believer confesses Jesus Christ as his Saviour and Lord he is *presenting* the Gospel to the whole world. In keeping with His practice of sharing with His disciples, Jesus told them that one of them would betray Him. This may reflect that believers do have some responsibility about the attitudes and conduct of each other. It is the responsibility of the group when one of the number becomes disloyal to Jesus Christ personally.

> When Jesus had thus said, he was troubled in spirit, and testified, and said, Verily, verily, I say unto you, that one of you shall betray me. Then the dispiples looked one on another, doubting of whom he spake (John 13:21, 22).

DISCIPLES UNSUSPECTING

It is interesting that not one of them suggested Judas as the culprit: nobody seemed even to suspect him. Judas Iscariot was an honored person in their midst, the treasurer of their little group. This was a position of trust and honor. Thus, when this matter of betrayal came up, nobody suspected the man they had put in a position of trust. Each man was ready to suspect himself first, turning to the Lord to ask "Is it I?"

In John's report of this incident there is a reference to himself when he writes: ". . . there was leaning on Jesus' bosom one of his disciples, whom Jesus loved" (John 13:23). This is commonly understood to refer to the Apostle John, the writer of this book. John never speaks of himself as *John,* but calls himself, *the disciple whom Jesus loved.* One can sense that to John this was the all-important, humbling, breathtaking and distinguishing fact. Certainly this could be highly commended to anyone as a worthy opinion of oneself: this is actually what makes the difference: "he, whom Jesus loved."

In response to a direct question by John, Jesus indicated how the betrayer would be known: ". . . to whom I shall give a sop, when I have dipped it . . ." (John 13:26). And when Jesus had broken off a piece of bread and dipped it into the contents of the dish, He handed it to Judas. At that point a very suggestive comment was made by John: "And after the sop Satan entered into him . . ." (verse 27). What would be the meaning of those simple yet profound words *Satan entered into him?* Earlier John had remarked that "the devil having now put into the heart of Judas Iscariot, Simon's son, to betray him." Here it would seem Satan not only put the evil thought and intent into Judas' heart, but himself took possession of that heart, mind, and will.

After this Jesus said, ". . . That thou doest, do quickly." None of the disciples knew what Jesus meant. Since Judas was the treasurer, it might have been an order to purchase food for the poor. The account tells us that "He then having received the sop went immediately out: and it was night" (John 13:30). Here again so much is implied by John's few simple words. When Judas walked out from the presence of Christ, it was indeed night for him, even as it always is for any who turns away from the invitation to come to Him and accept salvation.

It was truly night for Judas. But for men and women today, the door stands open. The decision is yet to be made, and God who sent Jesus to die and raised Him from the dead, is calling men to come now without delay, and accept this gift of eternal life.

GLORIFICATION BEGUN (13:31-38)

As before noted, the word *glorify* had little meaning in popular language, being largely confined to scriptural usage. The idea is common in the Old Testament where it is used in referring to harvest. The glory of anything was not in its appearance but in the fulfilment of its purpose or interest. Thus the word *glorify* primarily refers to harvest, completion, the finishing of a certain matter. To glorify is to bring *to full completion* whatever was possible in a given situation or task. In simple words it means, to *get the job done.*

> Therefore, when [Judas] was gone out, Jesus said, Now is the Son of man glorified, and God is glorified in him. If God be glorified in him, God shall also glorify him in himself, and shall straightway glorify him (John 13:31, 32).

Substituting the phrase "get the job done" for the word "glorify" may sound awkward and crude, but it will make sense: "Now the Son of man is getting the job done, and God is getting the job done in Him. If God is getting the job done in Him, God shall also get the job done in Him for Himself and shall straightway get the job done about Him."

Jesus was to be glorified after He had been crucified, which means: Jesus was to have the job done in Him after He had been crucified. This emphasizes the necessity of the crucifixion. And this makes sense because the time of the crucifixion was drawing nearer and nearer. Judas had gone out to betray his Master to the Jewish authorities, and Jesus knew how swiftly events would move after that. Jesus was to be taken into court, just as a common criminal. After His arrest He was going to face condemnation and then death. But this was not the end. His body would be taken down from the cross and put in a tomb. Then He would arise out of that tomb and ascend into heaven where He would be at the right hand of God interceding for His people. He would send the Holy Spirit into the hearts of all who accepted Christ as Saviour. All this would be the natural result, the full fruition, the accomplished work of Christ. This would be the glorification which was to follow. This is how God "got the job done" in and through Jesus Christ.

It is as if a woman were making a dress. How does this begin? The woman purchases a piece of material. The type and color of material may have been discussed, and the decision may have been difficult to reach; but eventually cloth and pattern are in hand and the work begins. A sewing machine is necessary. As a rule a woman plans the time carefully. "I will work this afternoon, tomorrow morning, and Tuesday evening. This should be sufficient to complete the dress." Making the dress had to have a beginning, the planning, the purchase, the cutting, the stitching. All of these worked together into the finished garment.

Now bring this illustration over into spiritual things. Here too there is the beginning and the fulfillment of a task. Jesus Christ came into this world to seek and to save the lost. He came to give His life a ransom for many. He was born as a babe in Bethlehem; He grew up as a child under the care of Mary, His mother, in the home of Joseph. When he became a man He began to teach and work miracles of one kind or another. But all of this was not the real purpose of Jesus Christ coming into this world. He came to die for sinners, but not just to die; He came to be raised from the dead, not just for Himself, but that believers might be saved. The whole thing was beamed at the believer. And "the job is done" afresh every time a man or woman is saved. God is thus glorified in every soul won back to Him.

The day He comes again is the day of the final and complete fulfilment, when He gets the job done with His brethren in the presence of God, the Father. That will be the final harvest.

Now all this process toward fulfilment began at the moment Jesus was arrested as He said: "Now is the Son of man glorified . . ." which means to say "Now is the beginning of getting the job done in the life of the Son of man." The final fulfilment lies ahead, but there are truths to be learned even here as children.

> Little children, yet a little while I am with you. Ye shall seek me: and as I said unto the Jews, Whither I go, ye cannot come; so now I say to you (John 13:33).

The Lord Jesus Himself was to die, and be raised from the dead, but that is not to be the procedure for believers now. Christians do not die in the flesh now that they might be raised in the flesh. When a soul accepts Christ, he has the experience of being led by the Holy Spirit to die in the flesh, to rise *in the Spirit,* but all that is not in the physical realm. The physical resurrection lies in the future for these mortal bodies of ours.

A New Commandment

A new commandment I give unto you, That ye love one another; as I have loved you, that ye also love one another. By this shall

all men know that ye are my disciples, if ye have love one to
another (John 13:34, 35).

When Jesus said "a new commandment," He did not mean a new one
in place of any old commandment. This new commandment is not a
replacement but an additional truth. Taking the Scriptures as a whole,
and thinking only in terms of commandments, one would probably say
the great commandment ". . . Thou shalt love the Lord thy God with
all thy heart, and with all thy soul, and with all thy mind. This is
the first and great commandment. And the second is like unto it, Thou
shalt love thy neighbour as thyself. On these two commandments hang
all the law and the prophets" (Matthew 22:37-40). Now Jesus adds a
further commandment, "Love one another."

One valid reason for taking this to be an additional commandment is
that a new situation faced the disciples, even as it now faces all believers. Believers are always in the presence of God and live in this
world under the law of God.

But living in this world they must mingle with other people. They
will see them in distress and need, and they will strive to help them;
they will feel impelled to act in obedience to the Word of God: "Love
thy neighbour." However, there is now a further step into which they
are led.

When a person accepts Christ, he joins a church; he belongs to the
Church, the body of Christ. This will mean that other Christians are
bound with him as the Word tells us. One believer may be the hand,
another the foot, another the eye, but all are members of the one
body. They now belong together. In this fellowship of the Church,
they must love one another. During the time that each Christian is
here in the world, he must show love toward all the other members of
the body of Christ in a more intimate way then. This commandment is
strengthened by the result Jesus says will take place when this is done:

> By this shall all men know that ye are my disciples, if ye have love
> one to another (John 13:35).

Such mutual interest in and concern for each other will win recognition on the part of the world. Jesus said, "By this shall *all* men know."
This recognition from the world will both honor the name of Jesus
Christ and incline people to listen to the message Christians set forth
in their Gospel.

> Simon Peter said unto him, Lord, whither goest thou? Jesus an-
> swered him, Whither I go, thou canst not follow me now; but
> thou shalt follow me afterwards. Peter said unto him, Lord, why
> cannot I follow thee now? I will lay down my life for thy sake.
> Jesus answered him, Wilt thou lay down thy life for my sake?
> Verily, verily, I say unto thee, The cock shall not crow, till
> thou hast denied me thrice (John 13:36-38).

As Jesus had been teaching His disciples He had indicated He was about to leave them. Peter did not want to be left behind and volunteered to go with Jesus wherever He was going. When Jesus said Peter would not now be able to follow Him, though he could do this later, Peter confidently said that he was willing to lay down his life for the sake of his Master. But living in obedience to Jesus Christ requires more than a personal intention to obey: no man is good enough nor strong enough to walk with the Lord in his own human nature and strength, and Peter was going to learn the truth of this in what happened to him in the next few hours.

Chapter 15

LET NOT YOUR HEART BE TROUBLED

THE REALITY OF HEAVEN (14:1-12)

Jesus left no room for doubt as to the reality of heaven in His public teaching as reported by the gospel writers.

> Let not your heart be troubled: ye believe in God, believe also in me. In my Father's house are many mansions: if it were not so, I would have told you. I go to prepare a place for you. And if I go and prepare a place for you, I will come again, and receive you unto myself; that where I am, there ye may be also. And whither I go ye know, and the way ye know (John 14:1-4).

Someone could ask a Christian, "Have you seen heaven?" The believer would have to reply, "No, I have not seen it." Such questions might continue: "Are you sure there is a heaven? How can you know? What does it look like? Where is it?" In reply, the Christian would need only to quote these verses. These words do not specifically answer such detailed questions, but they give positive assurance to the believing heart. If anybody in the world wants to know what Jesus of Nazareth thought about heaven, John 14:1-4 gives the answer! Stop and think for a moment. Who made this profound statement? Surely if anyone who had ever lived on earth was in a position to know what heaven is like, where it is, and what to expect there, it would be the One who came down from heaven, the Son of God, Jesus of Nazareth.

Realizing that human beings are so limited in their natural experience Jesus spoke a word of assurance: ". . . if it were not so, I would have told you." The believer is just a human being, living his life here on earth by faith in the Son of God, and by His grace. He can have no opinion or explanation about heaven, but he can stand on the ground Jesus has given him: "In my Father's house are many mansions . . . I go to prepare a place for you." These words have spoken peace to many a heart, even as Jesus meant that they should, when He began His message by saying, "Let not your heart be troubled." Ten thousand, ten million men might admit they had not seen heaven, but that does not change it. Why should anyone pay attention to such as admit they do not believe? ". . . I know whom I have believed," wrote Paul, "and am persuaded that he is able to keep that which I have committed unto him against that day" (II Timothy 1:12). The believer is committed to the Lord Jesus Christ. Every confidence he has is in Him.

The Christian feels that he can step out and tell the whole, wide world that heaven is real. "If it were not so, I would have told you!" And so believers can join in to sing with others of like faith about another world, "far, far away."

> Face to face! O blissful moment!
> Face to face — to see and know;
> Face to face with my Redeemer,
> Jesus Christ, who loves me so.

So many beautiful songs have been written about heaven, and the joys that await the saved souls. How heartily they can join in singing about the "golden bells"; about being "Safe in the arms of Jesus": and perhaps one of the loveliest of all:

> When all my labors and trials are o'er,
> And I am safe on that beautiful shore;
> Just to be near the dear Lord I adore,
> Will through the ages be glory for me. . . .
> Oh, that will be glory for me, . . .
> When by His grace I shall look on His face,
> That will be glory, be glory for me.

Anyone who gives serious thought to the reality of heaven will be brought back to one central idea: Jesus Christ talked about heaven with all assurance. It is not necessary to decide whether heaven is north, south, east, west, below, or above. Suffice it to say that no matter where its location, it belongs to God. It is adequate for a Christian to know that heaven is where God is. Jesus taught His disciples to pray, ". . . Our Father which art in heaven, Hallowed by thy name" (Matthew 6:9). Wherever it is, God is there! And that is where the mansions are to be found.

In thinking about heaven, there is a more important aspect to be considered. Anybody thinking or talking about heaven would surely want to go there. Certainly he would want his loved ones to go to heaven. The mind may have reservations about the reality, but the heart has no question as to its desirability! !

It is worthy to note that people feel the same about hell. Many will say they don't know anything about it; they have no idea where or why it exists. And many will firmly insist they do not believe in hell. Actually they may not be sure about this or that, but there is one thing about which they can be sure: they don't want their boys and girls to go to hell.

The Way to Heaven

Jesus went on to say, ". . . the way ye know." Thomas questioned this. "We don't know where you are going, Lord, and how can we know the way, wherever it is?" At this point Thomas was being practical, not actually doubting, yet wanting to keep things clear and above board. Jesus answered in the famous utterance known among all believers:

> Jesus saith unto him, I am the way, the truth, and the life: no man cometh unto the Father, but by me (John 14:6).

It is important to notice the way this is written: "I am the way" — *the* way, not a way or any way — *the* truth, *the* life. There is only one way and that is through Jesus Christ our Lord. "No man cometh unto the Father, *but by me.*"

Jesus was not talking about God as Creator or as the Almighty One with sovereignty over all things. Every human being on earth has dealings with God the Creator, and every man or woman will have dealings with God as Judge. Every living creature is under the supervision of God and sustained by God. But none of these considerations bring the thought of God as Father. When one considers God as Father, he is in the position of a child: this person is His son or daughter, begotten of Him; through the Son of God, brought into newness of life. If anyone wants to come to know the Father, the avenue of approach must be through the Son. ". . . no man cometh to the Father but by me."

At that point, Philip spoke up. ". . . Lord, shew us the Father, and it sufficeth us" (John 14:8). If the disciples could just see the Father, Philip felt that would be enough to content them. This request brought forth the amazing wonderful statement by Jesus Christ, expressing the relationship between the Father and the Son:

> Jesus saith unto him, Have I been so long time with you, and yet hast thou not known me, Philip? he that hath seen me hath seen the Father; and how sayest thou then, Shew us the Father? Believest thou not that I am in the Father, and the Father in me? the words that I speak unto you I speak not of myself: but the Father that dwelleth in me, he doeth the works (John 14:9, 10).

Seeing Jesus Christ would not be so much seeing the Judge of all the earth or the Creator of all living things, but rather seeing God as Father, sending His own Son to die for sinners. Jesus of Nazareth was actually indwelt by God: He was God. "He that hath seen me," Jesus of Nazareth, has actually seen God as Father.

In other words, these men were to understand all that Jesus had done before their very eyes, all the miracles He had worked, all the deeds performed on behalf of others, all that was said, were all done, worked by the mighty processes of God at work within Jesus of Nazareth. "Believe me that I am in the Father, and the Father in me: or else believe me for the very works' sake" (John 14:11). The works performed by Jesus of Nazareth were and are from God. In the last analysis, this is the best proof, the ground for our faith.

GREATER WORKS

This was followed by a truly amazing statement, which is hard to understand even today.

> Verily, verily, I say unto you, He that believeth on me, the works that I do shall he do also; and greater works than these shall he do; because I go unto my Father (John 14:12).

These words express a profound truth. God will work in and through His people. This could well be the source of the power manifested in great evangelistic meetings so blessed, with countless men and women coming to find Christ as Saviour. Such may well be the *greater works* done, after Calvary and the Resurrection have made them possible!

"ASK IN MY NAME" (14:13-26)

> And whatsoever ye shall ask in my name, that will I do, that the Father may be glorified in the Son. If ye shall ask anything in my name, I will do it (John 14:13, 14).

When this statement is seen in context with what was written just before, the more complete truth is brought into view. Here Jesus tells in unmistakable terms that if believers ask anything in His name, that is, in accordance with His will, He will do whatever is so asked.

This was by way of encouraging the disciples to pray for guidance and blessing that they might find themselves in the will of God, and do the "greater works" He had predicted they would do.

Jesus then continued His teaching by indicating the way of answered prayer: "If ye love me, keep my commandments" (verse 15). When He says, "If ye love me," He is saying in effect: "If you want to please Me, if you want to do My will and bring honor to My name, then keep My commandments." This word *keep* means to cherish, heed, and follow after: it means to guard the commandments carefully lest they be broken.

THE HOLY SPIRIT

> And I will pray the Father, and he shall give you another Comforter, that he may abide with you for ever; Even the Spirit of truth; whom the world cannot receive, because it seeth him not, neither knoweth him: but ye know him; for he dwelleth with you, and shall be in you. I will not leave you comfortless: I will come to you (John 14:16-18).

The words *another Comforter* imply that Jesus Himself was a Comforter; and the Holy Spirit is to be another such person, bringing God's blessing to our hearts. The word for "Comforter" in the Greek is *paraclete,* which actually means *someone called alongside of.* The account of an actual incident written in New Testament Greek shows the meaning of the word. A small boy, perhaps four years of age, had fallen and hurt himself, and was crying because of his pain and fright. His mother came running to his side, picked up the little lad, hugged him, wiped his face, and dusted off his clothing. In short, she had come along side of him with love and care. That is what the word *paraclete* means. This is exactly what the Lord Jesus Christ had done during the days of His ministry on earth and what the Holy Spirit does for believers now. He actually watches over them, and when they need special care, He is there to meet that need. He will wipe the tears from their eyes and ease their hurts.

Since He is always with them, they are never alone. He is their "Paraclete." Always, moment by moment and day by day, believers have the Comforter. What a wonderful provision the Lord Jesus promised for each one of His people when He told His disciples He would ask the Father to send another Comforter.

Jesus next speaks of the ". . . Spirit of truth; whom the world cannot receive, because it seeth him not, neither knoweth him . . ." (verse 17). It is natural to think that this inability to receive the Holy Spirit is because the world was in sin, wicked, disobedient to the will of God, and not recognizing God as the Father. But this is not altogether a true statement. In this passage it is put very clearly. The world cannot receive the Spirit of God because ". . . it seeth him not, neither knoweth him . . ." In other words the world does not understand about the Spirit, and because of this lack of understanding and of esteem, He can do nothing in the world.

This is an amazing truth. Actually the Holy Spirit will come to a man who has sinned, to a person who is weak or wayward, or to someone who is ignorant of the truth. There is only one condition required of a believer in Christ Jesus to have indwelling in his heart the blessed Paraclete: He must understand who the Holy Spirit is and treat Him for what He is. If any person will honor Him and allow Him entrance, He will come into his heart. Enthroned there, He will show the believer the things that will strengthen his faith and incline his heart to obey the will of the Father. This is the work of the Holy Spirit. When our Lord Jesus Christ was here, that is what He did. He called men unto Himself, and said, "Follow Me," then He guided them along the way. The Holy Spirit will guide believers in the things of the Lord, and will comfort and strengthen them daily as they live and serve.

This whole truth of the continuing companionship of the Holy Spirit is confirmed in a promise which is precious to many believers: "I will not leave you comfortless: I will come to you" (verse 18). The underlying thought of the words, in the original, are "I will not leave you orphans." Anyone who is without a family knows how special this promise is.

After this Jesus discussed in some detail the close identification of believers with Himself. "Yet a little while, and the world seeth me no more; but ye see me: because I live, ye shall live also" (verse 19). Here is the blessing of eternal life: life here on earth in the power of the indwelling Holy Spirit, and life everlasting in that glorious place He has prepared for us. To be forever with the Lord is the joy of the Gospel.

What a marvelous thing it is to become a Christian! The sinner believes in the Lord Jesus Christ, and receives Him into his heart. God then adopts him as one of His children and sends the Holy Spirit, who makes the Father's will clear, leads the believer into the grace of the Lord Jesus Christ.

"He that hath my commandments, and keepeth them, he it is that loveth me: and he that loveth me shall be loved of my Father, and I will love him, and will manifest myself to him" (verse 21). In these simple words Jesus describes the frame of heart and mind prevailing in the believer.

This section closes with a summing up of the whole presentation of this glorious truth:

> But the Comforter, which is the Holy Ghost, whom the Father will send in my name, he shall teach you all things, and bring all things to your remembrance, whatsoever I have said unto you (John 14:26).

Here then, is the glorious work of the Comforter, to show the things of the Lord Jesus Christ, as He lives in and with the believers forever.

THE WAY OF PEACE (14:27-31)

How often someone expresses a longing desire for peace in the midst of this troubled world! Calamities beset the world, strikes, riots, and war increase month by month, so that those who are without the love of God and the indwelling grace of Christ Jesus through the Spirit, are beside themselves with worry and fear.

The word of Jesus speaks of assurance and comfort:

> Peace I leave with you, my peace I give unto you: not as the world giveth, give I unto you. Let not your heart be troubled, neither let it be afraid (John 14:27).

It certainly is never easy, even for a Christian, to live in such a troubled world. The Lord Jesus Himself was a "man of sorrows and acquainted with grief," and knew what it was to shed tears. Many events are disturbing, and there are many burdens which seem, at times, very heavy. Nowhere in the Word of God is it promised that burdens will cease, but there is the promise that He will supply strength and grace to bear the burdens as believers grow closer and closer to Him.

So many people *speak* of peace nowadays, but so few people seem to *have* peace of heart. The word "peace" is on almost every tongue, but so many different things are meant by that small word, *peace*. It is only possible to learn its true meaning as a person has some measure of it. The depth of peace a person has depends upon how deeply that one is calling upon the Holy Spirit. Many people seem to think "the peace of God" is something reserved for a far-distant future. They do not understand what it means to have peace of heart right now, today, this moment. To be at peace does not mean the cessation of all activity. Peace is not sitting idly, accomplishing nothing at all. A paralyzed man is still, absolutely still, but this does not qualify him to be called a man at peace. If a group of children on a playground were suddenly attacked by a mad dog they might run together and huddle closely, hardly daring to move, but they would be far from being at peace. No, peace is not cessation of activity, but rather the elimination of discord and discontent. There are no conflicts when the peace of God rules in heart and head.

Again, let it be understood that peace is not a matter of everybody being exactly alike. Men do not speak of a town being at peace because all the residents think, act, and speak in the same way. Nor is peace the total absence of danger. No one can walk down any street, nor travel anywhere, and not face danger. Danger is all about, moment by moment, in this world of ours. But a person can have peace in the midst of danger!

It can be further noted that peace is not complete freedom from frustration. There will be things a person cannot do and possessions which he cannot have. There may be aspirations to church or civic authority, or promotion in business, which are not realized. But even under such circumstances of frustration, it is possible to have perfect peace of heart.

PEACE IS LIKE HARMONY

Perhaps the best way to describe peace is by likening it to perfect harmony. Harmony in music seems simple enough. It is possible for a person to play perhaps six or eight notes on a piano or organ, and the effect will be very pleasing to the ear. When these different notes blend agreeably with each other, the result is *harmony*. Harmony may be produced by one musician at a keyboard, or by a hundred musicians in a great symphony orchestra.

Peace may be compared to health. What does it really mean when someone is said to be healthy? How does he know? Teeth and ears are healthy, in good condition, when there is no ache or pain in them. So it is when the organs are in a healthy condition, and so with the other members of the body. When all are working together, and are able to do a good day's work, with some strength left for some recreation as well, the body is at peace. But does this mean it is inert, inactive? No, men are constantly using the body twenty-four hours a day. The heart never stops beating, the lungs continue to breathe regularly, evenly, and the blood pumps through every part of the circulatory system. But because of a certain regularity in rhythm a certain measure of peace pervades throughout the body.

The full meaning of this statement of Jesus is suggested by the phrase "my peace" and the further statement "not as the world giveth, give I unto you." How could the world give anything like the "peace of God which passeth understanding?"

The world considers "peace" as being the state of having everything one could desire. All a person wants to eat and drink, all of the possessions he covets, all the opportunity for fun, games and other pleasures. In short, the complete gratification of every sensual appetite is what the world considers "peace." But is that it? To have one's own way in everything? Too many of the world's own children have found out, to their sorrow, that such is far from peace!

And certainly this is not the way peace comes from the Lord Jesus Christ. *"My* peace I give unto you." *My* peace? Remember that this is what He said immediately before going to the Garden of Gethsemane. Remember how Jesus Christ went into the Garden, and prayed until He sweat, as it were, great drops of blood. Remember that He lay on His face and prayed to His Father with a deeply burdened heart. His soul was exceedingly troubled, nigh even unto death. This was no light burden that He carried. He, the sinless One, was facing the experience of taking upon Himself the sins of the world! And He who knew what was to come in that Garden, the agony of prayer, said to the waiting disciples, "Peace I leave with you, my peace I give unto you: not as the world giveth, give I unto you. Let not your heart be troubled, neither let it be afraid."

THE PEACE OF GOD

This is peace that comes when all has been yielded to the will of God. The believer yields everything to God, and in turn, God takes care of him. Yield into His gracious care everything which bothers and causes heartache. Let Him have His way: let Him solve the problem; and the soul will be quiet and at peace. *This is the peace of God!* And truly, it does pass all human understanding. It was this peace which flooded the heart and mind of Jesus Christ as He faced

Calvary, with its burden of the sins of the world. Coming out of that agony of prayer in Gethsemane, knowing all that lay immediately ahead of Him: betrayal, torment and persecution by His accusers, the long road to Golgotha, and then the lingering death in agony, and yet He had a deep and abiding peace! This is "My peace," His peace! !

How could Jesus have such peace, just before Calvary? Perhaps full understanding is not possible, but in part the truth is indicated in Hebrews 12:2: ". . . for the joy that was set before him endured the cross, despising the shame, and is set down at the right hand of the throne of God." In other words, the peace Jesus had was grounded in the promise that His Father would keep Him even through death. And this is the kind of peace the believer can have. God can give believers a peace that is free from the world and all its problems, fears and burdens. Christians don't have to have the pleasures; they don't need positions of affluence or influence; they don't need to have their own way; they don't have to gratify every impulse of the flesh — none of that is the way to peace. Christians want the fellowship of God. They want to live in His presence and be pleasing in His sight. He can achieve this peace in their hearts and lives as they yield themselves to Him. He assures them that He will forever keep them and forever live within them through the power of the indwelling Holy Spirit. The world can go its own way. Christians are free from its power and influence. They have a peace within, which the world cannot give and can never take away.

Jesus knew this joyful experience to the full.

> Ye have heard how I said unto you, I go away, and come again unto you. If ye loved me, ye would rejoice, because I said, I go unto the Father: for my Father is greater than I (John 14: 28).

In other words, the Lord Jesus was telling them not only of the suffering unto death which lay ahead: His arrest by the soldiers after the betrayal, the shame and humiliation at their hands, the cross with its agony, and His death, but also of the glorious resurrection morning, and victory! He also was trying to make clear to these men, whose eyes were still darkened by the tragic suffering He must endure, that if they really cared about Him, they would be glad that this process was under way and would rejoice because through all this grief He was going to the Father. Being with the Father forever with no future prospect of separation was a prospect of joy so wonderful it made any suffering seem bearable.

> Hereafter I will not talk much with you: for the prince of this world cometh, and hath nothing in me. But that the world may know that I love the Father; and as the Father gave me commandment, even so I do. Arise, let us go hence (John 14:30, 31).

There comes a time in the affairs of men when there is nothing more to be said. There may even be the feeling that Satan seems to have control of the circumstances. A person living in his own home, where he might expect peace and joy, instead finds hard, difficult situations in his own family. Even here the hand of man seems raised against him. Perhaps another will face envy and malice in his place of business, or a threat to his interests because of his stand for Christ. These things could be inspired by Satan, and the devil may be expected to find delight in bringing dishonor upon the name of God through this Christian. The Bible reveals that he is constantly striving to thwart the purposes of God in the life of a believer. At such a time there is not much that a follower of Jesus Christ can say.

There is not much to be said in the face of Satan's operation. The sure defense of the Christian is to wait quietly and trust. Let Satan go on, for whereas all he can do is destroy the body, God can raise the dead. Satan with permission from God can take away the things of material importance, but he cannot touch the spiritual wealth which is in Christ Jesus and belongs to every believer, who is a "joint heir with Christ."

Jesus understood exactly why He was submitting to Satan's actions. "But that the world may know that I love the Father; and as the Father gave me commandment, even so I do. . . ." What more can be done? This "even so I do" did not refer to Jesus going on with His daily life, with the tasks which faced Him, as He dealt with crowds of needy and suffering men and women. He was going straight to the trial, the false accusations, the spitting and shame, the unjust condemnation, and the agonizing death by crucifixion. This is what Jesus Christ *accepted* that the world might know that He loved the Father. Jesus' testimony to His love for His Father was expressed in accepting sorrow, pain, and death such as no man has ever known. Loving the Father meant the full performance of the Father's will in His life and death and resurrection!

Jesus ended this period of instruction with a ringing call to action, to face whatever would come in the will of God: ". . . Arise, let us go hence." Forward to face the suffering and death, forward to demonstrate that He loved God: this was the course of action Jesus took with power and peace in His heart. This is the peace Jesus Christ offers to believers today, every day, as they walk in this world with their trust and confidence fully in Him.

Chapter 16

THE GREATER COMMANDMENT

ABIDING IN JESUS (15:1-11)

There is much more to the Christian life than the acceptance of Christ Jesus as Saviour. Listen to what Christ Himself said about this life.

> Abide in me, and I in you. As the branch cannot bear fruit of itself, except it abide in the vine; no more can ye, except ye abide in me (John 15:4).

This clearly states the necessity for living in communion with Jesus, day by day and moment by moment. He spoke these words to His disciples as He was explaining to them that their spiritual life would come from Him, that there was no such thing as living, walking, and serving apart from Him. He told them plainly that they were unable to do the will of God in their own strength.

A further step beyond the initial acceptance of Jesus Christ as Saviour is even more than having the Holy Spirit actually living in the life of the individual Christian, although it includes that. This is the concept of walking in the will of God, following the guidance of God, being inwardly led by Christ Jesus and motivated by the Holy Spirit.

Jesus knew He was soon to be crucified, and knowing that He had only a short time left with His disciples, He took this time to prepare them for the experience they must face after He was gone from them in the flesh. When His bodily presence would be gone, what could they do? They were accustomed to turning to Him day by day for answers to their questions. He would never again sit with them at the table, sharing mutual fellowship as they shared the food. So Jesus took this time to teach them what life would be like and what resources would be available to them when His personal presence was no longer with them.

Jesus began His explanation by using a simple figure of speech: "I am the true vine, and my Father is the husbandman." The word *husbandman* is not common in today's vocabulary. It is an old English term easily understood. Today men say *farmer,* or possibly *gardener.*

THE NECESSITY OF PRUNING

Every branch in me that beareth not fruit he taketh away: and every branch that beareth fruit, he purgeth it, that it may bring forth more fruit (John 15:2).

Careful pruning is necessary in any successful fruitgrowing, and Jesus is making use of his disciples' knowledge of that here. An unfruitful branch will simply be cut off.

Young Christians can easily have an inadequate idea of what to expect as they enter into their new life and because of that may walk right into situations which cannot possibly produce fruit. They may feel that now nothing should distress them, there surely should be no serious problems: life should be a time of glad triumph.

But anyone who has walked the pilgrim way for any length of time knows that such is not the case. The Christian may be called upon to face experiences which are hard to bear. He may, for example, be called upon to give up something which He considers precious. When this treasure is removed, he may feel the Lord is against him. But the Lord may be merely pruning, that the believer might bring forth more fruit to His glory! By taking away the thing which was engrossing the attention and absorbing the heart's affection, God was actually pruning so that the energies of the believer may more completely be used in accord with His will. Pruning is done again and again as the gardener sees a certain tree or plant which needs this treatment in order that it may produce the very best fruit.

Jesus continued His teaching to point out what happens after the pruning has taken place. "Now ye are clean through the word which I have spoken unto you" (verse 3). "Cleansed" means that the believer has been "pruned." ". . . the word which I have spoken to you," meaning the Scriptures, are useful in pruning. Reading and thoughtful studying of the Bible will actually have the effect of cleansing out some things in the life of a Christian which are not in accord with the will of God. This is a necessary and natural process in growth. Many habits and ways, some of which may not be evil in themselves nor harmful in other persons, are not fruitful and do not help toward Christian character. God wants these to be cut out.

It should also be recognized that in some cases the pruning may be done in some act of Providence. Some calamity, or disaster, or perhaps some trouble with other persons may make it necessary or at least advisable to cease from certain practices. The believer may not even be aware that this change in his way of living was actually important for his growth in spiritual living. The result can be more fruit to the glory of God who brought such change or changes to pass through His providence in order that the believer might be more blessed.

THE FRUIT FROM ABIDING

Jesus speaks of being "the vine," and of believers as "the branches," and says, "Abide in me, and I in you. . . ." He adds that no branch can bear fruit by itself, it must be a part of the vine. Thus the relationship between the believer and Christ is clearly set forth. They are members of Christ as the branches are members of the vine; and when this is true, the branch brings forth fruit, even as believers when they abide in Him. The words ". . . for without me ye can do nothing," simply mean "separated from me you cannot bear fruit." This does not mean that the believer cannot do a day's work, putting in a full eight hours in the office or shop, to earn a decent living for his family. Nor does it mean he cannot drive a car or engage in any ordinary forms of activity. But it does mean that he can do nothing to bear fruit in the will of God, apart from the Lord Jesus Christ. The believer cannot live the full Christian life apart from the strength of God operating in him, that is to say, without "abiding in the vine."

As a master teacher, Jesus repeated His idea by further use of this figure of speech.

> If a man abide not in me, he is cast forth as a branch, and is withered; and men gather them, and cast them into the fire, and they are burned (John 15:6).

Everyone has seen plants like that, even bushes and trees, when a certain portion was dead, dry, brown, withered up. Such sections were still on the main stem or trunk. The gardener will come along and prune, or cut off, those dead twigs or branches, and burn them. This truth can easily be seen in the spiritual realm when the professing believer who is not abiding in Christ and bearing fruit to His glory is cast forth as a withered branch. The life shows no joy, no self-denial, no love for God or for others, no service — in short, no fruit.

Again the Teacher's skill is seen in His use of contrast:

> If ye abide in me, and my words abide in you, ye shall ask what ye will, and it shall be done unto you (John 15:7).

When the believer puts his whole trust in God, when His words abide in the heart, that is, if the believer seeks to let his life conform to the Lord's guidance, and lives entirely in His will, following the Scriptures in yielding to the suggestions of the Holy Spirit, he will ask what he wills and find that God will grant his request. Obviously this does not mean he can ask *anything, everything.* His petitions will be guided by the Spirit, if he is truly abiding in Christ. He will soon find out that what he wants will in some way have come to be what the Lord wants! What really makes the difference is whether the Lord is working in the heart of the believer according to His word.

Herein is my Father glorified, that ye bear much fruit; so shall
ye be my disciples (John 15:8).

It is the purpose of God to produce fruit in the lives of those who
accept Christ Jesus. God is getting this job done on earth, through believers, through all those who abide in Christ and let the Holy Spirit
guide and inspire them. To say they will "bear much fruit" is just
another way of expressing the achievement of God's purpose, and "so
shall ye be my disciples."

FULL JOY

There are even deeper meanings in the fellowship with God through
Christ as Jesus went on to point out:

As the Father hath loved me, so have I loved you: continue ye in
my love. If ye keep my commandments, ye shall abide in my love;
even as I have kept my Father's commandments, and abide in his
love. These things have I spoken unto you, that my joy might
remain in you, and that your joy might be full (John 15:9-
11).

It seems incredible that Jesus loves believers as the Father loves Him.
This is a remarkable tribute to the grace of Jesus Christ and lays a
heavy responsibility upon the Christian to respond with all the dedication that he is able to give. This is the source of whatever joy the
believer may have: it is the joy of the Lord in his own heart: "that
my joy might remain in you." This joy is not grounded even in the response in service on the part of the believer, but in that fact that God
in Christ loves him.

This wonderful truth means that Christian people will trust completely in their Lord. They will look to God for building up in the faith
and for guidance day by day and will yield their lives to Him. The
results will be that their lives will manifest things pleasing to God, such
as ". . . love, joy, peace, longsuffering, gentleness, goodness, faith,
Meekness, temperance [self-control] . . . ," the fruit of the Spirit out-
lined by Paul in Galatians 5:22, 23. These characteristics of the true
child of God will grow in the Christian. The Lord will be pleased and
satisfied, and the believer shall glorify the Father!

JESUS PREPARES HIS DISCIPLES (15:12-19)

It is important for Christians to note how Jesus was preparing His
disciples for living in this world without His bodily presence. Believers
today live without seeing Him, except by the eyes of faith. They
cannot see His face, nor hear His voice; they cannot reach out to
touch Him, though they depend utterly upon Him. Because the Christian believes in His teaching and His promises as recorded in Scrip-

ture, he knows Jesus Christ is alive, loves him and speaks to him daily through His Word.

Certain definite guidelines are drawn for all believers, and John has recorded for all to see and to learn:

> This is my commandment, That ye love one another, as I have loved you. Greater love hath no man than this, that a man lay down his life for his friends. Ye are my friends, if ye do whatsoever I command you. Henceforth I call you not servants; for the servant knoweth not what his Lord doeth: but I have called you friends; for all things that I have heard of my Father I have made known unto you. Ye have not chosen me, but I have chosen you, and ordained you, that ye should go and bring forth fruit, and that your fruit should remain: that whatsoever ye shall ask of the Father in my name, he may give it to you. These things I command you, that ye love one another (John 15:12-17).

This is the way of life Jesus was setting forth for all who accept and seek to serve Him. He says explicitly, "This is my commandment, That ye love one another, as I have loved you." This is a high standard. He had emphasized its importance when He said earlier:

"LOVE ONE ANOTHER"

> By this shall all men know that ye are my disciples, if ye have love one to another (John 13:35).

The word "love" should be closely noted for it has degrees of meaning. In the New Testament "love" is not a matter of the *emotions* at all. It is more a certain *attitude* which governs thoughts, impulses, and actions toward others. As Christians strive to do things on behalf of their brothers, they seek to contribute to the blessedness and happiness of other Christians. It is not that any believer considers his fellow Christians to be perfect, but in any time of need the Christian comes to them to help, to bring encouragement or advice. The love of God fills the heart of the believer and makes him considerate of others, so that one can say he acts in love to other men and women when he is led to show them an expression of God's grace.

It is difficult to describe what is meant by this word *love*. It cannot be seen with the physical eye, any more than one can see the wind which stirs the leaves of the trees. Love is a descriptive term to designate the way in which a person acts toward others. A mother expresses love for her child in the care she gives it; a young man gives things to the girl of his choice and thus shows his love; a husband loves his wife in the way he provides for her welfare, her needs, and by his consideration of her plans and desires, as well as his own. Any person can *say* "I love" but it is conduct that will disprove or prove the statement, even as it is demonstrated in action.

The basic meaning of love in the New Testament use of the word is to be interested in the happiness and the welfare of the person loved. To love anyone is to try to make his experience in the world a happy one, to make his welfare a particular concern. ". . . love . . . as I have loved you," said Jesus. "Greater love hath no man than this, that a man lay down his life for his friends." This is what Jesus did for men. No one can give more than his life. That is the ultimate offering on the altar of love.

FRIENDS OF JESUS

Jesus carried this analogy of relationships a step further. He tells His disciples they are no longer servants, but friends. They are not living only to obey Him, they are to have fellowship, for He says ". . . I have called you friends. . . ." He makes them understand that He will keep them advised as to what He is going to do so that they can willingly cooperate with Him in getting His work done.

Not only did Jesus show His grace by emphasizing that His disciples were His friends, but He went a step further, with a most amazing and heart-warming statement, "Ye have not chosen me, but I have chosen you. . . ." Their friendship with Him was not something they had achieved by their wisdom or strength, but something He had done. The truth was He sought them out, He chose His friends! This truth means He comes to believers today that He might have fellowship with them, and then ordains them to go out and become fruit bearers.

That word *ordained* does not refer to a church ceremony in which a minister or an elder is "ordained." The word as used here really means to *prepare*: to prepare for a given task or service. Jesus told them that He had not only chosen them but also prepared them in the very place where He wanted them to be. And this is what He continues to do with His own: He prepares the field in which they work. He gives an assignment for each of them.

As one grows in grace and knowledge as a Christian, one becomes conscious of the fact that any good he has done was — and is — all the Lord's idea, not his own. It is not that the Christian gropes around blindly and finds Him: rather He seeks and finds the believers: "I have chosen you, and ordained you, that you should go and bring forth fruit, and that your fruit should remain. . . ."

It is sometimes hard for a believer to grasp this, particularly when he is young in the Christian life. Perhaps it can be more readily seen if the statement of Jesus is paraphrased using the name of *Tom Andrews*. (If by chance a real Tom Andrews reads this book, may he be blessed by this illustration in full measure!) Then the passage would read: "Tom Andrews did not choose Me, but I have chosen Tom Andrews and prepared him by ordaining him, that Tom Andrews might bear fruit, and that his fruit might remain: that whatsoever Tom Andrews asks of the Father in My name, He will do for Tom Andrews."

In setting forth the truth of the vital relationship between the Lord and the believer, Jesus pointed out also the hatred of the world outside of Christ.

> If the world hate you, ye know that it hated me before it hated you. If ye were of the world, the world would love his own: but because ye are not of the world, but I have chosen you out of the world, therefore the world hateth you (John 15:18, 19).

This can express itself in many ways: in the shop, the school, the office, even in the home, or among one's own circle of friends. James tells us that ". . . whosoever therefore will be a friend of the world is the enemy of God" (James 4:4). But the same thing is true in reverse, it can be said that whosoever will be the friend of Jesus Christ will find enmity from the world active against himself.

Christ Jesus chooses believers out of the world, and calls them unto Himself. When John uses the term "the world" he is referring to the way of life which is based on human interests, desires and purposes. It is natural living in the will of man as over against spiritual living in the will of God. The world can be any place where people are living according to their own ideas and seeking their own good by their own efforts. Thus the world is composed, in this particular use of the word, of those who either oppose or are indifferent to the Gospel of Christ, and with all that is involved in His call and anointing for service.

WHAT BELIEVERS CAN EXPECT (15:20-26)

Having described the close relationship that exists between the believer and His Lord, Jesus went on to point out the treatment the believer may expect since he is now openly identified with Christ.

It is a sobering fact that Christ Jesus left the public proclamation of His love, His sacrifice, His redeeming grace to His disciples after His return to the Father. Therefore this is the task of all believers who accept Him and serve Him with faithful and loving hearts.

And so He pointed out to them that

> . . . The servant is not greater than his lord. If they have persecuted me, they will also persecute you; if they have kept my saying, they will keep yours also (John 15:20).

Thus He warned them that they need expect no better treatment than He had received and would receive, and He was speaking of Calvary in the immediate future. He went on to say that He was suffering rejection, and He warned His disciples that rejection would be their lot for the very reason that they were His disciples.

This is something Christians need always to keep in mind. If believers intend to be faithful to the Lord Jesus Christ in their personal relationship with Him, and faithful in their witnessing for Him before the world, they can expect that the same world that rejected Him will turn a deaf ear to their testimony and will reject them. This the people of the world will do, not because of the Christians themselves personally, but because these witnesses are setting forth the things of God, and it is true now as it was then, ". . . now they have no cloak for their sin" (verse 22). Hostile rejection and violent opposition are to be expected.

REJECTION AND PERSECUTION

Despite the certainty of such rejection and such persecution the Gospel must be preached. Christ Jesus died for men that are lost. He came to do all that was necessary to reconcile sinners to God. Because this is true, the Gospel must be preached in all the world. Christ Jesus Himself gave the Great Commission (Matthew 28:18-20). Missionaries must go out everywhere and preach the good news that Jesus died for the sins of men.

It is most important to realize, to accept, and to act upon, the solemn fact that such preaching is what parents do in the home; what a preacher does in the pulpit and in his daily life; what a Sunday school teacher does in the Sunday school class and during the week. At all times and in every place Christians are either preaching the Gospel or they are hindering this truth about salvation. Some people who do not know Christ develop their opinion of Him by noting the actions and attitudes of His followers. A human being is born with the capacity for faith, just as he is born with an innate readiness to worship, but he needs to be told about the love of God as this is manifested in Jesus of Nazareth.

No doubt the reason many do not know Christ Jesus is that no one has ever told them the story of Jesus and His love. There is a real responsibility to witness upon each believer in the Lord Jesus Christ.

Teaching about Christ, telling the message of the Gospel, is not sufficient. There must be an invitation to come, to believe and to accept. It is not only the giving out of information, it is the personal and immediate concern that the person or persons listening shall respond and commit themselves to the Saviour, that is important. No one is truly preaching the Gospel unless his hand is outstretched with an invitation to sinners to come. Unless there is an urgent appeal in the message, until there is a sincere personal concern that the hearer should come and turn to the Lord, whether from a pulpit or in a Sunday school class, or in a casual encounter in school, office, barbershop, dress shop, the Gospel has not really been preached.

It has been noted above that Jesus warned His disciples that Christians who go out to tell of Jesus and His love must accept one fact: they will face opposition from certain elements of the world's population. The Christian is to be His witness, he is to share in His life, and so he can expect to find acceptance or rejection, even as He did and still does.

When people receive the Word of God, they are apt to consider the man preaching it a wonderful friend; if they reject the message, they are apt to speak of the preacher in the most unkind terms. This is equally true for the man in the pew who testifies to the grace of God in his life. He may find many new friendships in Christ, or he may find himself called a fanatic, or a man unworthy of friendship. The same is true with a parent who stands out in the midst of a family for the Word of God. A father may find his son or daughter opposing him, and even expressing hatred for him. The same thing can happen to a Sunday school teacher who is truly teaching the Word of God and attempting to lead pupils to know Christ as Saviour. The Lord Jesus has one word for all who suffer shame for His Name.

> But all these things will they do unto you for my name's sake, because they know not him that sent me (John 15:21).

What Jesus was actually saying was that when people reject the Christian because of his witnessing, they are not really rejecting him, but Christ: it will not be the believer personally, but what he is saying about Christ Jesus and the sin of the world. This makes the rejection not personal, but actually spiritual, since it is inspired by an aversion to God.

WHY CHRISTIANS ARE REJECTED

In His explanation Jesus went still deeper into the explanation of the opposition of the world. He tells His disciples that because He had come, sinners now have "no cloak for their sin." This means they will hate to be brought out into the open, they will dislike having their opposition brought into the light. It is possible to find such a condition among church members, and even among teachers in the Sunday school. It is not at all unusual to have someone in a church or Christian circle who really seems to know the Lord show aversion and perhaps even resentment if another should venture to present the deeper things of Christ to him. This hostility to Christ has a deep origin: "He that hateth me hateth my Father also." This is a useful insight for those who witness for Christ, for it helps to understand the conduct of others: it is when men hate Christ that they express that hatred in their attitude toward those who are witnessing for Him.

Jesus Himself understood very well why men hated Him!

If I had not done among them the works which none other man did, they had not had sin: but now have they both seen and hated both me and my Father (John 15:24).

One of the reasons why sinners will hate the witnessing Christian today is because the Gospel's power has been shown, and the Lord Jesus has been presented over and over again as the only Saviour, Keeper, and Friend. Christian witnessing has made a tremendous impression around the whole world. When people in pagan lands find Christ, the results are even more striking than here in our land. Such consequences are manifest to all, and put those who reject Christ in the position of being wrong in their attitude. This they resent. This is what Christians — and their Lord — must bear.

Chapter 17

PREPARATION

JESUS GIVES STRENGTH (15:27—16:4)

It has been noted that John has recorded how Jesus was preparing His own for what would happen after His death, resurrection and ascension. He knew what was ahead for them, and He wanted to give them knowledge and strength to face the days that were coming. After taking time to warn and to prepare them to face opposition with understanding, He made it very clear that witnessing will be their task.

> And ye also bear witness, because ye have been with me from the beginning (John 15:27).

He knew He would be taken out of the world, He knew He would have to leave them, He knew He would be killed, and He knew His sheep would be scattered. But He also knew that blessings would come after He was at the right hand of the Father, and He wanted His disciples to understand this. He wanted them to be ready for co-operation with Him, even though they would see Him only with the eyes of faith.

He made it a definite promise that they would not be left alone when He told them about the Holy Spirit. Jesus also assured the disciples that this Spirit would make clear many things which they were not able to understand as yet. God intended, in His great plan of salvation, that the whole world should know the Gospel. These disciples were to begin the ministry of reconciliation by sharing with the world the testimony of what Calvary and the Resurrection meant. They were especially equipped to do so, for they had been with their Lord from the very beginning of His ministry, and now His Holy Spirit would show them more of the true meaning of all that God was doing in Christ.

> These things have I spoken unto you, that ye should not be offended (John 16:1).

The word *offended* carries a meaning based on the idea of a *stumbling block*. He explains that He had spoken the sober words of warning because He did not want them to stumble when the opposition appeared. Persecution was coming, and He wanted them to be prepared through previous knowledge about its occurrence.

> They shall put you out of the synagogues: yea, the time cometh, that whosoever killeth you will think that he doeth God service (John 16:2).

Christians will live in the world with other people. Here they must maintain relations with employers, fellow employees, and neighbors. It will be their responsibility to talk with them, to witness to them, and to tell them the Gospel of Christ. But there will be resistance to this message. There are people everywhere who are sensitive about the Gospel, who do not want to hear about it, talk about it, or think of it. This is, of course, tied up with the fact that such persons have rejected Jesus Christ, and they are conscious that their hearts are not right with God.

A believer may be faithful in prayer, in Bible reading and study, in church attendance, in giving of his means to the Lord's work; he may be seeking the guidance of God, trying to be humble and co-operative with his neighbors, and gentle with all whom he meets. Why then such intense opposition? Jesus answers that question before it can be asked because He knew everything there is to know about persecution.

Jesus warned His disciples that "They shall put you out of the synagogues . . ." and it is possible even today that accusations could be lodged against a faithful witness to Christ Jesus which would cause him to be brought before the discipline of his own church! Jesus went on to predict: "yea, the time cometh, that whosoever killeth you will think that he doeth God service." Opposition may come from sincere religious leaders, who think they are doing the right thing by opposing what they consider extreme teaching. As a matter of fact even the simple matter of praying faithfully may have the result of antagonizing people, even within one's own household.

Jesus explains how such opposition can occur; this is His answer to the believers' "Why?"

> And these things will they do unto you, because they have not known the Father, nor me (John 16:3).

Jesus is giving the disciples assurance so that they may not falter in their witnessing even though they are sharply opposed.

> But these things have I told you, that when the time shall come, ye may remember that I told you of them. And these things I said not unto you at the beginning, because I was with you (John 16:4).

As long as He was with them in person He could protect them directly from the opposition. But now that He was leaving them He wanted them to be prepared so that they might not be demoralized when such unreasonable persecution befalls them.

What Jesus told His disciples is always true. Any time that the faith of a Christian seems to be unduly tested, it should be remembered that the living Lord knew all about it before it happened. He suffered many of the same oppositions and sorrows Himself, and He gives His followers strength to endure.

For this reason the Christian may take courage, for when it seems he is all alone in his service or in his witnessing he is not really alone.

JESUS MUST GO AWAY (16:5-16)

> But now I go my way to him that sent me; and none of you asketh me, Whither goest thou? But because I have said these things unto you, sorrow hath filled your heart. Nevertheless, I tell you the truth; It is expedient for you that I go away: for if I go not away, the Comforter will not come unto you; but if I depart, I will send him unto you" (John 16:5-7).

It would be hard to see how anything could be better for living than to have Jesus walking beside a person in the flesh, day by day. Yet Jesus Himself said, "It is expedient for you that I go away. . . ." As long as the Lord Jesus Christ was here in person, walking and talking with them, the Holy Spirit would not be sent to them. (As a matter of record the Holy Spirit did not come into the hearts of believers until Pentecost, which was about fifty days after Jesus had departed into heaven.)

> And when he is come, he will reprove the world of sin, and of righteousness, and of judgment: Of sin, because they believe not on me: Of righteousness, because I go to my Father, and ye see me no more: Of judgment, because the prince of this world is judged (John 16:8-11).

The word *reprove,* in the original, conveys the meaning of *convince.* Thus the Holy Spirit will convince or convict the world of sin, righteousness, and judgment.

By making the things of Christ Jesus plain and actual the Holy Spirit can show sin by contrast, to what is utterly right in Jesus. The Holy Spirit would be showing the perfect example of righteousness. In the light of a perfect illustration anybody can understand what true righteousness really is. By His death Jesus revealed the judgment of God upon sin. By looking at Calvary any person anywhere can know what God will do with sin. It is part of the work of the Holy Spirit to so present the things of Jesus Christ that men may know for sure what the truth is, about sin, righteousness, and judgment.

"THINGS TO COME"

After this Jesus told them that there were yet many things to be said, but they could not bear to hear them at this time.

> Howbeit when he, the Spirit of truth, is come, he will guide you into all truth: for he shall not speak of himself; but whatsoever he shall hear, that shall he speak: and he will shew you things to come (John 16:13).

"Things to come" — what a promise! They knew the past: His birth through a virgin mother; the *Lamb of God that taketh away the sin of the world*. They had seen His baptism and the Holy Spirit coming to rest upon Him; they had heard the preaching, and the teaching; they had seen the miracles; they had heard Him promise that people who trusted in Him would never perish — all these things had been said and were done. Yet now there are things to come.

When Jesus said, "I have many things to say unto you," He did not mean that these things would change what had already been said. He then said, "When the Spirit is come He will be the guide into all truth." He will not speak of Himself but of Christ. How similar to what Jesus said of Himself: "The Son can do nothing of himself, but what he seeth the Father do. . . ." "My Father worketh hitherto, and I work." He also said that the Son says nothing of Himself. The Father speaks the words, and the Son repeats them.

> He shall glorify me: for he shall receive of mine, and shall shew it unto you. All things that the Father hath are mine: therefore said I, that he shall take of mine, and shall shew it unto you. A little while, and ye shall not see me: and again, a little while, and ye shall see me, because I go to the Father (John 16:14-16).

The meaning of the word *glorify* has been discussed before: "to get the job done." Jesus here tells His disciples the Holy Spirit will come and glorify Him, will bring to pass what Jesus came to do. He shall receive the things of Jesus, things that the Son and the Father hold in common and show them unto the disciples and unto all believers. Everything the Holy Spirit reveals will belong to the Lord Jesus Christ.

It may have seemed strange to the disciples when Jesus told them that for a little time they would not see Him, then again they would see Him "because I go to the Father." Death by crucifixion, then the three days in the tomb are just about to take place. After that the Resurrection would occur, followed by forty days of occasional fellowship with His risen body, and the final separation from human vision, when He ascended to the Father. After that would come the gift of the Holy Spirit, who would reveal the things of Christ to His followers for all time to come.

Believers become far more conscious of righteousness, and have a much stronger desire for holiness, when they realize that God is not only alive, but they are constantly in His presence. This insight becomes a challenge to a life of holiness and dedicated service!

"A Little While" (16:16-33)

As Jesus continued to teach He spoke of what would happen to Him and of its effect upon the disciples: There would be sorrow, but joy would come afterward. "A little while, and ye shall not see me" — that is sorrow: ". . . and again, a little while, and ye shall see me, because I go to the Father" — that is joy! The disciples were puzzled, their eyes were darkened, and their understanding dim as to the future. They said,

> . . . What is this that he saith, A little while? we cannot tell what he saith (John 16:18).

Sorrow to Joy

They simply could not grasp His meaning. Jesus did not predict in detail how things would happen, but He gave them strong assurance that their sorrow would be turned into joy.

> Verily, verily, I say unto you, That ye shall weep and lament, but the world shall rejoice: and ye shall be sorrowful, but your sorrow shall be turned into joy (John 16:20).

This seems to be the usual pattern for spiritual experience. Jesus used the illustration of a mother's joy in her newborn child to show how things would go with the disciples. She has sorrow and pain in her labor, but when the baby is in her arms, she forgets the pain and suffering, and rejoices in the tiny newborn, ". . . for joy that a man is born into the world." The Christian too shall rejoice when he sees what lies ahead in blessing and glory. Thus he can forget the difficulties which beset his human experience.

As Jesus went on with His teaching He described the sort of experience which would bring joy to those who believed in Him.

> And in that day ye shall ask me nothing. Verily, verily, I say unto you, Whatsoever ye shall ask the Father in my name, he will give it you. Hitherto have ye asked nothing in my name: ask, and ye shall receive, that your joy may be full. These things have I spoken unto you in proverbs: but the time cometh, when I shall no more speak unto you in proverbs, but I shall show you plainly of the Father. At that day ye shall ask in my name: and I say not unto you, that I will pray the Father for you: For the Father himself loveth you, because ye have loved me, and have believed that I came out from God. I came forth from the Father, and am

come into the world: again, I leave the world, and go to the Father (John 16:23-28).

This was the prospect set before the disciples, and it is valid for believers today. As Christians walk with their Lord, in the light of the Bible, their prayers will be answered. Jesus told His disciples that in their praying it would not be necessary to ask Him, for the Father Himself loved them and would hear and answer them. "And in that day ye shall ask me nothing." Then He went on to encourage them with the assurance: "Whatsoever ye shall ask the Father in my name, he will give it to you." In this way Jesus was giving them encouragement to go into the very presence of God the Father. They were to remember their Lord and Saviour had given Himself for them, and using His name they were to press their claim for answered prayer. It is this teaching which gives believers the blessed assurance that, as they live in fellowship with Jesus Christ through faith in Him they may look for answered prayer, according to His will.

As Jesus came to the end of teaching He took time to show them that the events about to take place were all involved in His whole purpose of coming to save them. When Jesus spoke of coming from the Father He was referring back to Bethlehem.

When He used the phrase ". . . again, I leave the world, and go to the Father," He referred to Calvary and the events that followed. The authorities thought they were putting a man to death and putting an end to His career. They did not know He was the Son of God, and that they had no power over Him without the Father's permissive will and His own acceptance of His Father's will. All that happened was in His plan. "It is finished" signaled His going back to His Father.

Jesus foretold the disciples of their own fright and betrayal which He knew was coming by telling them ". . . ye shall be scattered, every man to his own, and shall leave me alone . . ."

NOT ALONE

Then He pointed out the further truth that He would not really be left alone: ". . . and yet I am not alone, because the Father is with me" (verse 32). In this way He taught that Christians can always count on the presence of God with them. Whenever they may be left alone, whether through the home-going of loved ones, or because of persecution, they are not really alone. The gracious presence of the Father is ever with them and His loving care surrounds them.

As He comes to the end of His time of instruction, Jesus gives His disciples the assurance that all is under God's hand. His purpose will be carried out even in the events that distress: in fact they will actually be strengthened by them.

These things I have spoken unto you, that in me ye might have peace. In the world ye shall have tribulation: but be of good cheer; I have overcome the world (John 16:33).

And so the final and full victory belongs to the Christian. Jesus was victorious in His hour of trial, and the peace, joy and victory of the believer are grounded in the eternal, spiritual victory of Jesus Christ. It *is* possible to have peace and joy in this sinful, contrary world today. It is natural to expect that in becoming a Christian a believer could await everything to work out for his good. This is true enough in the end, but the journey through life may be complicated by many trials, much sorrow and suffering. That was the clear teaching of Jesus Christ as He faced His hour of anguish and death.

Chapter 18

THE PRAYER OF JESUS

THE HOUR IS COME (17:1-8)

These words spake Jesus, and lifted up his eyes to heaven, and said, Father, the hour is come; glorify thy Son, that thy Son also may glorify thee (John 17:1).

The will of God has a purpose and an objective. God moves matters to that point of conclusion. The plan for the life of Jesus of Nazareth had been fulfilled. Now death lay ahead, and it would be the death of dishonor: the death of a common criminal on a cross. Not only did Jesus have full knowledge of all this but also a willingness to accept the plan of God, His Father. He could say "Father, the hour is come," and bring to completion the purpose of God.

This seventeenth chapter of John is the chapter of *prayer*. In it is recorded what has been called the "high priestly prayer of Jesus Christ." It is proper to read it with a sense of awe and reverence because here is the report of what the Son of God said to His Father. Here is actually a revelation of pure communion with God. He spoke it for our benefit, so that we might know of the relationship between Him and His Father.

If the question is asked, "What did Jesus Christ come to do?" the answer will come at once to every Christian: ". . . that he should give eternal life to as many as thou hast given him" (verse 2). The words *life eternal* refer to the life that comes only from God. This is not an extension of the life a person has now, as he goes about his natural existence. It is a new life imparted by God, the very life of the Father Himself. This is the life of God in the soul, as believers come to know the only true God and Jesus Christ, whom God has sent for this very purpose.

Jesus called His Father "the only true God." Many people have other gods of their own creation and thought. Man is clever in thinking up his own gods to worship, but *there is only one true God*. He is not the combined opinion of several cults or religions. He is real, true, ". . . the King eternal, immortal, invisible, the only wise

170

God . . ." (I Timothy 1:17). He is in Himself what He is, apart from the opinion of anybody else.

GLORIFYING THE FATHER

Jesus again makes use of the idea of glorifying God:

> I have glorified thee on the earth: I have finished the work which thou gavest me to do. And now, O Father, glorify thou me with thine own self with the glory which I had with thee before the world was (John 17:4, 5).

These are parallel statements, the one means the other. This brings out the clear teaching that the actual work of Jesus Christ on earth was to finish what was in the mind and heart and purpose of God, the Father. Paul wrote about this:

> For we are his workmanship, created in Christ Jesus unto good works, which God hath before ordained that we should walk in them (Ephesians 2:10).

Redeemed persons then are the plan of God brought to completion, and in them God and Christ are glorified.

> I have manifested thy name unto the men which thou gavest me out of the world: thine they were, and thou gavest them me; and they have kept thy word. Now they have known that all things whatsoever thou hast given me are of thee. For I have given unto them the words which thou gavest me; and they have received them, and have known surely that I came out from thee, and they have believed that thou didst send me (John 17:6-8).

Christ Jesus is, as it were, making an account to God of those entrusted to Him by God. "They have kept Thy word"; "I have given unto them the word thou gavest me," "They have received them," "and they have believed that thou didst send me." These words bring joy and comfort to believers, for all of this belongs to every Christian, to all who accept Christ Jesus as Saviour and Lord. Here Jesus is saying, "Father, these have followed along and have been responsive to the message. They are worthy of this glory."

JESUS PRAYS FOR HIS OWN (17:9-14)

As this record by John is reverently studied, it becomes clear that Jesus Christ prays for believers in a way in which He prays for no others. Christians are in a special circle of His care, love and intercession. He lifts His heart to God, and says,

I pray for them: I pray not for the world, but for them which
thou hast given me; for they are thine. And all mine are thine,
and thine are mine; and I am glorified in them (John 17:9, 10).

In these words, so comforting and sustaining to the hearts of all who
believe, lies a truth which is almost shocking when recognized for
what it involves.

The Christian Gospel is commonly known to the general public.
At Christmas men and women sing carols which convey some meaning even to the careless heart. Everywhere there are churches. Probably there are few people in the country who have not heard praying or
singing of hymns. Although the Bible is often unknown and unread,
most educated people feel that they "know" what is in the Bible.
Right or wrong, just from common consensus of opinion, worldly
people have built up an image of Jesus Christ. They have ideas about
Him, not very exact, but nevertheless, quite definite in their minds.
The disturbing factor is that often the image of Jesus Christ, so popular and common among people, is simply not true to the actual reality
of Jesus Christ as portrayed in the Scriptures.

It is such an easy assumption to hold that Jesus Christ will treat all
men alike. Men can "interpret" Scripture to mean what they like.
Someone will say, "God is no respecter of persons," and others will point
out that Jesus Christ will treat all men, women and children alike, rich
or poor, young or old, big or little: all this is true after a fashion. It
is certainly true in reference to the sins of men and in respect to the
call to return to God. The invitation goes out to every person in the
world today, *Whosoever will may come.* That is true! But the work
that is done by Jesus Christ, the actual result of believing in His atoning
work on the cross, and the consequences that follow, are not for everyone. These benefits are only for those who accept the offer, who confess their sins and look to God for cleansing through the shed blood of
Jesus Christ, specifically to *those who believe.* John carefully detailed
that in the prologue to this book (John 1:12).

Glorious truth for believers! Jesus is praying for them. If Christians could only grasp this fully, believe it implicitly, rest on it confidently, what a change in their experience! Nothing could be plainer
in its meaning: "pray for them — I pray not for the world." He
promises to "get the job done," to be glorified in His followers. How
humble Christians should be to know that He will use them as instruments in His hands for the accomplishment of His holy purposes! Surely no greater incentive is needed for a life of devotion and
obedience.

ONE IN CHRIST

And now I am no more in the world, but these are in the
world, and I come to thee. Holy Father, keep through thine own

name those whom thou hast given me, that they may be one, as
we are (John 17:11).

Believers are to be one in Christ. They are to be blended into one
unit in Him. If a man adopts a child, and he already has three children, the adopted child takes his name, receives the same treatment
as the other three and is considered as his very own. The family
now has four children. This communion is what Jesus was praying for,
as He looked ahead to the time of His departure.

> While I was with them in the world, I kept them in thy name:
> those that thou gavest me I have kept, and none of them is lost,
> but the son of perdition; that the scripture might be fulfilled
> (John 17:12).

By way of showing how the disciples were kept together in unity
He said, "I have given them thy word. . . ." This was the great means
of keeping them as one. The Bible is far more important than people
commonly think. It is the very life food of believers. The real Christian is the one who seeks the truth as found in the Scriptures and feeds
upon it, to the edification of his spirit.

OUR RELATIONSHIP TO THE WORLD (17:15-26)

The Lord Jesus Christ did much more praying than is recorded.
There were times when He spent the whole night in prayer. His
communion with His Father was, for the most part, private and
apart. Even the intimate group of twelve known as His disciples did not
always have knowledge of His prayer time. This prayer is the only
long one given in the Scriptures. However, now at the right hand of
the Father in heaven He prays constantly for the believers.

Some idea of what He is praying for can be gained from John's
record.

> I pray not that thou shouldest take them out of the world, but
> that thou shouldest keep them from the evil. They are not of
> the world, even as I am not of the world. Sanctify them through
> thy truth: thy word is truth (John 17:15-17).

The word *sanctify* actually means to set apart. So Jesus asked His
Father to set apart His own who are in the world to keep them for
Himself. It is obvious that Jesus sees His disciples in the world
"as strangers and pilgrims." He does not expect them to share in the
things of the world, as if they belonged in the world. Being in the
world they will face the evil, but Jesus asks that the Father may keep
them from being involved in it.

Christians can be recognized as persons who strive to serve God
and do His will. How should they feel about the world? It could be

helpful if they thought of themselves as a ship in the ocean. There need be no alarm about the depth of the ocean nor even about the waves which may toss the ship about, as long as the ship does not let the ocean leak into the ship. The ship *on* the ocean presents no problem, but it is the ocean *in* the ship that would bring disaster. Christians can live with God in the world just as long as the world does not get into their hearts.

Christians must live in the world. This need not bring any harm to the church or to its individual members. But if, in the course of every-day association with the people of the world, worldliness creeps into the church, so that worldly matters are esteemed in the spiritual fellowship of the group, then the Christians have "sprung a leak," as it were, and their life and the testimony will suffer. Apparently this is what Jesus meant, when He said, "I pray not that thou shouldest take them out of the world," but "keep them from the evil." Evil habits, associations, thoughts, acts come from fellowship with worldly men. "Sanctify them through thy truth: thy word is truth." Faithfulness to the truth of God, as expressed in the Bible is the safeguard for the Christian ship as it sails the worldly seas.

SENT INTO THE WORLD

As thou hast sent me into the world, even so have I also sent them into the world (John 17:18).

Jesus was truly the "sent one" of God, sent for our redemption, to achieve salvation for all who believe in Him. He was sent into the world to redeem all who would come to Him. Jesus does not intend to have His people come out of the world, to draw apart and live in some ivory tower. He sends them into the world with His purpose, with His mission, with His message. The Lord Jesus did not come to enjoy Himself, to make anything out of Himself, to acquire riches or fame. He painted no picture, wrote no book, built no empire, invented no machine, and led no armies. There is nothing, so far as the world is concerned, that Jesus was sent to do other than "to seek and to save" all the lost ones. This same Jesus says to His followers, "As God the Father sent me, so I send you."

When a person receives Jesus as Saviour, he becomes a child of God. God counts him as one of His own. Since the Christian is truly God's child, why should not God take him at once home to Himself? Since He has saved the believer from sin and the things of the world, why not take him right out of this present evil world into His own presence forever? God has others whom He wants to win. There are men and women who need to know His plan of salvation, whom He wants for His own, too. The only way to reach them is through the witness of believers, who have been born again into the new life in

Christ Jesus. When a person comes to Him as he is, accepts Christ, and is now saved by grace, believing in Him, trusting Him, and seeking His will, God will also use that person. He will send him out into the world, as a shepherd is sent out after lost sheep, to bring others to Him.

Jesus went one glorious step further in explaining His own involvement with believers:

> And for their sakes I sanctify myself, that they also might be sanctified through the truth (John 17:19).

Though He was Lord of all, yet as Head of the Church, He set Himself apart for the task of saving the lost. He committed Himself to this one thing deliberately, and as members of His Body, believers share in this commitment.

> Neither pray I for these alone, but for them also which shall believe on me through their word (John 17:20).

"THAT THEY MIGHT BE ONE"

Even at that time when He was facing the cross He was thinking of all who were to believe on Him through the ages.

He continued to have the whole company of all believers in mind as He explained about the unity that would be in their experience.

> That they all may be one; as thou, Father, art in me, and I in thee, that they also may be one in us: that the world may believe that thou hast sent me (John 17:21).

It might be said that because this was written by men centuries ago it would have no bearing upon believers today. But the language in verses twenty and twenty-one leaves no room for doubt. He prayed for all believers. Oh the wonder and the joy of that knowledge! He still prays for all who believe in Him.

> And the glory which thou gavest me I have given them; that they may be one, even as we are one: I in them, and thou in me, that they may be made perfect in one; and that the world may know that thou hast sent me, and hast loved them, as thou hast loved me. Father, I will that they also, whom thou hast given me, be with me where I am; that they may behold my glory, which thou hast given me: for thou lovedst me before the foundation of the world. O righteous Father, the world hath not known thee: but I have known thee, and these have known that thou hast sent me. And I have declared unto them thy name, and will declare it: that the love wherewith thou hast loved me may be in them, and I in them (John 17:22-26).

Jesus concluded this period of praying with one general theme, the idea of unity in Christ. This is not external unity, such as is achieved by fitting pieces of a jigsaw puzzle together. It would be the inward unity which comes from the presence of the Holy Spirit within each believing heart, binding all into one glorious whole in Christ, their Head. Believers should think of themselves as branches grafted into one parent tree, of which they are now a part. When a child is adopted, it becomes one of the family and takes the family name, with all the rights and privileges. And so it is with believers.

In the closing portion of this prayer His great love for His followers is shown by the concern He expresses for their personal experience. He wants them to be blessed with unity with Him and among themselves. Such harmony will give great joy. As the world sees this unity in communion it will recognize the same spirit in them that was manifest in Him as He did all things pleasing to the Father. For the disciples themselves He prayed that they might be with Him to share His glory throughout eternity. He wanted them to enjoy the blessedness of the love of God forever, and this would be possible in the communion they could have in perfect unity with the Father, with Him, and with each other.

Chapter 19

JESUS BEFORE PILATE

Christians should enter the study of these last days of the earthly career of Jesus with hearts filled with gratitude, wonder, and praise. And yet, the study of the record of what happened to Jesus reveals what might be expected to happen to His followers. The servant is not greater than his Master. What happened to Him could happen to any Christian who is dwelling in Him.

THE ARREST (18:1-11)

John gives a simple, factual account of what occurred. Jesus was on the eve of betrayal and arrest. The arrest must have been a very humiliating experience. How hard for God to accept! Not only was He taken into custody, but His betrayal to the officers of the law was by one of His own chosen men — the crowning humiliation of all.

Although Jesus knew He was on the verge of betrayal, He continued doing the usual things. When He had completed His teaching, He took His disciples with Him and went out to a certain garden for rest and prayer:

> . . . for Jesus ofttimes resorted thither with his disciples (John 18:2).

Thus He continued in His customary routine. Nothing is worse than betrayal at the hands of a close friend but Jesus knew it would happen:

> Jesus therefore, knowing all things that should come upon him . . . (John 18:4).

Thus it was no surprise to Jesus of Nazareth. He was prepared for this.

When the soldiers came to Him and said they sought Jesus, He did not hide. He said calmly, "I am he." This was as if He had said, "Arrest me, I am the one for whom you seek." His calm announcement had a most unusual effect upon these Roman soldiers. They stepped backwards and fell to the ground.

They answered him, Jesus of Nazareth. Jesus saith unto them, I am he. And Judas also, which betrayed him, stood with them. As soon then as he had said unto them, I am he, they went backward, and fell to the ground. Then asked he them again, Whom seek ye? And they said, Jesus of Nazareth. Jesus answered, I have told you that I am he: if therefore ye seek me, let these go their way: That the saying might be fulfilled, which he spake, Of them which thou gavest me have I lost none (John 18:5-9).

There was no reason why His followers should be taken to prison by the soldiers. In effect Jesus said, "I am the man for whom you look. Let these others go free."

PETER TRIES TO HELP

At this moment Peter rushed forward ready to defend His Lord. He took out his sword and hit the servant of the high priest, cutting off the man's ear. But Jesus turned to Peter with a quick word of restraint.

. . . Put up thy sword into the sheath: the cup which my Father hath given me, shall I not drink it? (John 18:11).

In this fashion Jesus refused deliverance. Matthew points out how this was the free voluntary decision of Jesus.

Thinkest thou that I cannot now pray to my Father, and he shall presently give me more than twelve legions of angels? (Matthew 26:53).

In preparing His disciples Jesus had said that when the time came for His death they should remember that He would lay down His life and take it again. Now that He was arrested, in the permissive will of God, He refused to accept any deliverance, thereby yielding up His life, as He had said He would do.

Christians can learn much from this incident of the arrest of Jesus. In their obedience to Him believers may have to face hostility in a similar way. They may face opposition and even betrayal of one kind or another. He was betrayed by one of His own, and this may happen to any Christian. Such opposition need not be in any sense the fault of the believer. Judas was personally responsible for his act of betrayal.

It is quite probable that Judas was aware of His Master's custom of going to the Garden of Gethsemane for prayer in the cool of the evening. He could lead the enemy to the very spot!

STANDING WITH THE ENEMY

Matthew reports that Judas betrayed his Master and Friend with a kiss, using the gesture of real friendship to give Him over to the enemy! John's observation that "Judas also . . . stood with them . . ." may actually tell the story of what happened to this man.

Whenever a Christian finds himself standing in fellowship with the enemies of God, he is in real trouble. Association with enemies, in the world, will certainly result in less Bible reading, less praying, less time spent in the worship of God. A Christian today cannot betray his Lord to death, as Judas did, but he can betray His loving friendship.

Apparently the love of money was an inherent weakness in the nature of Judas. In the lives of some Christians, too, are inward attachments, things loved or desired beyond measure, not necessarily sinful in themselves, but not in the will of God for them. Such a desire or habit can actually be a snare in hindering the believer from following the Lord.

PETER'S DENIAL (18:12-27)

Not only is it enlightening to watch Jesus of Nazareth in these last hours before His death for sinners, but there is also much to be learned by looking carefully and thoughtfully at some of the men who were with Him, such as Simon Peter, already well-known because of his habit of speaking up whenever he felt the impulse to do so. At this time of betrayal and arrest, John reports,

> And Simon Peter followed Jesus, and so did another disciple
> . . . (John 18:15).

Very few followed Jesus that night! Most forsook Him and fled. But Peter followed Him, showing both love and courage. It seems clear the other disciple was John. Hundreds of people were round about but only these two followed.

It appears it was John who had an acquaintance in the court and was instrumental in getting Peter admitted into the inner precincts of Caiaphas' palace.

> . . . Then went out that other disciple, which was known unto the
> high priest, and spake unto her that kept the door, and brought
> in Peter (John 18:16).

Students have noted that John refers to himself as "that other disciple." He may have been a family acquaintance, or a relative of the high priest, but John was permitted to go into the palace and take a friend with him. It will be helpful to remember that this was a compound, surrounded by four walls, with a main gate. The Temple stood in a similar compound, in which its various buildings were located. The Temple then was not one single building, but a group of buildings surrounding a courtyard. Peter had been left standing outside because he was an unknown stranger, and it was very early in the morning. John was therefore Peter's sponsor into the palace yard.

The girl who had opened the outer gate for Peter immediately asked him a question: "Aren't you one of the disciples of Jesus?" Then came the first denial, "I am not."

CAIAPHAS AND JESUS

In that inner room on the other side of the courtyard, Caiaphas, the high priest, was questioning Jesus about His doctrine, and His claims about being the Son of God. Jesus gave clear answers.

> . . . I spake openly to the world; I ever taught in the synagogue, and in the temple, whither the Jews always resort; and in secret have I said nothing. Why asketh thou me? ask them which heard me, what I have said unto them: behold, they know what I said (John 18:20, 21).

His open candor infuriated the officers who had arrested Him.

> . . . when he had thus spoken, one of the officers which stood by struck Jesus with the palm of his hand, saying, Answerest thou the high priest so? Jesus answered him, If I have spoken evil, bear witness of the evil; but if well, why smitest thou me? (John 18: 22, 23).

Although Jesus' personal conduct had been characterized by meekness and humility, He did not hesitate to answer His accusers. As the high priests asked further questions, they tried to trap Jesus into admitting wrong doing of one kind or another. But Jesus avoids this snare by reminding them He had preached openly: everyone had heard Him; nothing had been done under cover. For this frankness He was abused as the officer struck Him. Sometimes a false accusation, justly denied, sheds light on the evil intentions of the accusers. So it was here. The rulers knew in their hearts He had done no wrong but this did not check them from their aim to destroy Him.

PETER'S MISTAKE

While Jesus was thus being abused in the court Peter was warming himself at the fire with the men who had arrested his Master. The dramatic course of Peter's attitude and actions with the soldiers shows that he was being affected and influenced by his companionship with these strangers. There is a real lesson for all Christians in this unhappy experience. In the world people have all manner of ways in which they ease their feelings. They use devices for relieving tension and trying to escape trouble. It can be a temptation to a Christian to join with them in some of these actions which seem harmless in themselves. There need be no doubt that Peter's cold body was warmed at that fire, but at what a price! Here Peter was confronted by a relative of the man whose ear he had wounded. He certainly had not expected that, and in the face of the true accusation, he denied his personal relationship to Jesus. And immediately the cock crew just as Jesus had predicted. What had been for Peter just a way of keeping warm without attracting attention suddenly became a situation in which he denied His Lord.

Just a few short hours before, Peter had been standing with Jesus before those same soldiers, and his attitude had been one of hostility in conflict. He had used his sword against a servant of the high priest. But now he joins them in friendly fashion. How can one understand such conduct?

Some understanding of Peter's mind can be gained by recalling how he had always been inclined to see things from a human point of view. When he tried earlier to prevent Jesus from going into Jerusalem, Christ called him Satan (Matthew 16:21-23). Here was the beginning of the trouble for Peter, thinking naturally, as sinful man thinks, and not spiritually. How great is the warning to Christians today!

In addition to thinking in human fashion Peter was so filled with self-confidence that he replied,

> . . . Though I should die with thee, yet will I not deny thee
> . . . (Matthew 26:35).

Believers in Christ are surrounded with temptations, faced daily with suggestions to deny the Lord in subtle ways. The Christians's only protection against such things is a confident trust in Christ's complete victory, inspired by the indwelling presence of the Holy Spirit.

JESUS BEFORE PILATE (18:28-36)

After being tried before the high priest Jesus was taken to the court of Pilate, the Roman Governor. Thus He was taken out of the ecclesiastical court, the religious court of the Jews, to the civil and political court of the Romans. The Jewish leaders had a reason for wanting this to happen. The Feast of the Passover was just about to begin, and because of their ceremonial laws the Jews would not go into the court of Pilate at this time. Considering what they were planning to do to Jesus such caution on their part seems strange. These people were so careful about their conduct that they would not go into that courtroom because it would make them unclean; yet they were actually planning the death of an innocent man! It reminds one of the chief priest who hired Judas and paid him thirty pieces of silver to betray His Lord, but then was too ethical to accept this money when Judas returned it!

Pilate went out to the Jews (since they would not come into his court to him) and asked point blank, "What do you have against this prisoner you have sent in to me?" Their reply was carefully evasive. In effect they said, "Do you think we would bring a man to you if there was not something wrong about him?" But their real reason soon became apparent: they wanted to destroy Jesus but were forbidden by Roman law to inflict the death penalty.

> Then said Pilate unto them, Take ye him, and judge him according to your law. The Jews therefore said unto him, It is not lawful for us to put any man to death: That the saying of Jesus might be fulfilled, which he spake, signifying what death he should die (John 18:31, 32).

JESUS' KINGDOM

When Pilate went back into his judgment hall and called Jesus to stand before him, he began to question Him, asking "Art thou the King of the Jews?" (verse 33). In his examination it was evident that Pilate did not feel harsh, but was trying to arrive at the truth.

> Jesus answered him, Sayest thou this thing of thyself, or did others tell it thee of me? Pilate answered, Am I a Jew? Thine own nation and the chief priests have delivered thee unto me: what hast thou done? Jesus answered, My kingdom is not of this world: if my kingdom were of this world, then would my servants fight, that I should not be delivered to the Jews: but now is my kingdom not from hence (John 18:34 - 36).

Jesus of Nazareth standing before Pilate made clear a very important truth when He said "My kingdom is not of this world." The real truth of the matter is that the Gospel of the Lord Jesus Christ is something which did not begin in this world, is not going to end in this world, and operates day after day with forces and factors that are not of this world. When Jesus referred to His Kingdom, He spoke of all He had done, does and will do as the Son of God: all that which is under His control and direction. When souls are born again, they become subjects of His Kingdom, members of the Body of Jesus Christ, the Church. They are under His rule as members of that Kingdom which is spiritual. Paul, in writing about this says:

> Now this I say, brethren, that flesh and blood cannot inherit the kingdom of God . . . (I Corinthians 15:50).

The work of Christ Jesus in the soul is not a human work. What the Lord does in anyone who is willing to receive Him, does not begin here, will not end here, is not being carried on by any power of this world. The world does not understand this, nor did it understand when Pilate faced Jesus and received His answer, "My kingdom is not of this world. . . ." The mission of Christians in this world is to tell men and women that Jesus Christ came to save them. This is not so much a matter of *helping* the world. Christians should be thinking in terms of individual, lost sinners, who need a Saviour from sin. If a person lived on the ocean shore and had ever watched a lifeboat launched in the face of a tremendous storm to reach a sinking fishing vessel, he would realize how unrealistic it would be to expect the captain of the lifeboat to take along paint and brush to paint the cabin doors! If a fire department were called to a burning house, and found three children trapped on the third floor, they would not carry window polish up the long ladder, so they could clean the window before they rescued the children! ! They would get the children out, not seek to improve the house. Christians are passing through this world as pilgrims and strangers with a definite mission of winning the lost to Jesus Christ.

The average man of the world feels free to criticize the church and to make suggestions about its mission and conduct. His feeling of adequacy to do this is based on the fact that he thinks of religion in terms of good works: of helping the poor, getting sick people into clinics and seeing that orphans are provided for. Good works, in themselves, are quite all right. Christians have tender hearts. They will seek to help those who need help. But their chief task is to reach people with the saving Gospel of Jesus Christ. "My kingdom is not of this world" is still true today.

PILATE'S DILEMMA (18:37-40)

Pilate therefore said unto him, Art thou a king then? Jesus answered, Thou sayest that I am a king. To this end was I born, and for this cause came I into the world, that I should bear witness unto the truth. Every one that is of the truth heareth my voice. Pilate saith unto him, What is truth? And when he had said this, he went out again unto the Jews, and saith unto them, I find in him no fault at all. But ye have a custom, that I should release unto you one at the passover: will ye therefore that I release unto you the King of the Jews? Then cried they all again, saying, Not this man, but Barabbas. Now Barabbas was a robber (John 18:37- 40).

John highlights the awful responsibility of Pilate, focusing attention on him, upon whose shoulders rested the decision of what would be done with Jesus of Nazareth.

Pilate is an example of a politician, a business man, who does not want to be involved in any religious argument. His kind are legion to-day around the world. His only interest throughout the whole incident was to protect or advance his own interests.

Pilate was the Roman Governor of Palestine. To represent the great and powerful government of Rome was quite an achievement. It meant not only that Pilate was a good politician. To reach this post a man must have proven himself an able and desirable citizen at home in Rome. This then was Pontius Pilate, a man not especially opposed to religion, but rather wanting to be left out of religious debate or decisions. But Pilate had the experience so many people have had. He found that it is impossible to ignore Jesus Christ.

When God sent Jesus into the world, it was as if God had reached out to shake hands with man. If a person meets another on the street and holds out his hand, he is challenging that second person to respond. If such a one does not take the outstretched hand, he has already made a decision, a decision to reject this gesture of friendship. Ignoring the hand is that same decision. But Pilate was forced to deal with Christ.

When Jesus answered Pilate, "Thou sayest I am a king," the Greek idiom He used had the same meaning as if today one would say "You said it! What you say is the truth." Then Jesus went still further to emphasize who He was: "To this end was I born, and for this cause came I into the world. . . ." This is a complete and concise picture of the Son of God and His mission!

In the course of affirming His mission in the world Jesus told Pilate He had come to "bear witness unto the truth." Pilate asked Him "What is truth?" Jesus did not reply, and there is no clue as to why He did not answer. It may well be that when Pilate phrased his question in the form of a perennial philosophical issue Jesus held His peace because Pilate's question would lead into fruitless discussion.

When Pilate had asked his question, he went out and told the Jews that as far as he was concerned their prisoner was guiltless. He could find nothing wrong. In each of the gospel narratives, the record of Pilate bears testimony to his own belief in the innocency of Jesus. Mark, however, adds a comment which throws an interesting light on Pilate's final action:

> And so Pilate, willing to content the people, released Barabbas
> unto them and delivered Jesus . . . to be crucified (Mark 15:15).

Pilate tried to have Jesus released but the aroused crowd demanded that Jesus be condemned. The man who was released in His stead was a robber. Other gospel narratives tell us that the chief priests and the scribes had aroused the people and urged them to cry out against Jesus. So the loud cry of "Crucify Him! Crucify Him!" rang out on the morning air. Pilate endeavored to get out of this load of responsibility, but he could not. The decision was made: "to content the people."

Certainly Pilate did not want to make a wrong decision here. He understood full well that the Jews had delivered Jesus to him because of their hatred for Jesus. He felt their cause was unjust, that this prisoner before him had done nothing amiss, and he tried, as best he could, to get Jesus freed. It must be realized that whatever desire he had not to do wrong was wiped out by the fact that he did do the wrong thing. Yet it was not what he would have wanted. The account seems to show that had Pilate been left alone to make his own decision, Jesus would have been freed.

In this situation Pilate is a true example of a man who does not want to commit himself about going to church. Such a man might not come out to say he opposes the preacher, but he is being influenced by some inner consideration. He will not say he does not want to become a Christian, but he will avoid in every way possible any direct issue as to whether he will accept Christ. In effect, he is saying, "This is my business, leave me alone! I am not bothering you, why do you bother me?" God, in His providence, and in the working out of His plan of salvation, had permitted His Son to be brought before Pilate. Even though this person did not want the responsibility of passing judgment and condemnation upon Jesus, he could not escape that very issue.

As Pilate faced Jesus that morning it looked as if he were deciding what was to be done with the Lord. What he did not recognize was that he was actually condemning himself. When, to "content the people," Pilate gave Jesus over to the soldiers for crucifixion, he actually "wrote out his own ticket." This is a word of sober warning to all. Each person needs to face the issue about Jesus Christ honestly and squarely. What he does about Jesus and His invitation will indicate exactly what God Almighty will do with him.

Chapter 20

THE CRUCIFIXION

SCOURGED (19:1-17)

It would no doubt be a good thing for every Christian to read at least once a week one of the gospel narratives about the trial and crucifixion of Jesus. It would help him to read it in several versions. A modern speech version which does not lull the reader with the beautiful language of the King James may shock him into a realization of the brutality involved. This would be especially helpful for anyone whose personal interest in Jesus is not as strong as it should be. Such a person may not fully appreciate what was involved in the atonement, by way of physical suffering. Taking one gospel after another, reading aloud, will help a person to realize what Jesus suffered, and it will stir his heart to realize that it happened *for him.*

John continues his account into chapter nineteen with: "Pilate therefore took Jesus, and scourged him." This was not, of course, because Jesus had been guilty of some crime or evil deed, because He had misbehaved Himself in prison, because He had been in any way impudent to Pilate. This was apparently just routine procedure with the declaration of guilt.

> And the soldiers platted a crown of thorns, and put it on his head, and they put on him a purple robe, And said, Hail, King of the Jews! and they smote him with their hands (John 19:2, 3).

Evidently word had gotten about that Jesus had claimed to be a king. And so the soldiers went beyond procedure in their cruelty. In a crude kind of horseplay, they wove a crown of thorns and jammed it down upon His head. Purple is the color of royalty, so someone obtained a purple robe. Then they knelt before Him, mocking Him, "Hail, King of the Jews!" They struck Him with their fists and slapped Him with their open hands.

> Pilate therefore went forth again, and saith unto them, Behold, I bring him forth to you, that ye may know that I find no fault in him. Then came Jesus forth, wearing the crown of thorns, and

186

the purple robe. And Pilate saith unto them, Behold the man!
(John 19:4, 5).

Pilate tried once more to win freedom for Jesus, but his efforts were
to no avail. Jesus was brought before that riotous mob, wearing the
crown of thorns and the purple robe, before the gaze of His enemies.

"CRUCIFY HIM!"

When the chief priests therefore and officers saw him, they cried
out, saying, Crucify him, crucify him. Pilate saith unto them,
Take ye him, and crucify him: for I find no fault in him. The
Jews answered him, We have a law, and by our law he ought
to die, because he made himself the Son of God (John 19:6, 7).

That was the crux of the whole situation, "he made himself the Son
of God." This was their chief accusation, the thing for which they hated
Jesus most. Once again Pilate told them that he found no fault in this
Man whom he now presented to them.

But this comment by Pilate certainly accomplished nothing: it made
no difference. He was the governor, the man whose word counted,
and he had allowed the Jewish authorities to take Jesus. For this he
was personally responsible. The reply of the Jews to Pilate that Jesus
ought to die, according to their law, was their way of taking advantage
to get their wishes done. They had to give some reason to the Roman Governor and this suited their purposes very well, because Jesus
had affirmed the fact that *He was the Son of God*. When Pilate heard
that, he was uneasy. He did not like any part of this whole affair, and
he did not trust the Jews. He felt the shallowness of the arguments but
did not see how to stop the proceedings without jeopardizing his own
political future.

Even so Pilate tried again:

And went again into the judgment hall, and saith unto Jesus,
Whence art thou? But Jesus gave him no answer. Then saith
Pilate unto him, Speakest thou not unto me? knowest thou not
that I have power to crucify thee, and have power to release
thee? Jesus answered, Thou couldst have no power at all against
me, except it were given thee from above: therefore he that delivered me unto thee hath the greater sin. And from thenceforth
Pilate sought to release him: but the Jews cried out, saying, If
thou let this man go, thou art not Caesar's friend: whosoever
maketh himself a king speaketh against Caesar (John 19:9-12).

But the Jews were using every argument they could think of, including this suggestion to Pilate about not being "Caesar's friend." They
were well acquainted with Roman politics and knew this would have a

telling effect upon the Roman Governor. The result of their pressure was that finally Pilate yielded, and turned Jesus over to them.

The Romans involved had no way of knowing the full meaning of what was happening, but any believer reading this account knows that Jesus endured all of this torment, shame, suffering, the mocking and abuse for the sake of sinners. God permitted this to happen. Heaven must have looked down on this scene with anguish and horror. It must have hurt the heart of God the Father to see His Son suffer. And yet salvation was being wrought out in the plan of God, as the Son was carrying out the will of the Father. Not only was the Son of God put to a shameful death by men not worthy to tie His shoelaces, but God had allowed this to come to pass. This was the measure of the grace of the Lord Jesus Christ who came to give His life a ransom for many.

To the Cross

When Pilate therefore heard that saying, he brought Jesus forth, and sat down in the judgment seat in a place that is called the Pavement, but in the Hebrew, Gabbatha. And it was the preparation of the passover, and about the sixth hour: and he saith unto the Jews, Behold your King! But they cried out, Away with him, away with him, crucify him. Pilate saith unto them, Shall I crucify your King? The chief priests answered, We have no king but Caesar. Then delivered he him therefore unto them to be crucified. And they took Jesus, and led him away. And he bearing his cross went forth into a place called the place of a skull, which is called in the Hebrew Golgotha (John 19:13-17).

After Pilate had reluctantly made his decision to condemn Jesus of Nazareth for treason as the Jews demanded, things moved quickly toward their end. Having taken his place on the judgment seat to pronounce sentence Pilate brought Jesus before him to hear the public announcement. It was about noon when he tried to settle the matter by turning Jesus over to the will of the Jews saying "Behold your King." One can almost feel that Pilate is trying once more to avoid being responsible for condemning this person. But the Jews did not want to handle the matter of condemning Jesus. They wanted Him to be killed and as has been pointed out by their law they could not inflict the death penalty. So they cried out, "Away with him," urging the Roman government to execute Him according to Roman law. As a final effort, Pilate asked, "Shall I crucify your King?" This brought forth a prompt clever reply, "We have no king but Caesar," leaving Pilate no alternative: he would now be obliged to proceed to the destruction of this man as a traitor.

The decisive action ending this trial was the simple turning over of the prisoner Jesus of Nazareth to the soldiers for the execution of the death penalty by crucifixion. This was not an unusual event. On this very day two other men were to be so put to death. That this prisoner should carry his own cross to the place of execution was also the usual procedure.

The tragedy of this whole affair can be felt in the account as John has written it. The soldiers themselves who actually crucified Him had no idea who He was. They were only carrying out a routine task. Pilate who authorized the crucifixion was not at all convinced that the prisoner deserved this penalty, nor was he personally satisfied with what he felt he had to do in condemning Him. The people who shouted for His destruction had been led into this emotional mob action by artful rabble-rousers. The chief priests who were responsible for insisting on the death penalty were seeking to safeguard their own positions as leaders by maintaining the status quo at the cost of destroying this good man, whose teaching had become a threat to their whole system. And so this whole affair moved along in a steady stream of events until He went on His way to Golgotha carrying His cross — despised, rejected.

All those responsible for His crucifixion may not have truly known what they were doing or what was happening, but Jesus knew. He understood very well that His willing death for sinners was precious in the eyes of His Father in heaven, and that in this death He did what was necessary to redeem the souls of all who believe in Him.

And so in all this welter of confusion, with people doing certain things for a good or a bad reason, for a short or a long reason, for their own benefit or just in the doing of their duty: in all of this, God's will was carried out! There is no indication that God's will varies because of circumstances or the selfish ideas of men. God always carries out His purpose, and the believer may share in that with Him, if he will but trust Him.

It is proper for us as Christians to rejoice in eternal life. However, we should remember what it cost. Each time Christians come to the celebration of the Easter season, they should keep in mind the awful suffering, the agony of body and anguish of heart, which Jesus bore for them. It is wonderful beyond understanding, that believers can enjoy the peace of sins forgiven, but that inner peace is real because Jesus Christ hung on that cross for us. It cost the blood of the precious Lamb of God. No Christian should ever forget that the source of his joy was the pain and suffering of his Lord.

THE SIGNIFICANCE OF A TITLE (19:18-22)

Where they crucified him, and two other with him, on either side one, and Jesus in the midst. And Pilate wrote a title, and put it on the cross. And the writing was, JESUS OF NAZARETH THE KING OF THE JEWS. This title then read many of the

Jews: for the place where Jesus was crucified was nigh to the city: and it was written in Hebrew, and Greek, and Latin. Then said the chief priests of the Jews to Pilate, Write not, The King of the Jews; but that he said, I am King of the Jews. Pilate answered, What I have written I have written (John 19:18-22).

When Jesus of Nazareth was put to death on a cross on a hill outside the city wall, He was treated as an ordinary prisoner. The record shows there was no preferential treatment there — just three criminals on three crosses. This is a factual account of what happened, with no attempt by John to arouse emotion in the reader. It is a simple, modest report, and could not have been stated more concisely.

And yet this death of the Son of God was most remarkable. Nothing like this had ever happened before, nor ever will again. It was so amazing that the angels in heaven "desire to look into" the matter and understand it (I Peter 1:12). Although the record is so simply stated, the underlying will of God is very plain. God could have acted at any moment to prevent the death of His Son. God's hand was in every detail of that period of suffering. It is the mark of God's gracious dealing with sinners that He permitted the soldiers to carry out their orders, so that men might be saved through Christ Jesus (Romans 5:8).

CONQUERING DEATH

The deaths of the other two men, one on either side, carried no significance for the world. But the death of Jesus of Nazareth was different. He had announced that He would be put to death, but also that He would not stay dead. He said He came into the world to die, but He died in order to be raised in new life. By the power of God all who believe in Him can expect to be raised, so that for them death has lost its sting.

No doubt many people look upon death as a deep, black hole in the ground where they place the remains of someone dear to them, who is now gone forever. But death is not like that for the believer. Death is more like a tunnel: it may look deep and dark, but there is a glorious light at the other end. Passing through the darkness, the soul comes into the glorious presence of God Himself. This is now the Christian understanding of death, and every believer in the Lord Jesus has this hope in his heart (I Thessalonians 4:13-18).

It is the will of God that whosoever will follow Jesus Christ must die to self. The Christian in his believing must actually experience this death. This is not always easy. Satan will try to cause anyone who seeks to follow the Lord to stumble. Satan tempted Jesus at the very beginning of His public ministry (Matthew 4:1-10) and again just at the close (Matthew 16:21-27), and anyone who will turn to the Lord in faith can expect similar temptation to stop short of full surrender. When a Christian thinks about being crucified, he expects to yield himself to God to allow this to happen. But God may provide human means to do the crucifying. The Lord Jesus said "I lay down my life," but it was the callous soldiers who carried out the crucifixion with all its preparations and its final anguish. Jesus walked all the way, carrying His cross, submitting to the nails in hands and feet, but it was the soldiers who actually drove in the nails. It is this aspect which is often so hard to accept.

CRUCIFIED WITH CHRIST

Just as Jesus of Nazareth yielded to allow His body to be put to death that He might rise from the dead, so must the believer in Him yield his human nature to the will of God and let the self be crucified. Only in this way can he be raised from the dead. The actual experience will not be the same for any two people. Each has his own individual nature, but there is always the matter of denying one's self and of reckoning one's self to be dead to the world but alive unto God.

This matter of being turned over to others is a price the believer pays. It is a matter of humiliation. This crucifixion of self is not related to the salvation of anyone else, but is a part of the believer's own spiritual experience. It is necessary to go through it so that the Christian might be raised to newness of life.

Even the Jews had to give up the *complete* "victory" over Jesus. Pilate thwarted their pride at its very center by refusing to change his inscription. Perhaps it was his way of paying some tribute to a person he personally could not help but admire. But there were greater deeds to come. The Jewish leaders were to discover that God is greater than their status quo.

THE SOLDIERS FULFILL PROPHECY (19:23-30)

Normally the will of God is performed in the lives of men and women who accept and serve Jesus Christ, but the will of God is also wrought out in the world by sinners, by those who are truly His enemies. This is what is meant by God's power to overrule and to make even the wrath of men to serve Him.

> Then the soldiers, when they had crucified Jesus, took his garments, and made four parts, to every soldier a part; and also his coat: now the coat was without seam, woven from the top throughout. They said therefore among themselves, Let us not rend it, but cast lots for it, whose it shall be: that the scripture might be fulfilled, which saith, They parted my raiment among them, and for my vesture they did cast lots. These things therefore the soldiers did (John 19:23, 24).

These soldiers were acting just the way they wanted to act, and yet they were doing exactly what God had known they would do. Prophetic foreknowledge does not force a man into an act, but God knows what that person will do at any time. People who do not have God or His ways in mind or heart will yet carry out His will unwittingly. This is a sobering thought for anyone. These soldiers were used of God to carry out the death of the Lord Jesus Christ and when they afterward disposed of the clothing of the crucified prisoner, they fulfilled the will and prophecy of God, for David recorded this event centuries earlier in Psalm 22.

One very moving example from this crucifixion psalm is the cry of Jesus Christ on the cross: "My God, my God, why hast thou forsaken me . . .?" (Psalm 22:1). And again the last phrase of this Psalm, at the close of verse thirty-one, in the Hebrew expression, "he hath done this" comes very close to the cry of our Lord from the cross, "It is finished." It is the idea of completion of the work of redemption. "He hath done this," said the Psalmist, and Jesus cried, "It is finished!" The entire twenty-second Psalm is prophetic in nature. It seems possible that Jesus may have been repeating this Psalm to Himself as He hung on the cross. To have this possibility in mind will make the Psalm more vital in a remarkable way.

JESUS, MARY, AND JOHN

Now there stood by the cross of Jesus his mother, and his mother's sister, Mary, the wife of Cleophas, and Mary Magdalene. When Jesus therefore saw his mother, and the disciple standing by, whom he loved, he saith unto his mother, Woman, behold thy son! Then saith he to the disciple, Behold thy mother! And from that hour that disciple took her unto his own home (John 19:25-27).

Here is seen the care and love and consideration of Jesus for His mother. Even in the midst of the pain of this awful form of death, and in the midst of the agony of bearing the sins of the world Jesus provided for the future of His sorrowing mother. This gives a glimpse of His loving care of His people: His consideration for the needs, His concern for their sorrow! He is ". . . touched with the feeling of our infirmities . . ." (Hebrews 4:15).

There is something significant in the report of the faithful women who were present at the crucifixion. How often during Christ's earthly ministry the women were of help to Him! And it has been true in the spread of the Gospel that the great ministry of women through participation and in sympathy is of tremendous value in the church. These women could do nothing at the cross until Jesus was dead. Then they assisted in preparing His body for the tomb. They were not able in any way to change the course of events, but they had the courage to gather about their Lord at this time.

Jesus of Nazareth had been ignored, disowned, despised and rejected of men. "His own received him not," yet there were the women at the foot of the cross, heartbroken, faithful, and adoring Him in their smitten hearts. He had been rejected and humiliated. The authorities, Jewish and Roman, had made a public spectacle of the Son of God. He had been treated with ignominy, but here were the women who loved Him, and who were worshiping Him humbly even now at the moment of His shame and death. All the good Jesus had done seemed to have been forgotten by the multitudes. He had healed so many, opened blind eyes, given life back to the dead and made the lame to walk. All seemed to have been forgotten as multitudes scorned Him, but the women stood fast.

What an example is set by these few sorrowing women who stood loyally by!

> After this, Jesus knowing that all things were now accomplished, that the scripture might be fulfilled, saith, I thirst. Now there was set a vessel full of vinegar: and they filled a spunge with vinegar, and put it upon hyssop, and put it to his mouth. When Jesus therefore had received the vinegar, he said, It is finished: and he bowed his head, and gave up the ghost (John 19:28-30).

John emphasizes that Jesus was careful in His conduct to do all things in fulfilment of what the Scriptures predicted. This implies that He was concerned that our confidence in Himself and in His mission might be strengthened by His actions and experiences. The use of vinegar may have been a common custom, but He made it a point to let it be seen that this had been given to Him as predicted in Psalm 69:21.

"It Is Finished"

Finished! The whole program God had begun with His people before creation: the atonement which had been planned from before the foundation of the world. Finished! Redemption from sin and the new life in Christ. Finished! The gift of eternal life, the assurance of the "place prepared for us" when this life is over. All this confirmed as Jesus said, "It is finished!" These were the last words of Jesus of Nazareth. When next He speaks He will be the risen Christ in the new body of His resurrection.

When Jesus said, "It is finished," He may have been referring to His incarnation in a human body. But of course, as the Son of God He was going on in the eternal purpose of His Father's will.

When Jesus died, He set in motion a whole train of events: the Resurrection, the many appearances to His disciples and others, the ascension, the coming of the Holy Spirit, and the beginning of the proclamation of the Gospel of salvation to the whole world which is continuing until this very day and will continue until He comes again!

PROOF OF DEATH (19:31-37)

The Jews therefore, because it was the preparation, that the bodies should not remain upon the cross on the sabbath day, (for that sabbath day was an high day,) besought Pilate that their legs might be broken, and that they might be taken away. Then came the soldiers, and brake the legs of the first, and of the other which was crucified with him. But when they came to Jesus, and saw that he was dead already, they brake not his legs: But one of the soldiers with a spear pierced his side, and forthwith came there out blood and water. And he that saw it bare record, and his record is true: and he knoweth that he saith true, that ye might believe. For these things were done, that the scripture should be fulfilled, A bone of him shall not be broken. And again another scripture said, They shall look on him whom they pierced (John 19:31-37).

Men have proposed the theory that Jesus of Nazareth fell into a sort of coma on the cross and was taken down and put into the tomb, but did not truly die. However, there can be no doubt in the mind of anyone after reading this account by John. The evidence is too clear, couched in correct medical terminology. Because it was the time of Passover preparation, the Jews were anxious to have the bodies taken down from the crosses. Therefore, they asked Pilate to have the soldiers break the legs of the three men. The soldiers broke the legs of the first man, then of the other man crucified with Jesus, but when they came to the body of Jesus "and saw that he was dead already, they brake not his legs." This was a testimony by the soldiers, in effect, that death had come to Jesus.

A BROKEN HEART

The account written by John supports the idea that Jesus actually died of a broken heart, that literally His heart had burst within Him. When the spear pierced His side, blood and water gushed forth. Medical authorities say that this careful description indicates that the great blood vessel of Jesus' heart had burst while He was hanging on the cross; then when the spear opened His side, it was natural there would come out blood and water.

There are many terms used by Christians which bring this event to mind. It is common to refer to the "blood of Christ," and this means His death, of course. Believers sing about a "fountain filled with blood, Drawn from Immanuel's veins," and their minds go back to Calvary, and the fountain of blood which gushed out, to "wash us whiter than snow." Christians sing "There is pow'r, pow'r, Wonder working pow'r, In the precious blood of the Lamb." Again and again they are remembering the "Lamb of God, who taketh away the sin of the world." In this death the love of God for the whole world was demonstrated.

In this is to be seen the great truth of the gospel message: Jesus was ordained of God to die for the sin of all men. This is important beyond words to describe. It is called vicarious suffering, and is spoken of as a substitutionary death. The Lord Jesus substituted His sinless life for the life of the sinner atoning for his sin. Jesus of Nazareth died in order that God might deal with the sinner on the basis of His atonement.

JESUS BURIED (19:38-42)

> And after this Joseph of Arimathaea, being a disciple of Jesus, but secretly for fear of the Jews, besought Pilate that he might take away the body of Jesus: and Pilate gave him leave. He came therefore, and took the body of Jesus. And there came also Nicodemus, which at the first came to Jesus by night, and brought a mixture of myrrh and aloes, about a hundred pound weight. Then took they the body of Jesus, and wound it in linen clothes with the spices, as the manner of the Jews is to bury. Now in the place where he was crucified there was a garden; and in the garden a new sepulchre, wherein was never man yet laid. There laid they Jesus therefore because of the Jews' preparation day; for the sepulchre was nigh at hand (John 19:38-42).

From the very moment the death of Jesus was established, all harsh and cruel treatment was ended, and all that was done with that lifeless body was done in reverent, loving care. It was the hands of Joseph of Arimathaea that took His body down from the cross. He was joined by Nicodemus as together they prepared the Lord's body for burial. The body was wrapped in linen cloth, with the customary spices being used, and then laid in the tomb.

The other gospels make it plain that Joseph was a young man, rich, and well known, a member of the council of the highest governing body of the people. This young and influential man was a secret follower of Jesus. He believed in his heart but never openly confessed because of fear of the Jews. His conduct proves that he was a true believer, but he was also a secret believer, which almost seems a contradiction in terms. It may be questioned if such a state of mind and lack of action is ever possible, but it is. The expression of faith in Christ is not as it should be, but under the circumstances his failure to confess can be understood. Now he came openly and asked for the body of Jesus.

Jesus had only that morning been condemned as a common criminal and then executed. The high priest was the highest official of that community, and he had testified against Jesus in such a way that death was inevitable. The chief priests had aroused hostility against Jesus of Nazareth among the people. The council as a whole had condemned Him. Joseph of Arimathaea was a member of that highest governing body. He had kept his personal faith a secret, but now he did that which has forever honored his name.

Apparently the sum total of abuse, cruelty and humiliation poured out upon Jesus had come to a point at which Joseph could no longer keep silent. It was as if he had said out loud, "Now this has gone far enough! If you are going to treat Jesus in this way, I will admit now before you all that He is my Lord and my Saviour." When no one else was showing any loyalty, this young man stepped forward and claimed the body, as if to say, "I belong to Him, so let me take care of His body." He carried that request straight to Pilate.

Joseph's Witness

Joseph of Arimathaea could be considered the first witness to the crucified Jesus Christ. This is the beginning of that testimony which now goes around the world. This is what every Christian believer does now — witness to the saving and keeping grace of Jesus Christ.

Today the repudiation of the Bible and the questioning of the Gospel has resulted in mounting confusion and the widespread rejection of Jesus Christ. Now is the time for believers to step forward and say, as did Joseph, "I belong to Him, I believe in Him, He is the Son of God and my Redeemer!" Such testimony and witness bring glory to His name.

No doubt there are many reasons for discouragement in Christian witnessing, and at times it seems as if almost the whole world were turning away from the Gospel. Actions on the part of the leaders in the churches can fill the heart with dismay, even as men called ministers of the Gospel openly admit they do not believe in the Scriptures. But then in the darkness of unbelief, like a sudden ray of light on a dark and stormy night, one finds a layman rising up to testify to the love and power of the Son of God!

What an opportunity for men and women to rise up and be counted! How refreshing it is to hear someone get up and testify that he was saved by believing in the Lord Jesus Christ, and that he is rejoicing in fellowship with Him now. In any community, in school or shop, office or wherever the Christian spends his working days, the open door is before him to step out and identify himself with the name of Jesus Christ. Just as Joseph stepped forward to witness openly to his own faith in Jesus at a time when all had fled, so can a Christian today openly confess his faith in Christ Jesus and join that courageous and faithful band who are not afraid to stand up and be counted!

Chapter 21

THE RESURRECTION

MARY COMES EARLY (20:1-18)

The first day of the week cometh Mary Magdalene early, when it was yet dark, unto the sepulchre, and seeth the stone taken away from the sepulchre (John 20:1).

These familiar words are read around the world each Easter Sunday in many countries and many languages. Hearts rejoice to think of the triumph they convey, and there will be people singing "Up from the grave He arose, With a mighty triumph o'er His foes." It is wonderful that God *is* able to raise the dead to life.

Looking at the crucifixion one can marvel at the humility of God, the meekness and lowliness of God, as He sent His Son into this world. That same meekness and humility can be seen in the Resurrection. The risen Jesus did not walk into the presence of Pilate, nor did He confront the high priest, or even the group of Roman soldiers who had pounded the nails into His hands and feet, or the soldier who had pierced His side with the spear. Such action would have been dramatic and might suggest to some a graphic way to emphasize the Gospel.

Jesus revealed Himself only to believers. If the world had not been impressed by the Scriptures, if men had not believed the miracles, the signs and wonders, the Resurrection would not have impressed them. Some story about an unconscious body being placed in the tomb would have been told and nothing would have been accomplished. This is what Abraham told the rich man when he requested that Abraham send someone back from the tomb to warn his brothers, lest they come where he was, in hell. The rich man argued that if somebody was to rise from the dead and return to their community, people would pay attention to that, and heed what was told them. Abraham said the brothers had Moses and the prophets, and if they were not heeding them, they would pay no attention if one rose from the dead (Luke 16:31).

Mary Magdalene was the first to discover that the body of Jesus was no longer in the tomb. Why did she come so early? This may have been because she loved Jesus. She had been delivered from so much, and her gratitude was so great that she had to come. That may well be, but it is not the whole story. Jesus' body was taken down from the cross just before sundown. The preparation for the Passover was about to begin. So they took the body down, wrapped it with spices in linen, and put it in the tomb. In accord with their custom, it would take a longer time to prepare the body for burial and permanent embalming. After the period of Passover was over, they could come and complete the embalming process. Mary Magdalene was one of those who would want to come and help. In fact she was the first one to arrive.

PETER AND JOHN

Then she runneth, and cometh to Simon Peter, and to the other disciple, whom Jesus loved, and saith unto them, They have taken away the Lord out of the sepulchre, and we know not where they have laid him. Peter therefore went forth, and that other disciple, and came to the sepulchre. So they ran both together: and the other disciple did outrun Peter, and came first to the sepulchre. And he stooping down, and looking in, saw the linen clothes lying; yet went he not in. Then cometh Simon Peter following him, and went into the sepulchre, and seeth the linen clothes lie, And the napkin, that was about his head, not lying with the linen clothes, but wrapped together in a place by itself. Then went in also that other disciple, which came first to the sepulchre, and he saw, and believed (John 20:2-8).

Someone has pointed out that John, being younger than Peter, ran at a faster pace and so reached the grave first. There is no reason given as to why John did not go in. He waited outside. Peter went in, then John followed. This is in keeping with the character of Peter who was always the first one to speak or act.

The linen clothes were lying in one place; and apart from them, "wrapped together in a place by itself" was the napkin that had been placed around the head of Jesus. There is no explanation offered, yet this would be an indication that He was really alive. It may also be an indication of how careful our Lord was in His personal habits during His life on earth. This may have been such a characteristic trait as to serve as evidence that Jesus had personally folded the napkin in this fashion. It was not flung down upon the ground, but "wrapped together."

The record states that when John went in and looked, "he saw, and believed." Apparently John, who characterized himself as "the disciple whom Jesus loved," did not fully see nor believe until that moment! It seems that John shared the common experience of all the disciples at that time.

For as yet they knew not the scripture, that he must rise again from the dead. Then the disciples went away again unto their own home (John 20:9, 10).

Not knowing what the Scriptures taught about the Resurrection, the disciples were unable to realize the significance of this event. They may have been stirred by the empty tomb, but they turned quietly away and went home! Jesus had told them He would rise from the dead. He had explained that if His body were destroyed, in three days He would rebuild it, but even so, they had not understood nor believed. They were not convinced even now. Calvary had been a time of shock and sorrow. They were probably completely shaken by the amazing turn of events, and so they went quietly away, and told no one.

He Is Alive

Verses eleven to sixteen tell a wonderful story of the deep love of Jesus for His own:

> But Mary stood without at the sepulchre weeping: and as she wept, she stooped down, and looked into the sepulchre, And seeth two angels in white sitting, the one at the head, and the other at the feet, where the body of Jesus had lain. And they say unto her, Woman, why weepest thou? She saith unto them, Because they have taken away my Lord, and I know not where they have laid him. And when she had thus said, she turned herself back, and saw Jesus standing, and knew not that it was Jesus. Jesus saith unto her, Woman, why weepest thou? whom seekest thou? She, supposing him to be the gardener, saith unto him, Sir, if thou have borne him hence, tell me where thou hast laid him, and I will take him away. Jesus saith unto her, Mary. She turned herself, and saith unto him, Rabboni; which is to say, Master (John 20:11-16).

Mary's action in looking down into the sepulchre was the natural thing a sorrowing person would do. Her heart was heavy: she was weeping both because of His death, and because His body had been removed in some unknown way. Then as she stooped lower for a better look at the place where His body had been placed, behold, two angels! When she had answered their question she turned away, and saw the form of a man outside.

Mary did not recognize Jesus. Whether God prevented her from recognizing Him, or whether her eyes were blinded with tears, is not explained, but she did not know her Lord. Love is not always practical: a woman could not carry the dead body of a man, but her loving heart was concerned only with giving that body the proper preparation for final burial, so she said, "I will carry the body away, if you will tell me where you have laid Him." At that point He called her by name — "Mary!" He probably used the Hebrew form of that name and spoke her name in the accent she would have known so well: "Miriam!" Her response came in one word, "Rabboni!"

Mary's experience is suggestive of what is always true. The Lord Jesus will always reveal Himself to the humble, adoring heart.

> Jesus saith unto her, Touch me not; for I am not yet ascended to my Father: but go to my brethren, and say unto them, I ascend unto my Father, and your Father; and to my God, and your God. Mary Magdalene came and told the disciples that she had seen the Lord, and that he had spoken these things unto her (John 20: 17, 18).

It has never been clear to students of Scripture what Jesus meant when he restrained Mary Magdalene from touching Him at this time. Just how this was related to His ascending to His Father is beyond understanding based on revelation in the Bible. Whether Mary Magdalene understood Him in this comment is not recorded, but His instruction to her is plain and clear.

MARY'S MESSAGE

Mary Magdalene was given a message which included two significant items. He called His disciples "my brethren" which would not only be very reassuring but was also most gracious. In His dark hour on the cross they had fled, forsaking Him in dismay and fear. Their action revealed weakness and perhaps even doubt. But now He calls them "my brethren," reminding them of His grace and of their high privilege in belonging to Him.

When He sent them word that He was ascending to His Father and His God, He included them by saying, "your Father, and your God." In this is to be felt how graciously He lifted them in Himself into the very presence and communion of Almighty God. In Him they also belonged to God and would be with Him forever.

John reports that Mary Magdalene did as she was told. He offers no comment as to the reaction of the disciples. In the other three gospels there is some reference to the fact that they could not believe He was actually alive. But John makes no reference to this whatever. He says that they were given the message and omits any reference to their thoughts or their actions in response.

The next important matter was His first appearance to the company of disciples that very evening.

> Then the same day at evening, being the first day of the week, when the doors were shut where the disciples were assembled for fear of the Jews, came Jesus and stood in the midst, and saith unto them, Peace be unto you. And when he had so said, he

shewed unto them his hands and his side. Then were the disciples
glad, when they saw the Lord. Then said Jesus to them again,
Peace be unto you: as my Father hath sent me, even so send I
you (John 20:19-21).

This plain and simple record reveals the group of disciples gathered
— one might almost say huddled — behind closed doors, in fear of
the Jewish authorities. Their leader had been Jesus, but He had been
publicly condemned by the high court of the Jewish nation. He had
been openly treated as an ordinary criminal. The Roman court had
delivered Him over to death. The disciples had watched as He had
died in agony on the cross. Everything Jesus had stood for seemed
to be in jeopardy. If the shepherd had been smitten, so might the
helpless sheep. Thus they gathered in bewilderment and terror.

"Peace"

Jesus had warned them that it would be difficult for them to believe,
and now stress and terror had wiped so much from their minds that
doubt and fear came naturally. As they were gathered in this fearful
seclusion, with the *doors locked,* suddenly a figure appeared in their
midst! His reassuring first words were "Peace be unto you." He knew
they were frightened, and that terror filled their hearts. He always
knows, this loving, gracious, tender Lord, what terrifies and troubles
His disciples!

As He comes His first word is "Peace."

This is how the Lord meets the disciples' need as they are confronted
with this new challenge to their faith. He does not rebuke them for
failing to recognize Him, nor chide them for not knowing His voice.
He has spoken, "Peace," and now He is going to build the groundwork
for their complete belief and acceptance of the reality of His resurrection. He holds out His nail-scarred hands, and exposes His spear-
pierced side. Then they know! There was no mistaking those hands
and that side wounded before their eyes. This was the Lord whom
they had seen dying on the cross. They had seen that side pierced,
and they had seen the blood and water flow out. There could be no
misunderstanding now.

". . . Then were the disciples glad, when they saw the Lord"
(verse 20). They had been disheartened, confused, and in the depths
of discouragement. Now they were glad, with all the joy and peace
that phrase implies. It was not just joy at seeing Him whom they
loved, it was that they knew now, of a surety, that God's Word was
true and His purposes would be carried out in the world. The sudden
appearance of their Lord, alive from the tomb, spoke wonderful things
to them. There was marvelous promise for the days ahead. All the
blessedness of communion with Him was now restored to them.

CONVICTION AND COMMISSION

Seeing Jesus alive brought conviction to the disciples. As soon as these men were convinced about Him, their sorrow turned into joy and their confusion became peace. At this moment Jesus said to them, ". . . as my Father hath sent me, even so send I you." In place of confusion came conviction, and with conviction, commission! This commission was to go out into all the world and preach the Gospel. God sent His Son into the world to seek and to save the lost. Now His disciples are sent, as His redeemed sons to seek the lost and bring them to Him that He may save them and then send them forth. This is an endless chain which will continue until the Lord comes.

How wonderful if every Christian would remember this! When the Son of God came into the world to do His Father's will, He did not take part in any worldly activities, good or bad. He sought no public or ecclesiastical office. He did not sponsor any local cause, however worthy. He spent Himself in the service of others. He accumulated no wealth or property. His whole life was to "do the will of Him that sent me." This is actually the pattern of procedure in service that Christians are commissioned to perform as they carry out His will. ". . . as my Father hath sent me, even so send I you."

> And when he had said this, he breathed on them, and saith unto them, Receive ye the Holy Ghost (John 20:22).

It is plain that this indicates there is more ahead. They were to receive richer endowment than they had ever had for their work. In the same utterance He gave them promise for their effectiveness as they would carry out their commission.

> Whose soever sins ye remit, they are remitted unto them; and whose soever sins ye retain, they are retained (John 20:23).

This is a remarkable statement, implying that believers will not only be doing what He wants them to in obeying the commission, but, by the power of the Spirit, men and women will actually be saved from sin. This is not giving Christians the power to grant a sort of "pardon or remission." Christians in their own preaching and teaching cannot forgive sin, but they have the message which can bring sinners to Jesus Christ who can and will forgive, so that they are justified in the eyes of God through His shed blood.

What a wonderful harvest has been reaped on the mission fields of the world through the carrying out of this commission by Christians! Wherever missionaries go, wherever preachers proclaim this wonderful news, anyone who believes and receives the Lord Jesus Christ is delivered from sin and brought into fellowship with the living God. The pastor, the evangelist, the missionary, the Sunday school teacher, the father or mother — anyone who carries this glad news to another person, is actually bringing that person into deliverance from sin, because of the grace of Jesus Christ. How humble this should make every believer, and how this can inspire faithful witnessing! How gracious is the God and Father of the Lord Jesus Christ to give His followers such privileges!

THOMAS BELIEVES (20:24-31)

> But Thomas, one of the twelve, called Didymus, was not with them when Jesus came. The other disciples therefore said unto him, We have seen the Lord. But he said unto them, Except I shall see in his hands the print of the nails, and put my finger into the print of the nails, and thrust my hand into his side, I will not believe. And after eight days again his disciples were within, and Thomas with them: then came Jesus, the doors being shut, and stood in the midst, and said, Peace be unto you. Then saith he to Thomas, Reach hither thy finger, and behold my hands; and reach hither thy hand, and thrust it into my side: and be not faithless, but believing. And Thomas answered and said unto him, My Lord and my God. Jesus saith unto him, Thomas, because thou hast seen me, thou hast believed: blessed are they that have not seen, and yet have believed (John 20:24-29).

"Doubting Thomas" is notorious wherever the gospel story is known. In this report given by John in his gospel there is a significant clue for understanding this unbelief in this one disciple. "Thomas . . . was not with them when Jesus came." It is possible all the disciples were filled with doubt before Jesus appeared in their midst. There is no explanation as to why Thomas missed being there. This absence cost him additional days of sorrow and doubt, for even though the disciples told him the joyous news of the Resurrection he refused to accept their testimony. They reported their fellowship with the Lord in actual personal communion, but Thomas stubbornly said he would not believe unless he himself could see and touch those scarred hands and that wounded side. There is an assurance which can be had only in personal fellowship with the Lord. Even the sincere testimony of other believers cannot give the conviction which could satisfy Thomas.

No doubt there are many like Thomas today. Unbelief and an unwillingness to respond to the Gospel is natural in the human heart. The witness of other believers is important and essential, but there is need for the work of God in the individual heart. Even as Jesus had told Peter that flesh and blood had not revealed that he was the Christ to him, but His Father in heaven, so it must be in the preaching of the Gospel. God must work in the heart by His Holy Spirit that conviction may come.

Jesus did not leave Thomas in his stubborn doubt. Since Thomas had stipulated that he would believe only after physical demonstration, the Lord graciously provided this special testimony. Thomas may not have been aware of pride, even though his determined attitude was a complete repudiation of the testimony of his fellow disciples.

Actually, Thomas was acting quite naturally. One cannot always trust one's eyes. In buying a suit a man may like the material in its appearance and yet reach out and rub it between his fingers to corroborate what his eyes have told him. It is the same when a woman selects some cloth for a dress. She will probably not purchase until she has tested the material with her hands, fingering it for softness or smoothness, pulling it to determine the weave, and making her decision by touch as well as by sight. No matter what a person is selecting the hands invariably come into use before the final choice is made.

When Jesus appeared the second time He uttered His greeting to all, "Peace be unto you." After this He spoke directly to Thomas. "Reach hither thy fingers . . . reach hither thy hand . . . and be not faithless, but believing." Thomas fell on his knees with the cry, "My Lord and my God!" manifesting complete faith and subsequent worship.

Jesus of Nazareth made this experience of Thomas the occasion for a profound announcement: ". . . blessed are they which have not seen, and yet have believed." Every Christian today whose faith is grounded in the Gospel as preached by believers shares in this blessing. There are persons today who seem to wait for some physical, psychological, or emotional experience before they can fully accept the Gospel. And there are those who testify that it was after certain manifestations that they were able to believe. Without questioning the validity of their experience and testimony, these words of the risen Lord distinctly affirm blessing upon such as believe without outward signs.

In any case it should not be overlooked that Thomas had all this experience because he was absent the first time Jesus showed Himself to His disciples after the Resurrection. There is no explanation of his absence, but the fact remains that he was not with the group, and right there lies an important truth. It is most important that a Christian be faithful in attendance at church services. He should be faithful in meeting with the Lord in his own "secret place." Sometimes a person will say, "Oh, I am too busy to come out on Wednesday night for Bible study. I don't spend much time with my Bible anyway. I cannot understand it, and so much of it was written about people so long ago." Faith actually "comes by hearing, and hearing by the word of God." Absenting oneself from fellowship with other Christians in the study of the Word of God is a sure way to weaken one's faith. To seek fellowship with others of like faith, to feed on the Word, and to be faithful in prayer, will cause faith to grow and become strong, to the Christian's own joy, as well as the joy of those with whom he associates.

Chapter 22

THE CONTINUING MINISTRY OF JESUS

JESUS APPEARS TO BELIEVERS (21:1-14)

After these things Jesus shewed himself again to the disciples at the sea of Tiberias; and on this wise shewed he himself. There were together Simon Peter, and Thomas called Didymus, and Nathanael of Cana in Galilee, and the sons of Zebedee, and two other of his disciples. Simon Peter saith unto them, I go a-fishing. They say unto him, We also go with thee. They went forth, and entered into a ship immediately; and that night they caught nothing. But when the morning was now come, Jesus stood on the shore: but the disciples knew not that it was Jesus. Then Jesus saith unto them, Children, have ye any meat? They answered him, No. And he said unto them, Cast the net on the right side of the ship, and ye shall find. They cast therefore, and now they were not able to draw it for the multitude of fishes. Therefore that disciple whom Jesus loved saith unto Peter, It is the Lord. Now when Simon Peter heard that it was the Lord, he girt his fisher's coat unto him, (for he was naked,) and did cast himself into the sea. And the other disciples came in a little ship; (for they were not far from land, but as it were two hundred cubits,) dragging the net with fishes. As soon then as they were come to land, they saw a fire of coals there, and fish laid thereon, and bread. Jesus saith unto them, Bring of the fish which ye have now caught. Simon Peter went up, and drew the net to land full of great fishes, an hundred and fifty and three: and for all there were so many, yet was not the net broken. Jesus saith unto them, Come and dine. And none of the disciples durst ask him, Who art thou? knowing that it was the Lord. Jesus then cometh, and taketh bread, and giveth them, and fish likewise. This is now the third time that Jesus shewed himself to his disciples, after that he was risen from the dead (John 21:1-14).

There is something very sobering to us in the fact that after Jesus rose He appeared only to those who believed in Him. Before that He had shown Himself to the world, He had called the men of the world to put their trust in Him, and they had crucified Him. They had shown that they would have nothing to do with Him and had cried, "Away with him!"

There is no record that the risen Lord ever showed Himself to an unbeliever. It was not for those who put Him to death to see Him in the glory of His resurrection body, nor to share in any way in the blessings of those who loved Him and rejoiced in His salvation. The next time the world will see Him, He will be coming in glory with ten thousand of His angels, taking vengeance upon them that do not know God (II Thessalonians 1:7, 8).

The fact that some of the apostles went fishing does not mean that they were disobedient to any commission which had been given to them. This was a natural activity, their daily livelihood. They had to work, they had to obtain food. On this particular occasion after a long night, their nets were empty.

They did not recognize Jesus as He was standing on the shore. He called to them, and they answered, still not recognizing His voice. When they were told to cast on the other side of the boat they obeyed what seemed to them to be a good suggestion. They responded readily to guidance. It was their willingness to be guided which directly led them to greater blessing than they had anticipated!

The disciple who recognized Jesus was John, and again he showed his characteristic reticence. In spite of his great love for his Lord, he made no move to approach Jesus. However, he did tell Peter who the person on shore was. It was Peter, in a manner characteristic of his own nature, who jumped into the sea in order to get to Jesus as quickly as possible. This Peter was the man who had denied that same Lord, but also the man who had been forgiven, and who was to become a great and mighty witness for the risen Christ. This contrast in the reactions of these two men is illuminating because it demonstrates that God can and does use all kinds of men and women in His service.

BREAKFAST

When the boat reached the shore, the disciples found a bed of coals with fish already on them, and bread. Jesus had prepared for a meal. Jesus said, "Bring of the fish which ye have now caught." This gave the disciples opportunity to share in the final preparation and in providing the food. Jesus Christ is ever willing to use the talents and the work of His disciples to accomplish His own purpose for the glory of His Father.

Simon Peter went to draw in the net and found an hundred and fifty-three fish. Despite this large catch of fish the net was not broken. This circumstance was unusual and impressed the disciples that Jesus was Lord even in the practical aspects of every work they performed. Without further comment Jesus invited them to share in the meal, and without any hesitation because of natural skepticism the disciples responded in obedience. This must have been a most impressive occasion to these men.

"Do You Love Me?" (21:15-25)

So when they had dined, Jesus saith to Simon Peter, Simon, son of Jonas, lovest thou me more than these? He saith unto him, Yea, Lord; thou knowest that I love thee. He saith unto him, Feed my lambs. He saith to him again the second time, Simon, son of Jonas, lovest thou me? He saith unto him, Yea, Lord; thou knowest that I love thee. He saith unto him, Feed my sheep. He saith unto him the third time, Simon, son of Jonas, lovest thou me? Peter was grieved because he said unto him the third time, Lovest thou me? And he said unto him, Lord, thou knowest all things; thou knowest that I love thee. Jesus saith unto him, Feed my sheep (John 21:15-17).

Here is a classic example of the call into service. The Lord Jesus wants our whole hearts devoted to Him, so that being fully yielded to Him, we can be used in reaching others. There may be something significant in the coincidence that as Peter denied Jesus three times on the night of His trial, so the Lord Jesus questions his love three times. But even more noticeable is the choice of words used by Jesus.

In the Greek language there are different words translated in English by "love." When Jesus said to Simon Peter, "Lovest thou me?" Peter's first answer used a word which meant, "You know I am your friend." In answering the question the second time, Peter replied using the same phrase. In His third question Jesus said, "Are you my friend?" Here He used the weaker word, the lesser word. Peter was grieved when he realized what Jesus was bringing to the surface and in his third reply Peter used the stronger word saying, "You know that I love you." By this method Jesus led Peter into complete commitment to Himself.

When John began his account of the life and work of Jesus he pointed out how Jesus called His disciples first to "Come and see," and then to "Follow me." As he comes now to the end of his story he reports Jesus saying to Peter, "Follow me." This is a very definite word of encouragement for believers. The Lord Jesus, as He ascended, was not leaving His disciples to work out their own lives, but when He was about to leave, He called them to a mission for Him. True, they were not to see His face during their earthly career, but in the person of the Holy Spirit they would have His presence in their hearts: a closer fellowship than they ever had when Jesus walked the roads with them. There would never have to be a time when Christians, as the heirs to these promises, would need to walk or work alone; nor would an occasion ever be faced without the knowledge that the Lord had said, "Follow me" — with the assurance that His presence and His guidance would be available to the obedient believer. He is never *behind* His servant, He is always going before to lead or walking beside to bless.

That promise is as valid today as on that day when He gave it. Nothing has changed in His power, His love, His will, nor has any word of His promise ever failed.

THE ROAD OF SERVICE

Verily, verily, I say unto thee, When thou wast young, thou girdest thyself, and walkedst whither thou wouldest: but when thou shalt be old, thou shalt stretch forth thy hands, and another shall gird thee, and carry thee whither thou wouldest not. This spake he, signifying by what death he should glorify God. And when he had spoken this, he saith unto him, Follow me (John 21:18, 19).

This is a statement of profound spiritual meaning for all believers. It is based on common human experience. When men are young they roll up their sleeves for work, tighten their belts, and start at their tasks with all their strength. They select their own equipment, go where they desire, and work largely on their own initiative. When they become mature they are more ready to work humbly under the direction of others.

This can be applied to spiritual living as well. Young Christians may receive a call to serve the Lord. They will be ready to undertake what He would have them do: teach Sunday school, prepare for full time Christian service, work hard in church, and give generously of their income that the Lord's work might prosper. It was all in their own hands. If they wanted to work, they felt they had the power to do so. Such freedom of action is a mark of being young.

When Jesus spoke to Peter about being *old* He did not necessarily mean eighty or ninety years of age. He meant the age of maturity, when a person is acting as an adult, taking whatever responsibility may come to him. When He spoke about stretching forth the hands, He was describing the position of crucifixion. In this way He told Peter there would come a time when he would not be his own boss. Someone else would guide, direct, and send him into whatever he was to do. Jesus included the words "and carry thee whither thou wouldest not." This implies Peter would be led into situations he would personally wish to avoid. This is the common lot of all who live the Christian life. Christians will find that other people will, as it were, take over. It is always sobering to realize that when Jesus was crucified, He was put to death by people who did not understand Him at all.

Christians can learn much from this statement of Jesus to Peter. There will be people in the community or home or church who will try to crucify the believer, and will not realize what they are doing. They will work against the Christian to hurt or harm him but may not be fully aware of the significance of their actions. The Lord was warning Peter about this very thing, and His remarks are valid today. When the Christian is young he may do as he pleases, but when maturity comes, when the Christian begins to carry responsibility, people will try to manage his affairs for him. This is a hard lesson to learn, and the believer can only let the Lord have His way and overrule in such situations.

John indicates these words of Jesus were also a prediction of the way Peter was to die. Tradition says that Peter was indeed crucified. But whatever may have been the physical fate of Peter the words set forth a spiritual prospect for every Christian. The only way to serve the Lord is by yielding in self-denial to the crucifixion of the personal ego.

> Then Peter, turning about, seeth the disciple whom Jesus loved following; which also leaned on his breast at supper, and said, Lord, which is he that betrayeth thee? Peter seeing him saith to Jesus, Lord, and what shall this man do? Jesus saith unto him, If I will that he tarry till I come, what is that to thee? follow thou me (John 21:20-22).

PERSONAL COMMISSION

Just after making this profound statement about the necessity of submitting in self-denial, Jesus made clear to Peter that each believer will have his own personal commission given to him. Christians will not understand their responsibility by looking at each other, but only by heeding the guidance which comes from the Lord Himself to each one individually. In a frank open manner Jesus indicated to Peter that John's commission for service was none of Peter's business. God does not authorize any Christian to watch the conduct of other Christians and then judge them. It is not the business of one church member to watch what someone else gives for the support of the church, or how often they lead in prayer, or how many souls they win. Such matters are between the individual and his Lord. Each Christian is accountable to God for the deeds done in the body, but it is not the privilege or the function of any other Christian to appraise or to judge such conduct.

> Then went this saying abroad among the brethren, that that disciple should not die: yet Jesus said not unto him, He shall not die; but, If I will that he tarry till I come, what is that to thee? This is the disciple which testifieth of these things, and wrote these things: and we know that his testimony is true (John 21:23, 24).

John includes in this report how a false rumor was begun because of unauthorized opinions expressed about the conduct of another believer. This carries its own warning.

This rumor affords at least one more observation. Preachers who would interpret any passage of Scripture should keep in mind that if the truth involved has not been experienced in their own spiritual life, they are simply not qualified to show its true meaning. A man should be humble enough to keep silent about that which he has not personally shared.

> And there are also many other things which Jesus did, the which, if they should be written every one, I suppose that even the world itself could not contain the books that should be written. Amen (John 21:25).

And how blessedly true it is that the Lord Jesus continues, day by day, year by year, to do great and mighty things! We can only praise Him, for our own salvation, and for that of the many who constantly seek Him, find Him, and then determine to live lives pleasing to Him.

In these words John makes it clear that he was not writing a biography, nor a comprehensive report of the ministry of Jesus of Nazareth in His public work. It will be remembered (John 20:30, 31) that John had a purpose in his writing this narrative account. He had selected certain items which he set forth to enable readers to accept Jesus of Nazareth as "the Christ, the son of the living God."

Chapter 23

A SUMMARY OF JOHN

"Full of grace and truth" was the judgment of John as he looked back on the years of fellowship and wrote the full impression made upon him and the other disciples by Jesus of Nazareth. These words probably were written years after John, the beloved disciple, walked with his Lord. But they summed up what he thought of the Son of God while He was in this world. If men would know truth, they must come to Jesus Christ; if they would apprehend grace, they must look to Him who is both Saviour and Lord.

Jesus is a teacher. In his gospel, John reported things that the Son of God did for men and women in His own country, in the days of His flesh as Jesus of Nazareth. John showed how He took care of His followers, training them, expressing His love for them. It was true they did not always understand, but later when the Holy Spirit came into their hearts the things which Jesus had taught were made clear to them. His procedure as Master deserves notice. Never did He send one of His followers to undertake a task. It was His practice to lead His disciples into their work. Invariably Jesus said, "Come after me, follow me." Always He had in mind they should be with Him: "That they all may be one: as thou, Father, art in me, and I in thee, that they also may be one in us: that the world may believe that thou hast sent me" (John 17:21).

He prepared them for the time when He would leave them, assuring them of the companionship of the Holy Spirit, who would abide in their hearts.

> But when the Comforter is come, whom I will send unto you from the Father, even the Spirit of truth, which proceedeth from the Father, he shall testify of me: And ye also shall bear witness, because ye have been with me from the beginning (John 15:26, 27).

Although Jesus would have to leave His disciples, He would not abandon them. This promise must have rejoiced their hearts, especially as they remembered it after the day of Pentecost. Christians are confident the Lord Jesus Christ will return in glory; and until then the Holy

Spirit comforts, guides, teaches, and sustains them by His presence in them.

In His last fellowship with His disciples Jesus showed thoughtfulness and loving care for His own. He spoke to encourage them as He said, "I will not leave you comfortless." In the Greek, the actual word means *orphan,* so His meaning could be translated "I will not leave you comfortless — as an orphan is alone." This record written by John becomes an encouragement as Christians meditate upon the provision of Christ Jesus for His own today.

Jesus Christ is the source of every precious thing in life right now. Every single day, morning, noon, and night, there are resources at the disposal of Christians: grace far beyond measure and far beyond our worth. This grace is sent by God Himself for the strengthening and the comfort of His own. The Lord Jesus Himself is a Comforter. The Bible says that the Holy Spirit was sent as the Comforter and it is the Lord Jesus moving and speaking through His Spirit who gives us a living sense of His presence and power. This is what He said: "Abide in me, and I in you." So Christ Jesus is the Source of all this for any believer, right now, today, as he may read these pages! Believe it and live it!

Christians can come to understand that the whole world is the creation of God, and that this life is in God's hands, not in the hands of the current rules or dictators who disturb and distress the world. The believer will realize anew that his life is in the wise and tender hands of God Almighty.

The Christian's knowledge will grow as he has fellowship with other Christians and as he reads his Bible and studies it, day by day. The Holy Spirit will take his hand and show him the things of Christ, guide his footsteps, and show him the mystery that hath been hid from other peoples.

In addition to all of this, *Jesus Christ has gone to prepare a place for His own* as He said in John 14:3, ". . . that where I am, there ye may be also." D. L. Moody once said, "Christ is as great a Saviour as we make Him." Believers are the ones who can withhold themselves, and thus make it impossible for Him to give all of Himself. This is the great loss some Christians suffer through failing to draw close to Christ.

With all that has been noted in these studies in John's gospel, the truth is that He is greater than everything that can be said about Him, His love is deeper than anything man can imagine. Only eternity will reveal the glories which imagination can never suggest, nor human earthly understanding grasp.

> And the Word was made flesh, and dwelt among us, (and we beheld his glory, the glory as of the only begotten of the Father,) full of grace and truth (John 1:14).

Hallelujah, what a Saviour!